RANK LADIES

Rank Ladies

GENDER AND CULTURAL HIERARCHY

IN AMERICAN VAUDEVILLE

M. ALISON KIBLER

The University of North Carolina Press
Chapel Hill & London

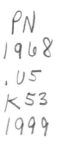

© 1999 The University of North Carolina Press

All rights reserved

Manufactured in the United States of America

Designed by April Leidig-Higgins

Set in Monotype Bell by Eric M. Brooks

The paper in this book meets the guidelines for
permanence and durability of the Committee on
Production Guidelines for Book Longevity of
the Council on Library Resources.

Library of Congress Cataloging-in-Publication Data

Kibler, M. Alison.

Rank ladies : gender and cultural hierarchy in
American vaudeville / M. Alison Kibler.

p.   cm. — (Gender & American culture)

Includes bibliographical references and index.

ISBN 0-8078-2483-6 (cloth: alk. paper).

ISBN 0-8078-4812-3 (pbk.: alk. paper)

1. Vaudeville — United States — History.

2. Women entertainers.   I. Title.   II. Series.

PN1968.U5K53   1999

792.7'082'0973 — dc21   98-47589

CIP

03 02 01 00 99   5 4 3 2 1

TO DENNIS

CONTENTS

ILLUSTRATIONS

Illustrations

ACKNOWLEDGMENTS

◆ ——————————————————————— ◆

I am pleased to thank the institutions that have supported this study by providing generous grants. A National Endowment for the Humanities Summer Stipend helped me revise portions of the manuscript, and an Andrew W. Mellon Foundation Fellowship gave me time to conduct research at the Harry Ransom Humanities Research Center at the University of Texas in Austin. A travel grant from the Research Council at the University of Wisconsin–Green Bay also helped with my travel expenses. At the dissertation stage, I benefited from the University of Iowa's four-year teaching/research fellowship as well as the Seashore Dissertation Fellowship. I am also honored to have received the Jane A. Weiss Dissertation Award in Women's Studies at the University of Iowa. A Smithsonian Graduate Student Fellowship, under the guidance of Charles McGovern, enabled me to take advantage of archival materials in Washington, D.C., during my ten-week residency at the National Museum of American History. I was also fortunate to receive a research grant from the Irish American Cultural Institute of St. Paul, Minnesota, through the Irish Research Fund endowment given by the Lawrence and Elizabeth O'Shaughnessy Charitable Trust. The Annette K. Baxter Travel Grant from the American Studies Association and the Albert J. Beveridge Research Grant from the American Historical Association helped fund travel to conferences and archives.

My former colleagues in the Social Change and Development Department at the University of Wisconsin–Green Bay gave me financial support and helped me combine research and teaching by providing good advice and the example of their own work. Thanks to Lisa Barlow, Francis Carleton, Mark Everingham, Tony Galt, Cheryl Kalny, Harvey

Kaye, Craig Lockhard, Larry Smith, and Lynn Walter. My former student Jill Duquaine graciously took time away from her graduate studies to help me with this project. The Centre for Women's Studies at the Australian National University (ANU) has generously supported this book by giving me an office and a computer. Even more important, faculty members Helen Keane, Rosanne Kennedy, Fiona Paisley, and Jan Jindy Pettman have made the center a friendly and intellectually stimulating place to work. Jill Matthews, in the Department of History at ANU, offered many helpful comments on gender and modernity.

I have benefited from the knowledgeable assistance of archivists at the National Records Center; the Motion Picture, Broadcasting, and Recorded Sound Division, Library of Congress; the Harvard Theatre Collection, Houghton Library, Harvard University; the Allen County–Fort Wayne Historical Society; the New York Public Library for the Performing Arts; and the Department of Rare Books and Special Collections at the University of Rochester Library. In addition, Ann Patrick promptly sent me sheet music from the Harris Collection at the John Hay Library, Brown University, and Melissa Miller helped me navigate the Theatre Arts Collection at the Harry Ransom Humanities Research Center. I also appreciate Annette Fern's willingness to locate photographs from the Harvard Theatre Collection for me. The staff members at the Special Collections Department at the University of Iowa Library deserve special thanks. Susan Hansen, Robert McCown, Judy Macy, and David Schoonover made my work with the Keith/Albee Collection there pleasant and productive. This book began in 1988 when I first opened the report books in that rich collection and started to read the theater managers' unpublished accounts of their weekly vaudeville entertainment. I have been grateful for the collection and the kindness and wisdom of its caretakers ever since.

I am also indebted to my dissertation committee: Linda K. Kerber, Tom Lutz, Kim Marra, Lauren Rabinovitz, and H. Shelton Stromquist. My dissertation adviser, Lauren Rabinovitz, has improved this study in many ways, from the very early stages when she pushed me to shape it into a more interdisciplinary project through her thorough review of every chapter. Linda Kerber provided important criticism of my work and generously offered advice on many personal and professional decisions. Linda Kerber and Lauren Rabinovitz have inspired me with their commitment to feminist scholarship and women's history as well as the high standards of their own work.

Many friends and colleagues have offered valuable comments on parts of this study: Richard Butsch, Janet Davis, Janet Greene, Laura Helper, Greg Kaster, William Mahar, David Roediger, Noliwe Rooks, Lillian Schlissel, Leslie Taylor, William Williams, and Leigh Woods. Robert Allen and Jane Desmond provided insightful responses to research I presented at a panel at the Berkshire Conference on the History of Women in 1996. Susan Glenn's detailed reading of the entire manuscript was an invaluable guide for revisions. I am grateful as well to the anonymous reviewers at *American Studies* for pointing out many ways to improve my interpretation of the Elinore Sisters. An earlier version of chapter 3 appeared in *American Studies* (Spring 1997), and the editors have kindly granted permission to reprint a revised version of that essay. It has been a pleasure to work with Kate Douglas Torrey, Ron Maner, and Paula Wald at the University of North Carolina Press. With patience and skill, they have improved this manuscript immeasurably.

Throughout my travels to archives and conferences around the country, I have enjoyed the hospitality of many friends and family members: Tina Chen and Hugh McElaney, Karen Edwards and Jim Merod, Virginia Kibler, Aaron and Aliza Menche, Anna and Gerald Seydel, and Tom and Connie Weck. Martha Campbell was a generous, friendly host in Austin, Texas. In addition, my parents, Austin and Pat Kibler, have supported this project by providing housing, extra money, and, more recently, babysitting during my research trips to Washington, D.C. They have aided me in facing the many challenges involved in moving to Canberra, Australia. They encouraged us to make the move and have been faithful, creative transcontinental parents and grandparents ever since. Thanks also to my grandmother, Ann Ogden Hoefle, who often said she thought I should write a book, and to Henry and Phyllis Deslippe for providing support in many ways throughout this project.

Thanks to my daughter Therese Deslippe for being a reasonable and flexible baby and for greeting each day with such delight. I dedicate this book to Dennis Deslippe. His style of work—"calm, cool, and collective"—helped make our household run smoothly and provided a model

Acknowledgments

for my own work. In the last two years, we have shared the challenge and joy of parenthood and have moved halfway around the world. Although these changes have not made finishing this book easier, they have enriched my life tremendously. I thank Dennis for being a true partner through these adventures and for his sense of humor, intellectual support, and love.

RANK LADIES

INTRODUCTION

On November 15, 1909, at B. F. Keith's vaudeville theater in Philadelphia, the matinee began with the usual vaudeville zing. Tom and Edith Arnold caught the audience's attention with a boisterous kangaroo dance and an ice-skating routine on top of a special elevated pedestal on the stage. After several other acts, the Howard Brothers juggled banjos, and magician Imro Fox followed with a "running-fire" of jokes during his feats of levitation.[1] Then the star attraction, French singer Madame Yvette Guilbert, took center stage, wearing a full-length, billowing gown and long white gloves, her hair swept up in a bun. The contrast between this act and the preceding performers was striking: Guilbert did not jump, shout, or shock the audience. Instead, as she sang in English and French, Guilbert shyly raised an eyebrow, shrugged her shoulders, and smoothly motioned with her hand. Publicity for her tour described the tall redhead as charming, quaint, and artistic. One critic remarked that "there is a demureness, a certain delicate and underlying humor . . . that makes Madame Guilbert's work most delightful."[2] Her foreignness also added to the aura of sophistication surrounding her: she was a "famous Parisian" artist.[3] First recruited to vaudeville in 1895, Guilbert was attractive to managers who were eager to embellish the respectability of their growing entertainment industry and to expand their audiences from the traditional base of working-class men. Charles Barnes, the manager of Keith's theater in Philadelphia, explained that he booked Guilbert in 1909 to draw in "society people."[4] Like other managers on this circuit, Barnes believed that her foreign identity, artistic reputation, and demure femininity made her the perfect symbol of vaudeville's new respectability.[5]

But the highly touted Guilbert flopped. Barnes noted that although she was "unquestionably very artistic in her method . . . [t]he majority of vaudeville patrons are not of a class that appreciates her work." A slapstick comedian, Jack Wilson, not Guilbert, actually emerged as the star of the show. Barnes explained that Wilson's comedy act (immediately after Guilbert's) ignited the audience: "It is unfortunate perhaps, but still true that this comedian following the mild success of Guilbert was a positive riot."[6] Although Guilbert's act brought only polite applause, Wilson had to make a speech to quiet the audience after he had performed for over thirty minutes.

Guilbert's chilly reception in Philadelphia was not surprising considering the nearly disastrous start of her tour in New York City a month earlier. When she opened her 1909 vaudeville tour in New York City on October 11, she was almost driven off the stage by the shouts and laughter of the patrons in the cheapest seats—the gallery. After cheering wildly for a troupe of slapstick comedians, the gallery crowd was so amused by Guilbert's old-fashioned costume that they hooted insults at her. Her ruffled dress with a wide hoopskirt and her formal gloves conveyed a "Victorian" persona. One critic remarked that her "oddly voluminous hoop skirt" reminded him of when "our mothers were maids."[7] The gallery patrons were not only amused by her Victorian costume but also angered because her second song was in French. Impatient and bored, they booed and hissed. Although visibly shaken by the hostile reception, Guilbert managed to hold the stage largely because of the persistent applause of a few patrons in the moderately priced orchestra seats. A few days later, Guilbert fought back by giving the vaudeville in-

Caricature of Yvette Guilbert, the French artist who battled
the gallery during her tour of the Keith circuit, by Marius de Zayas.
From Caroline Caffin's Vaudeville *(1914).*

dustry some unflattering publicity. "I cannot say that I like American audiences," she snapped; "[in France] you have a public educated up to realize the value of your art. Here the great public is not yet up to the mark." She believed American vaudeville patrons were unable to appreciate her subtle gestures, her slight vocal modulations, and her intellectual elevation.[8] Between Jack Wilson's success, the gallery patrons' revolt, and Guilbert's condescending reproach, vaudeville's campaign for feminine respectability and cultural uplift seemed dubious indeed.

The acrimony surrounding Guilbert's tour represented a pervasive struggle over who would lead vaudeville. Slapstick comedians, for example, complained about losing top billing and fancy dressing rooms to women like Guilbert. Dan McAvoy, a rough comedian, was angry about the star status of Miss Annie Irish, an actress from the dramatic stage, during her Detroit engagement in 1904. Irish received the headliner spot and ample praise from management: "It is women of this kind that have brought to this theater the very cream of Detroit society," explained the theater manager, John Finn. Irritated and resentful, McAvoy pestered the manager with complaints: "He kicked on his position on the bill, kicked because he was not billed over Annie Irish, kicked on his dressing room, and was on the whole disagreeable." But McAvoy got his best revenge onstage, where he overshadowed Irish as "the laughing hit of the bill."[9] Actresses and opera singers also had their share of temper tantrums about cultural hierarchy in vaudeville. Veteran dramatic actress Minnie Maddern Fiske made headlines in 1910 when she protested the appearance of a lithograph of her alongside a photograph of Lucille Mulhall, the Queen of Lassos, and actress Annie Yeamans left vaudeville allegedly "because she said she couldn't get on with the educated horse."[10] Leaders of the vaudevillians' labor union, the White Rats of America, also debated cultural hierarchy when they defended the artistry (and masculine honor) of male vaudeville performers, revising the common understanding of "legitimate" as a reference to the elite dramatic stage: "I know a lot of actors that are decent and honorable men that are not getting a fair deal; there are men walking the streets that ought to be working—good legitimate actors (when I say legitimate I mean vaudeville actors)."[11]

These struggles capture the focus of this book. This study shows how the contests over whether high or low taste would reign in vaudeville (whether performers like Guilbert deserved top billing) were buttressed by the symbolic weight of masculinity and femininity (as the traditionally masculine gallery rejected Guilbert's Victorian, feminine artistry). I examine the complexity of gender symbolism and cultural hierarchy in three areas of vaudeville: the audience, the careers of several female performers, and the labor movement. In the vaudeville audience, the masculine gallery often rebelled against the feminization of vaudeville, and women, contrary to managers' expectations, sometimes joined in the rowdy behavior. The case studies of women's careers reveal tensions among ranks of women (based on class, ethnicity, and race) as well as the ways vaudeville's ambiguous reputation undercut female performers' morality and feminine respectability. When women descended into vaudeville from such higher venues as the legitimate stage or moved into "low" styles of performance (masculine roles and racial masquerades, for example), they often faced questions about the proper boundaries of women's activity and influence. Should married women seek employment? Was women's moral influence destructive and stifling? Were women who entered male fields (such as athletics) sexually deviant? A sense of brotherhood and antipathy toward high culture united the vaudevillians' labor union, an organization that challenged the managers' equation of vaudeville's cultural improvement with the protection of white womanhood by arguing that greedy and immoral managers actually exploited female performers. In these ways, this study tells the story of disgruntled vaudevillians, disreputable patrons, unruly women, and the sometimes fearful ladies of vaudeville.

The controversy surrounding Yvette Guilbert was not simply an amusing oddity. This debate over gender and the mixing of high and low culture represents the primary growing pains and tensions in vaudeville, an industry that helped recast the social and cultural landscape of the United States at the turn of the century. From a scattered array of commercial amusements, vaudeville helped build a national system of entertainment. From a theater audience divided along the lines of class, ethnicity, race, and gender, vaudeville forged a heterogeneous audience. And from a raunchy, male-dominated popular entertainment, vaudeville crafted a respectable culture that catered to the female consumer. Vaudeville, therefore, was a key institution in the transition from a marginalized sphere of popular entertainment, largely associated with vice and masculinity, to a consolidated network of commercial leisure, in which the female consumer was not only welcomed but also pampered.

When vaudeville began, roughly in the 1880s, the theatrical audience was divided into relatively homogeneous groups, with working-class men dominating popular theaters, immigrants attending foreign-language theaters, and elite men and women patronizing expensive drama. Fifty years earlier, the theater audience in America had been a diverse crowd; the upper classes joined manual laborers and African Americans (although restricted to the upper balcony) joined white patrons to watch a variety of attractions, from Shakespeare to tumbling and juggling. But this common culture, this mingling of social groups in the theater and of types of acts onstage, gave way to a division between high and low culture, art and popular culture. In the second half of the nineteenth century, many highbrow cultural institutions emerged, including art museums, symphony orchestras, and foreign opera. The heterogeneous audience that had often dictated the range of a performance became divided into separate, homogeneous classes, and bourgeois standards of behavior replaced unruly activities in the theaters. Works of "art" were isolated not only from working-class, immigrant audiences but also from "popular" material. The Boston Symphony Orchestra, founded in 1881, briefly offered light music as part of its concerts but soon curtailed such "mixed" programs.[12] Opera in America followed a similar pattern. Opera of the mid-nineteenth century, often combined with variety acts like jugglers and blackface comedians, attracted a diverse crowd, well beyond an elite following. By the late nineteenth century, however, opera had been separated from other forms of entertainment and divided into high and low culture, with English-language opera remaining popular and foreign-language opera attracting a narrow, elite audience.[13] The cultivation of a rarefied realm of art was a historical process with far-reaching implications. Historians have shown that the new venues of high culture were, in large part, a means of conferring social power and defending a particular social order. They helped provide an "asylum" for elites from the urban disruptions of the day, such as immigration and labor unrest.[14]

The division of American culture into elite and popular levels in the middle of the nineteenth century depended heavily on the regendering of the traditionally all-male theater audience. "[T]he class transformations of theater," explains Richard Butsch, "were aligned with its gender transformation."[15] In the early nineteenth century, theaters threatened women's reputations largely because of the presence of prostitutes and actresses (usually considered no better than prostitutes). Middle-class white women held the key for theater entrepreneurs eager to establish a respectable reputation for their houses. These women, according to Victorian conventions, were the moral and spiritual guides of their families. Shaping others through the example of their selfless acts (not through direct confrontation or the assertion of authority), middle-class white women were supposed to be the saintly persuaders in their families.[16] Theater entrepreneurs knew that this domestic ideology of feminine influence could improve their industry's reputation. Beginning in the 1840s, theater managers promoted their attractions as educational, uplifting, and family oriented, particularly appropriate for mothers and their children, and eliminated many of the masculine elements of their houses. They silenced much of the audience's traditional combativeness and reduced the number of prostitutes in their theaters by requiring that women be admitted only with male escorts.[17] Often finding the new atmosphere stifling, many men sought other forms of entertainment that preserved a more masculine culture.[18] They turned to sports (such as boxing) in which they could watch heroic male competition and escaped to the minstrel show and the concert saloon, where they could enjoy drinking and lewd entertainment—all unfettered by female moralism.

Vaudeville, in many ways, seems to have been part of the sacralized, feminized culture that emerged in the second half of the nineteenth century. The leading vaudeville magnate, B. F. Keith, voiced a philosophy of cultural uplift ("catering to the best would cause the multitude to follow") that depended largely on attracting respectable female patrons and highbrow performers, from Shakespearean actors to learned lecturers.[19] Previous scholars have argued that vaudeville administrators eliminated coarseness from the stage, instilled feminine, "passive politeness" in their audiences, and upheld "genteel standards of refinement."[20] But, as Kathryn Oberdeck has demonstrated, vaudeville was actually a site of debate over cultural hierarchy and "refinement." Vaudeville's multilayered publicity and the variety of acts onstage upheld the ideal of a genteel culture cordoned off from the working classes but also mocked that refinement as "hackneyed Victorian prissiness."[21] Ultimately, vaudeville's "'refinement' was capricious."[22] Thus, vaudeville did not simply adopt the standards of high culture; it drew high and low together onstage and in the audience, uniting the fractured cultures (male and female audiences, art and amusements) in its theaters. Although vaudeville entrepreneurs sampled from many high-culture venues (from opera to the legitimate stage), they drew most of the raw material of vaudeville from nineteenth-century popular theater, namely, the tradition of "aggregate" entertainment: the heterogeneous offerings in the minstrel show, the concert saloon, the variety theater, and the dime museum.[23] These theaters were often associated with the working classes, and most were male dominated. Acts from these theatrical traditions were most likely to mock vaudeville's cultural pretensions and feminine restraint.

The blackface minstrel show, the most popular amusement between 1840 and 1880, was a combination of song, dance, and comic sketches and banter; like vaudeville, it was a "conglomeration of diverse parts in which each act was presented as a self-contained unit designed to stop the show."[24] The minstrel shows appealed to average Americans, primarily working-class men, by attacking women's rights, ridiculing the temperance movement, and making fun of a wide variety of intellectuals, experts, and authority figures.[25] Even the most marginal white patrons could place themselves above the black characters presented by white actors in blackface. Slaves were usually portrayed as childish, lazy, and contented, whereas free blacks were depicted as bumbling and unhappy outside of the plantation.[26]

Vaudeville pioneers relied even more heavily on the concert saloon, the variety theater, and the dime museum as the sources of vaudeville, frequently remodeling these houses into the new vaudeville palaces. Concert saloons and variety theaters (terms often used interchangeably) combined bars with cheap (or free) amusements in connected rooms or auditoriums. They were smoky, noisy, and crowded; patrons were likely to be drunk; and waitresses, jostling among the men, were often willing to sell sex along with liquor. Also associated with lewd entertainment, concert saloons were disreputable institutions. Moral reformers, for example, helped pass a law in New York State to eliminate concert saloons by prohibiting the employment of waitresses and the sale of liquor in these establishments. The legislature tried to take the saloon out of the concert saloon.[27] But proprietors' tricks, such as having waitresses dress as customers, and the lackluster enforcement of the law helped concert saloons survive. It is important to note that many concert saloons attracted middle-class men, "slumming voyeurs" who were eager to sample the city's mysterious underside and to mingle with poor or immigrant women.[28] As one observer noted in 1882, the concert saloon attracted a "motley crowd. . . . The men represent all classes of society. Some are strangers who have merely come to see the place; others are out for a lark; and others still have come in company with, or to meet, some abandoned woman."[29]

Similarly, many dime museums, a combination of pseudoscientific displays and stage entertainment, were housed in storefronts in inexpensive urban entertainment areas and attracted men only.[30] But the most famous dime museums, such as P. T. Barnum's American Museum, were an exception to the largely male-dominated working-class collection of amusements that formed the foundation of vaudeville. Entrepreneurs, beginning in the 1840s, added a variety show to the scientific exhibits and lectures of museums, using the educational reputation of earlier museums to draw customers who ordinarily would have been skeptical about the propriety of theater. In particular, Barnum lauded his museum as a morally impeccable public service; women and children would be safe in his museum, he claimed. Nevertheless, most dime museums did not follow Barnum's lead. Many disreputable dime museums, usually smaller than Barnum's, were clustered along the Bowery in New York City, "one of the largest and most notorious of the urban skid rows" in the late nineteenth century.[31] Dime museums in this area often attracted patrons with the bait of "the unclad female form in all its loveliness." The customers, however, were disappointed by the unclothed mannequins that awaited them.[32] Vaudeville entrepreneurs thus had to navigate deep fissures in late-nineteenth-century American culture, at a time when expensive theaters had become decidedly feminine whereas most variety theaters, concert saloons, and small dime museums were male dominated and often associated with vice.

From a divided theatrical world vaudeville forged a mass audience: a heterogeneous crowd of white men and women of different classes and ethnic groups. And the businesspeople of vaudeville organized theaters into national chains, developed centralized bureaucracies for arranging national tours and monitoring the success of acts across the country, and increasingly focused on formulas for popular bills that would please audiences beyond a single city or neighborhood. In these ways, vaudeville was an integral part of the growth of mass culture around the turn of the century.[33] After approximately 1880, a mass culture took shape in which national "leisure oligopolies" replaced family businesses, mass markets superseded local markets, and new mass media (namely, magazines, motion pictures, and radio) targeted large, diverse audiences.[34] As historian Robert Snyder says, vaudeville "arose in the middle of this transition [to mass culture] and helped it along."[35]

Vaudeville grew alongside many other mass culture industries, such as professional sports and department stores, and incorporated these kindred developments into its own success. Like vaudeville, professional baseball expanded and became consolidated in the second half of the nineteenth century. Establishing the National League in 1876, baseball owners drove out rival clubs, brought players under tighter control, and developed a bureaucracy to oversee the growth and evaluation of the game.[36] Similarly, in the late 1890s, massive department stores (some with as many as 125 departments) began to replace small, neighborhood stores. In 1896 in New York City, Henry Siegel opened Siegel-Cooper's, a six-story department store, selling a wide range of consumer goods, from pianos and tropical fish to coffee and clothing.[37] Like the entrepreneurs in sports and entertainment, department store owners created national chains. By 1901, for example, Siegel built a new Boston store, bought another New York City department store, and formed a circuit of retail houses from Manhattan to Chicago.[38] Vaudeville magnates not only used these trends to enhance the popularity of vaudeville but also helped promote baseball and department stores with their shows. Theater managers booked baseball stars, such as Babe Ruth, and provided patrons with the scores of important baseball games.[39] Owners also built vaudeville theaters near department stores (to attract women shoppers), advertised in department store windows, and even used department stores as theatrical venues.[40]

In this light, vaudeville's confusions and compromises over cultural hierarchy and gender are best understood as interlocking elements of a work in progress—mass culture. Victorian notions of gender coexisted (often uneasily) with the ideal of the New Woman (sporty and sensuous). The exaltation of gentility competed not only with a new celebration of sensuous consumerism and feminine display but also with cries for a truly egalitarian culture. In particular, vaudeville's varied and frequently ambivalent approach to cultural hierarchy casts further doubt on the description of mass culture as a process of homogenization and embourgeoisement. Many historical accounts emphasize the ways that mass culture grew out of the "disciplining" of low culture: religious leaders and social reformers attempted to clean up popular entertainment; early motion picture promoters, shedding their working-class, immigrant origins, began to "ape the physical trappings of high culture"; and, in general, mass culture consumers were more restrained and polite than the demanding and often raucous theater patrons of the early nineteenth century.[41] This portrait of mass culture is not complete without an examination of the other side of this process of uplift—mass culture's loosening of high culture around the turn of the century. Kathy Peiss, for example, argues that Coney Island became a "liberating experience for the middle class," and recent film scholars have shown that Vitagraph's highbrow films (of Shakespearean plays and biblical stories) were adapted to the experiences and tastes of the traditional working-class patrons of movie houses rather than aimed exclusively at new elite customers.[42] The accounts of mass culture as homogenization and embourgeoisement bear reconsideration on another level as well. Whereas many scholars have argued that mass culture subsumed local cultures into a middle-class norm, others have demonstrated that racial, ethnic, and working-class communities were "filters" through which consumers "encountered" mass-produced brands, chain stores, and movies.[43] This history of vaudeville clearly reveals mass culture's varied approaches to cultural hierarchy: it uplifted low culture and unraveled high culture; it aspired to bourgeois standardization but did not neglect working-class, immigrant pride.

Mass culture's expansive mixture of high and low relied on gender symbolism and had particular salience in women's lives around the turn of the century. The respectability of commercial amusements, including vaudeville and cinema, depended largely on their feminization (although their feminine identity was often duplicitous and ambivalent). Furthermore, the connotations of femininity proved to be slippery around the turn of the century. Early critics of mass culture linked women to a saccharine culture, not an educational and civilized culture. Scholars have explored the ideological underpinnings of the critique of mass culture as feminine, pointing to the ways critics throughout the twentieth century have used femininity to symbolize the passivity and decay they identify in mass culture.[44] In particular, recent cultural historians have linked this gendered rhetoric to the fears of male modernists and to broad uneasiness about mass production, conformity, and consumption at the turn of the century.[45] As this book shows, vaudeville, in the thick of these shifting meanings of feminization (from uplift to decay), is a rich arena for the investigation of the "dubious sexual analogies" framing the development of mass culture.[46]

Mass culture industries like vaudeville and cinema largely recruited female consumers by arguing that their theaters (safe and educational) complemented women's domesticity and their family obligations, but ironically, commercial entertainment also undermined this "domestic ideology" by drawing women into the public world of cheap amusements.[47] Promoters of popular entertainment had to break down the "ideological and material barriers to women's social activities in the public sphere" and transform the male audiences and masculine identity of their commercial leisure enterprises.[48] In these ways, amusements such as vaudeville were actually on the cutting edge of the dramatic transformations in women's lives around the turn of the century. The nineteenth-century doctrine of domesticity, passivity, and passionlessness for white women was crumbling by the end of the century.[49] Women pursued higher education and employment in greater numbers, the organized movement for woman suffrage gained momentum, and women expressed daring sensuality and assertiveness in new heterosocial institutions such as vaudeville.[50] Previous historians have shown, however, that amusement centers did not liberate women because the female consumer, usually not economically independent, had to rely on men in many ways for access to this world and women's patronage was often encouraged not as individual autonomy but as a part of a family or romantic partnership with a man. As women became part of the collective audiences of commercial leisure, they were also increasingly silenced as sexual objects on stages and screens.[51] Subsequent chapters of this book explore in greater detail the tension between tradition and novelty, constraint and freedom, for women onstage, in the audience, and in the labor movement in American vaudeville.

The nexus of gender and cultural hierarchy in vaudeville, and in mass culture, not only was structured by the dichotomy of masculinity and femininity but also depended on differences among women. This study explores the contrasts between the vaudeville industry's construction of a polite female spectator and the actual female patrons (often loose and raucous) and between the ultrafeminine artists recruited from opera and the legitimate stage and the "cyclonic" comediennes and animalistic acrobats.[52] The seemingly contradictory coexistence of these types deserves some explanation at this point. The female reformer—moral and pure—had always had a darker side, based on the Victorian notions of women's sexuality. Medical experts held that if a woman's sexuality was not channeled into domesticity and childrearing, her reproductive organs could be quite destructive, leading to disease and insanity.[53] The aesthetically and morally pure woman who symbolized vaudeville's reform was thus tied inextricably to the conception of a wild, sexually voracious woman who was ruled by her libido. The white Victorian woman was seen "as being both higher and lower, both innocent and animal, pure yet quintessentially sexual."[54] Historians have shown that the assumption that women are irrational and out of control sexually has been a source of women's symbolic power in popular culture. In early modern France, for example, unruly women—eating huge amounts of food and laughing loudly—played a role in parades, fiction, and drama in the subversion of a variety of hierarchical orders, including patriarchy. They took over male roles, sometimes dressing as men, and, in other cases, gained control over men, assaulting husbands and mocking male authority figures. Such fictitious and festive moments provided a symbolic reservoir for social protests against patriarchy, realignments of power in marriages, and some women's creation of unconventional lives.[55] But the penalties for women who stepped outside of the feminine norms in these comic spectacles were also clear, as these women often became the butts of misogynist jokes and the targets of violence.[56]

Along with exposing the internal instability of the pure and pious female reformer, the following chapters show that these contrasting models of femininity (the restrained lady versus the unruly woman) largely corresponded to different groups of women since many comic and unconventional women onstage were part of (or represented) marginalized social groups. Cora Youngblood Corson, a Native American, was odd because she played the "masculine" tuba, and Kate Elinore was a rare woman in slapstick comedy who portrayed Irish women as lascivious drunkards. The eccentric women in vaudeville were often outside of the ideals of feminine beauty: they were fat, dark-skinned, or "too mannish." In the playful, often novel world of vaudeville, the grotesque women who joked and cackled at prudish Victorian matrons, abused husbands in comic sketches, and took over male parts in athletic acts and slapstick routines were regularly labeled freaks, transvestites, and deviants.

In some cases, the wild women of vaudeville addressed and competed directly with the female artist and reformer, joining the "gallery gods" in challenging what they saw as the increasingly anemic feminine atmosphere of vaudeville.[57] Eva Tanguay, a singing comedienne who earned huge salaries for her sensual, frenetic, and often insolent performances, seemed to relish her battles with various "artists" for the title of top drawing card in vaudeville. In 1911 she defeated ballerina Adeline Genée, much to the dismay of theater critics who lambasted vaudeville patrons for having "no eye for aught but gaudy colors and no ear for anything but the noisy blare."[58] Perhaps as a way of savoring this triumph, Tanguay incorporated a burlesque ballet in later routines. Famous for her chunky physique, her frizzy, unkempt hair, and her two left feet, Tanguay appeared in a tutu and tried in vain to pirouette gracefully as she sang "When Pavlova Sees Me Put It Over" in 1915.[59] Not surprisingly, her spoof of the famous ballerina, Anna Pavlova, earned a particularly boisterous, enthusiastic reception from the gallery, Yvette Guilbert's old nemesis.

This study focuses on the most powerful chain of vaudeville theaters: the Keith circuit. Born on January 6, 1846, Benjamin Franklin Keith began his career in popular entertainment as a circus performer and promoter in the 1870s. In 1883 Keith and his partner William Austin opened a dime museum in Boston. Edward F. Albee, who also had previously traveled with circuses, worked for Keith in Boston, organizing the construction of new theaters in Providence, Rhode Island, and Philadelphia.[60] Albee eventually moved from being Keith's "general utility man" to the top ranks of Keith's administration.[61] Although Keith was the official head of the circuit, Albee was the power behind the scenes, handling all areas of Keith's booming enterprise. After Keith died in 1914, his son, A. Paul Keith, took his place until his death (from influenza) in 1918. Albee then gained full control of the Keith circuit and publicly displayed his authority in many ways, including his construction of new theaters bearing his name.[62] Looking back on their first venture in Boston, Albee recalled that their goal was "to offer family entertainment at an admission fee of 10 cents. At the time 10 cent shows were thick in the land—varieties, burlesques and the like. They were not the kind of entertainment, however, that a man would take his wife and children to. . . . The field for popular price amusement was obviously lying ready to be tilled."[63] At the museum, they displayed circus "freaks" for an admission charge of 10 cents, including Baby Alice, the Midget Wonder; the Tattooed Man; and the Dog-Faced Boy.[64] Keith soon opened a second-floor theater where he presented a series of singers and animal acts—his first vaudeville bill. He touted his clean variety and dramatic stage productions, such as a burlesque of Gilbert and Sullivan's *H.M.S. Pinafore*, to draw more middle-class patrons to his theaters.[65] In 1887 Keith transferred his entertainment to the Bijou Theatre in Boston and, in the following years, opened the Gaiety Theatre in Providence (1888), the Bijou Theatre in Philadelphia (1889), and Keith's Union Square Theatre in New York City (1893).[66] After combining light opera with variety acts in the late 1880s and early 1890s, Keith exclusively offered vaudeville after 1894.[67]

Whereas before 1900 vaudeville theaters were owned independently

THE ONLY DRAMATIC PAPER PUBLISHED IN RHODE ISLAND.

VOL V. PROVIDENCE, R. I., OCTOBER, 19, 1908 No. 8.

KEITH···NEWS

ANNIVERSARY NUMBER.

B. F. KEITH

EDWARD F. ALBEE

A. P. KEITH

1898

CHAS. LOVENBERG

1908

Cover of Keith News, *October 19, 1908, featuring B. F. Keith; his son,
A. Paul Keith; Edward Albee, who led the Keith circuit; and Charles Lovenberg,
who managed Keith's theater in Providence for almost thirty years. Although
the Providence theater first opened in 1888, this issue celebrated its tenth
anniversary because Keith reportedly inaugurated "high-class vaudeville"
in Providence after the theater was remodeled in 1898.
Courtesy of Special Collections, University of Iowa Library.*

or were part of small chains, after 1907 the control of vaudeville rested in the hands of a few vaudeville magnates, such as B. F. Keith. In 1923, according to *Equity*, a trade publication for actors, the Keith circuit included 34 big-time vaudeville theaters, 23 owned by Keith and 11 leased by Keith.[68] By this time, Keith's name was on the marquees of 8 theaters in New York City, 4 in Brooklyn, and 2 in Boston, as well as many others along the East Coast and in Ohio, Indiana, and Kentucky.[69]

Nevertheless, Keith's rising power in vaudeville was tied less to his ownership of theaters than to his control over the booking of engagements at an expanding circle of theaters. In 1906 Keith and Albee established the United Booking Office (UBO) to match performers and theaters more efficiently. Performers and theater managers subsequently worked through the UBO to arrange bookings and routes. The UBO had tremendous leverage over performers because it was the sole entryway to the most prestigious circuit in the country. If performers rejected a UBO salary, failed to appear for a UBO date, or played for UBO competition, they could be blacklisted from performing on the Keith circuit in the future. The Keith system deducted money from performers' salaries to pay the UBO for their bookings, and the Vaudeville Collection Agency, also a Keith business, processed these deductions, collecting 2.5 percent of the salary to pay for this service. Keith's position in the middle of the transactions between performers, booking agents, and managers was, therefore, quite profitable. When *Equity* surveyed the history of vaudeville in 1923, it emphasized the power of central booking agencies, including the UBO (the most prominent booking firm): "It is in the booking office that vaudeville is run, actors are made or broken, theatres nourished or starved. It is the concentration of power in the hands of small groups of men who control the booking offices which has made possible the trustification of vaudeville."[70]

The centralized authority of the Keith circuit is also evident in the weekly reports theater managers wrote to one another. They made suggestions about salaries and the best order for acts on the bill, described offensive material they had cut in performers' acts, and encouraged other managers to make sure that the offensive material did not reappear in a routine. The manager of Keith's theater in Boston concluded that "the performers are getting on to the fact that our theaters will not stand for anything vulgar, profane or suggestive . . . knowing full well they will get a call-down, and moreover that these cuts are reported from theatre to theatre."[71] Charles Lovenberg, the manager of Keith's theater in Providence, reflected on the importance of punishing performers who had upset circuit administrators when he described his problems with the Musical Simpsons in 1907. Refusing to appear because they were upset by their low status on the bill, the Musical Simpsons symbolized a broader issue for Lovenberg: "[I]t will only be a matter of time before all performers will tell us what time they go on, how they shall be billed, and where they shall dress and it seems to me that it is time that we disciplined a few of them by refusing to book them until they have thoroughly shown their repentance. For that reason I do not believe that this act should be booked on the Keith Circuit for another six months to come."[72]

Keith's control was strongest in "big-time," as opposed to "small-time," vaudeville. With expensive interior designs and stars who commanded high salaries, big-time theaters had higher production costs and, consequently, more expensive admission prices than small-time vaudeville did. Big-time theaters were also more attractive to performers because they offered two shows a day and maintained one bill for a full week. Small-time theaters, on the other hand, demanded a more grueling schedule from performers because they presented three to six shows a day and maintained a single bill for only half a week. For performers, therefore, "small-time was vaudeville's version of baseball's minor leagues."[73] Small-time theaters catered primarily to working-class or immigrant audiences, drawing particularly from local neighborhoods rather than attracting middle-class shoppers and suburbanites, who would frequently arrive at big-time theaters via trolleys and subway lines. One of the leaders of small-time vaudeville was Marcus Loew, who began to offer a combination of films and live performances in run-down theaters in 1905. Over the next decade, he improved his existing theaters and acquired new ones, establishing a circuit of 112 theaters in the United States and Canada by 1918. A 1914 article described Loew's theaters as houses where "the man with the wage or small salary looks for an evening's pleasure," establishments for "the filling of the poor man's hour with fun."[74] In particular, Loew's theaters on the Lower East Side of New York City catered to a working-class Jewish audience.[75] Big-time theaters, in contrast, attracted a more diverse audience of middle-class customers and some working-class patrons.

Although Keith continued to face competition in small-time vaudeville from Loew and others, he eventually achieved a monopoly over big-time vaudeville. With the development of his centralized booking authority, Keith brought more theaters and circuits under his control. One of the first significant mergers occurred in 1906 when Frederick F. Proctor and Keith combined their expanding circuits. Proctor began his vaudeville chain in the 1880s, and by 1906, he controlled seven theaters in New York State. Keith, his preeminent rival, purchased Proctor's Fifth Avenue Theatre in New York City in 1906 and negotiated a partnership with Proctor.[76] In February 1907, Keith and Proctor joined with William Hammerstein and Percy Williams, who owned several theaters in New York City. To combine with Keith and Proctor, Williams and Hammerstein abandoned the booking offices of William Morris, who, despite the desertion of these two preeminent managers, vowed to oppose the growing power of Keith's interests. Soon after the consolidation of Keith, Proctor, Williams, and Hammerstein, two leaders of the Theatrical Syndicate, a group of powerful entrepreneurs in legitimate theater, Marc Klaw and A. L. Erlanger, announced that they would offer vaudeville shows through the booking offices of William Morris. The *New York Times* reported that Klaw and Erlanger's presentation of vaudeville was the start of a "vaudeville war."[77] This battle, however, was short-lived. On November 8, 1907, a new merger between Klaw and Erlanger and Keith's circuit was announced, and Klaw and Erlanger agreed to stop presenting vaudeville for the next ten years. Thus, big-time vaudeville on the East Coast was consolidated under the guidance of Keith by 1907.

In 1910 the Keith circuit joined with Martin Beck's Orpheum circuit, the most successful vaudeville chain on the West Coast.[78] Performers signed contracts—often for several years of bookings—that combined Keith and Orpheum routes, and if one circuit rejected an act, the other followed suit.[79] Observers could thus confidently state that "[t]here is admittedly no big-time outside these two organizations."[80] In March 1911, the prominent managers, including Keith, Hammerstein, and

Proctor, formed the Vaudeville Managers' Protective Association (VMPA). The purposes of the association, claimed the directors, were to "encourage a higher standard of morality on the vaudeville stage, in the vaudeville profession, and in the conduct of the vaudeville theaters . . . and to protect [the members] and their business interests against unwarranted attacks."[81] The VMPA cast itself as a defense against the "attacks" of the vaudevillians' labor union, the White Rats of America, which had gained strength in the fall and winter of 1910. Despite their periodic challenges to Keith's centralized control, the White Rats never won any lasting concessions from vaudeville theater owners and managers.

With a monopoly in big-time vaudeville and a significant influence in small-time vaudeville, Keith controlled performers by threatening to blacklist them from the most lucrative tours in the big time, and he bullied managers of opposition theaters by forbidding acts booked on his circuit to perform at competing theaters. By the mid-1910s, Keith had established an extensive bureaucracy of administrators to monitor the quality of acts and maintain the uniformity of bills across the country. Nevertheless, some variation existed in the tastes and standards of theaters in different cities. The manager of Keith's theater in Boston explained why he wanted to keep an act another manager had fired: "Mr. [Edwin] Steven's work may be above the heads of Buffalo audiences for which reason I understand he was canceled, but it can be underlined from Boston that we will gladly welcome such an act every week in the year."[82] Whereas the audiences of big-time vaudeville in New York City were known for tolerating suggestive, flashy material, Boston's audiences seemed to have particularly strict moral standards. In 1909, for example, Carl Lothrop, the manager of Keith's Boston house, noted that he had to change the title of a dancer's routine from "'L'Amour de L'Artist'" to "'In the Artist's Studio' . . . on account of Boston's puritanical proclivities."[83] Despite some regional variation, Keith maintained a national reputation, and individual theaters and performers were largely under his control.[84] The standards established through Keith's extensive administrative hierarchy became the standards of national, big-time vaudeville, and Keith's central booking office assured his dominance of this industry. Keith vaudeville was big-time vaudeville in the United States.

This book focuses on three basic aspects of vaudeville: the audience, performers' acts, and labor relations. Chapter 2 explores the conflicting definitions of Keith's heterogeneous audience. Keith promoted his audience as a democratic mass, although he also emphasized that the mass followed the tastes of the elite. But in unpublished correspondence, managers described a divided audience, portraying patrons in conflict over Keith's standards of respectability and identifying separate segments of the audience based on class, race, and gender. Chapters 3, 4, 5, and 6 are case studies of individual performers and types of performances. These chapters explore the ways inversions of cultural and social hierarchies emerged in women's careers and acts, influenced their reputations, and shaped the definition of vaudeville. Chapter 7 examines the influence of gender and cultural hierarchy on the organization of the vaudeville labor movement. The vaudeville labor movement's identification with low culture initially encouraged performers to see themselves as laborers rather than as artists, and the masculine connotation of low culture contributed to the marginalization of women in the movement. Excluding women from membership for ten years, the White Rats formed a women's auxiliary only after female performers protested the union's policies. The tension between protecting female performers from sexual danger and advocating the equality of women and men in theatrical professions framed the formation of this auxiliary. In these ways, we can see how the eclectic nature of vaudeville and the industry's (sometimes ambivalent) pursuit of respectable women shaped the patrons of the vaudeville palaces, the entertainment onstage, and the labor relations behind the scenes.

LADIES AND NUTS

CULTURAL HIERARCHY AND MASS APPEAL
IN KEITH'S VAUDEVILLE AUDIENCES

In 1888 B. F. Keith opened a vaudeville theater in Providence, Rhode Island, the second house in his chain, and the entertainment proved so popular that he soon moved his operation to a larger theater. Although he was busy with his expanding business, Keith briefly turned his attention away from booking performers, negotiating salaries, and devising advertising schemes to settle a nagging problem in his theaters. Patrons in the gallery (the cheapest section of the theater) were frequently disheveled and drunk, and they often stomped their feet, rocked in their seats, and shouted their praise or condemnation at the performers. Keith was fed up with these patrons' disregard for the respectable reputation he was trying to cultivate, and he felt he had to assert authority over the gallery in his new theater. As he later recalled, sporting neatly trimmed hair and a crisp suit, Keith took center stage during the first performance, squared his shoulders, and glared up at the motley group in the gallery, announcing to them, "'You can't do that here. . . . I know that you mean no harm by it, and only do it from the goodness of your hearts, but others in the audience don't like it.' . . . As I walked off, I received a round of applause from the whole house, including the gallery. And that was the last of the noise from the gallery gods."[1] Written by Keith in 1912, two years before he died, this account of his apparent triumph over the gallery has been reprinted in several histories of vaudeville as a symbol of Keith's ability to draw a diverse audience together with passive, polite standards of behavior and moral, even instructive, entertainment onstage. Keith's congratulatory memory, however, provides only one version of vaudeville's history.[2]

An alternative, less well known incident in the history of the Keith circuit reveals the fragility of administrators' control over their audiences and performers. In 1920 the manager of Keith's theater in Philadelphia directed comedian Bert Fitzgibbon to stop addressing the audience as "ladies and nuts."[3] Fitzgibbon poked fun at vaudeville's pretensions—namely, its claims of uplift through the image of the refined lady patron—and drew attention to the rowdy elements of vaudeville (the nuts or slapstick comedians). Ladylike tastes and ladies did not control the vaudeville audience completely; rather, performers, patrons, and managers struggled over which social groups and tastes would actually rule in vaudeville.[4]

Whereas Keith's publicity emphasized that the audience was a refined, unified mass led by the ladies, in their unpublished reports managers described an audience fractured into many contentious segments: rowdy men and boys in the gallery, elite patrons in posh box seats, and women and children at matinees. Managers' perceptions of such strata in their audiences remained strong in the first two decades of the twentieth century, but the tastes and values of specific groups often surprised Keith administrators since different niches in the audience did not always behave according to the reputations associated with their identities and social status. Vaudeville's construction of a mass audience is therefore best described as the often-surprising combination of "ladies and nuts."

Keith frequently defined his campaign to broaden the vaudeville audience from its traditional base of working-class men (the patrons who had dominated variety halls, minstrel shows, and concert saloons) as an effort to provide democratic entertainment for the masses. He boasted that all patrons would be treated similarly in his theaters and that they could enjoy the same show.[5] Indeed, this circuit opened up new public avenues for white women and provided a common public space in which working- and middle-class patrons, immigrants and native-born citizens, watched the same entertainment. This expansion of the vaudeville audience, however, had clear boundaries at the outset. Keith invited all white patrons who could afford his modest ticket prices to enjoy the opulence of his theaters, the services of his ushers, and the wide range of amusements, whereas African Americans were segregated in Keith theaters and often excluded altogether no matter what they could afford or how respectable they appeared to be.

This analysis of vaudeville audiences builds on recent historical accounts showing that diverse social groups retained ethnic, class, and racial identities as they selectively and strategically participated in the growth of mass culture. Consumers of mass culture drew on the values of their local communities when they interpreted mainstream Hollywood films, listened to the radio, and bought new phonograph records; racial, ethnic, and working-class subcultures shaped the uses and meanings of mass culture.[6] The heterogeneous vaudeville audience, however, offers quite a different perspective on the attempt to incorporate a variety of social groups into a mass audience. Although segments of the vaudeville audience were indeed disruptive (often rebelling against the centralized authority of the Keith circuit), the persistence of ethnic, class, and gender divisions within the audience also bolstered Keith's plan for building a mass vaudeville audience. In fact, Keith and the many managers working for him often seemed to be more comfortable with the construction of their audience as a collection of distinct and varied social groups than with the construction of their audience as a homogenized mass. The persistence of divisions within the vaudeville audience was a precondition of mass culture, not a barrier against it.[7]

An examination of Keith's price scales is an important first step in assessing Keith's claims of democracy and in sketching the outlines of this heterogeneous audience. Although admission prices for Keith's theaters varied over time and from one theater in the chain to another, it is clear that the cost of Keith's vaudeville usually fell in a middle range, making it less expensive than the legitimate theater but more costly than early movie houses, the nickelodeons, which charged a nickel for admission. Generally not the cheapest theaters, Keith's houses were not a "poor man's entertainment" either.[8]

Despite being slightly more expensive than the cheapest amusements, Keith's theaters tried to lure patrons away from the lower-priced venues. Some Keith houses, for example, had ticket prices as low as a dime. Keith and Proctor's Union Square Theatre in New York City charged 10 cents in 1911 for some seats, and Keith's theater in Providence also advertised a price of 10 cents in 1915.[9] *Keith News*, the weekly publication of Keith's theater in Providence, asserted that the price of 10 cents made vaudeville accessible to the working classes and that "[w]e aim to attract and please them as much as we do the mon-eyed people."[10] Furthermore, even theaters with prices higher than 10 cents addressed publicity to patrons who usually paid only 10 cents for their entertainment, claiming that Keith's vaudeville was worth the extra money because "expensive shows such as [Keith offers] are very, very cheap at our prices."[11] Even with 15 cent rates, Keith theaters were clearly trying to attract the working-class patrons who were identified with the cheaper amusements.

Although many vaudeville theaters (particularly those with 10 cent seats) were accessible to some blue-collar laborers, the vaudeville audience was probably dominated by the burgeoning class of white-collar workers, as previous historians have claimed. The growth of salaried workers such as government employees, clerks, and managers helped expand and consolidate a middle class that first emerged in the early nineteenth century.[12] Comprising 2.4 percent of the work force in 1870, clerical and sales positions increased to 11 percent by 1920. It was this group of white-collar workers who, with more vacation time and usually more money than blue-collar employees, contributed heavily to the rise of commercial amusements around the turn of the century.[13] Surveys of wage earners' budgets in the early twentieth century provide some clues about the leisure pursuits of these workers. In her 1907 study of the spending habits of a group of New York City workers, Louise More found that the wives of postal clerks, tailors, and grocers—among the most prosperous workers in her sample—regularly bought

50 cent seats at the theater. The family of a draftsman in an architect's office was particularly invested in commercial leisure, spending money not only to attend the theater once a week during the winter but also to take summer trips to Coney Island. Furthermore, Robert Chapin concluded that although only 25 percent of families earning between $600 and $700 a year (including janitors, waiters, and teamsters) spent money on the theater, 51 percent of families earning between $900 and $1,000 (including tailors and city railroad operators) bought theater tickets. But even if the regular vaudeville patrons were white-collar workers or the most affluent wage earners, as the budget surveys suggest, vaudeville's admission prices, particularly the 10 cent charge, would not have prohibited unskilled, blue-collar workers from attending. Historian Kathy Peiss notes, for example, that female factory workers, who earned between $6 and $7 a week in the early twentieth century, often saved 10 cents for recreation by walking to work instead of paying for transportation and by skipping lunch.[14]

Along with looking at the costs of seats in vaudeville, it is important to consider vaudeville's organization of theatrical space in relation to other venues. Just as most seats in Keith houses were more expensive than seats in the nickelodeons and other 5 and 10 cent theaters, vaudeville theaters were also far more hierarchical than the motion picture houses. The nickelodeons did not offer the "sanctuaries" of reserved orchestra or box seats that vaudeville theaters did: "Any 'white' person with the price of admission could sit anywhere he or she pleased."[15]

Nevertheless, Keith's theaters came far closer to constructing an undifferentiated mass audience than legitimate theaters did, in large part because vaudeville theaters offered a narrower range of prices and made fewer distinctions within the price scale. The legitimate theaters in the Theatrical Syndicate were much more expensive than Keith's vaudeville, particularly in the upper range of seat prices. In New York City, the top syndicate price was $2—twice the highest Keith price between 1907 and 1910.[16] Furthermore, the gap between Keith's high and low prices was much smaller than the gap between syndicate theaters' top and bottom prices. In New York City, the Keith orchestra price was between 35 and 75 cents more than the gallery price, whereas the gap between orchestra and gallery seats in syndicate theaters ranged from

$1.00 to $1.50 from 1896 to 1910.[17] More accessible to working-class patrons than legitimate theaters and, at times, competitive with the "cheap" theaters of this period, Keith's vaudeville thus set prices that allowed a heterogeneous audience to assemble. But the organization and character of this audience remained an open question—the subject of discussion in the public and private accounts of vaudeville.

Promotional materials for the Keith circuit disclose the uneasy balance between cultural uplift and egalitarian goals, between an audience fractured by gender, class, and race and a unified audience. An advertising brochure for Keith's New Theatre in Boston, for example, called attention to the artwork in the theater, claiming that this house would appeal to the "most distinguished and most intellectual clientele that has ever assembled beneath the roof of a variety theater."[18] It compared the theater to an art gallery, emphasizing the "superb panel paintings by the eminent artist, Tojetti." The brochure described this artistic theater as a democratic institution, noting that the gallery was as exquisitely decorated and furnished as the orchestra: "On all sides can be seen evidences that the same careful attention has been given to the comforts of patrons in this section of the house as is bestowed occupants of the more expensive orchestra seats."[19] In an account of his visit to the B. F. Keith Palace in Cleveland, Archie Bell similarly described the theater as a "Palace for the Masses."[20] He marveled at the opulent environment, including artwork in the lobby, available to the masses: "A millionaire's playhouse, a gigantic poor man's clubhouse, one of the most interesting experiments in democracy imaginable!"[21]

Furthermore, Keith confidently claimed "instruction" as one of the purposes of vaudeville, and he emphasized that the tastes of regular patrons were uplifted to artistic standards. Drawn into vaudeville by ragtime, not classical music, the average patron could nevertheless be converted by the more refined offerings on the vaudeville bill. At first, the ragtime fan "fidgets and squirms during the classical selections," but soon the patron is unknowingly educated, explained the author of an article promoting Keith's vaudeville: "He wouldn't have come to hear the classical selections but coming to hear the popular songs and hearing the classics as well, he soon grows to like the latter, thus having his musical tastes improved without really realizing it."[22] Although intending to emphasize the common culture of vaudeville, the author suggested that class differences, emerging through contrasting tastes, endured in vaudeville, since despite some patrons' newfound enjoyment of the classics, they might remain somewhat ignorant, unaware of their own education.

Along with uplifting the masses to appreciate the artwork on the theater walls and on the varied bills of entertainment, Keith tried to bring the manners of the notoriously wild gallery patrons up to bourgeois standards. Keith's descriptions of comfortable gallery seats and well-behaved, feminine gallery patrons emphasized that this theatrical space would no longer be an affront to middle-class sensibilities. *Keith News*, for example, printed a letter from a "feminine patron" thanking the Providence staff for moving her to the gallery. She was "surprised to find how nice it was . . . and comment[ed] upon the honesty of the officer who returned her lost purse to her."[23] Referring to the Providence theater's gallery as the second balcony to avoid the negative connotations associated with the traditional term "gallery," *Keith News* claimed in 1908 that the theater's "second balcony and its patrons are decidedly above the average 'gallery.' . . . [T]he result is that we get an exceptionally fine class of people up there."[24] Keith administrators' problems with the gallery were not new, nor were they unique to vaudeville. In 1802 Washington Irving noted that patrons in the gallery at New York City's Park Theater expressed themselves by "stamping, hissing, roaring, whistling [and] . . . groaning in cadence." Irving added that they threw "apples, nuts & ginger-bread" at spectators below them.[25] This image of exuberant and rough gallery patrons continued throughout the nineteenth and early twentieth centuries. Most legitimate theaters built after 1920 did not include galleries, and the existing galleries were remodeled and renamed "second balconies."[26]

The desire to use the art of vaudeville theaters to cultivate highbrow tastes and polite modes of spectatorship among the masses resembled other campaigns to transform immigrants and the working classes through symphony concerts, foreign operas, and art museums. These attempts to use high culture to remake those who seemed strange and disruptive to elites were, however, often ambivalent. Elites, frequently craving distance from the lower classes, also used exclusive art institutions to protect themselves from the seemingly threatening urban masses. Although cultural arbiters craved an orderly world in which the tastes and values of laborers and immigrants matched their own, they were comforted by the social distinctions that contrasting cultural tastes and social spaces provided.[27] "Culture thus could be used as a force with which to proselytize among the people or as an oasis of refuge from or a barrier against them," explains Lawrence Levine; "the ambivalence that these conflicting urges created runs like a thread through the prolonged discussion of culture that became so prominent in the late nineteenth and early twentieth centuries."[28]

This tension is evident as well in the promotion of the Keith circuit. Although Keith claimed that the many groups in the vaudeville audience were blending together by sharing bourgeois tastes and manners, he also occasionally presented alternative portraits of vaudeville. First he advertised the separate compartments in his theaters, suggesting that elite patrons would be removed from any unsavory elements. A few accounts of Keith's audience emphasized the hierarchical distinctions of the theatrical space. *Keith News*, for example, described a typical vaudeville audience in 1906: an unemployed man and a busy mother, who "has hurried through a big washing maybe to bring her children to the matinee," occupy the second balcony, whereas the "envied social butterflies" sit in the orchestra and box seats.[29] However, Keith publicity sometimes hinted at the triumph of low tastes in vaudeville. According to Keith, even patrons who could afford high-priced seats might choose to buy a gallery seat: "The show is just the same, you can see and hear splendidly, and it's worth a lot to get up among the people who are not afraid to express their pleasure by a little applause. . . . Really, it's contagious."[30] In this case, the vigor of the gallery seemed more desirable than disreputable.

The celebration of art for vaudeville patrons, including the allegedly well-behaved gallery patrons, was part of Keith's attempt to recruit respectable female patrons. The "ideal" female spectator, in turn, became a multifaceted symbol of the elevation of Keith's vaudeville. "Vaudeville is kept wholesome by women," one actress declared in 1916 as she looked back on the early years of vaudeville; "[i]t was women who supported the late B. F. Keith in purifying vaudeville."[31] Publicity for vaudeville portrayed women as morally superior patrons; they were sensitive spectators who appreciated art, not vulgar jokes, and mothers who sought educational entertainment for their children.

Vaudeville's fare, according to much of the advertising, appealed to women's special aesthetic sensibility. Onstage, women of high social stature who performed highbrow acts mirrored the ideal female spectator imagined by circuit administrators. Mabel McKinley, the niece of former president William McKinley, offered opera selections in 1904, and four years later, theater managers marketed one female opera singer as a talented socialite, the Lady of the Green Veil. Charles Lovenberg, manager of Keith's theater in Providence, explained the reasoning behind this publicity gimmick: "This is a woman of grand opera voice or rather a woman who came to me to look for bookings and I adopted this method of presenting her as a mysterious singer appearing incognito. In our advertising we have led the public to believe that she is possibly a grand opera prima donna who needed the money but did not want her name identified with vaudeville or a society woman who did not want her set to know of her professional appearance."[32] The Lady of the Green Veil thus brought both art and elite social status to vaudeville, although her mysterious veil (suggesting her embarrassment) also indicated that vaudeville's refinement was still a work in progress. The presentation of such feminine opera singers was one way Keith extended the nineteenth-century notion that women had an innate ability to appreciate beauty in art. Although they were discouraged from using this emotional, artistic sensitivity to create art or earn any profits from art, women were supposed to use their knowledge of art to make their homes more attractive. A "mistrust of women's artistic capabilities" endured into the twentieth century, but women were increasingly accepted in a few artistic endeavors, such as music training and professional music careers.[33] Women from dramatic, opera, and concert stages often appeared in vaudeville to convey all of the overlapping elements of vaudeville's progress: femininity, art, and morality.

Keith linked women's supposedly domesticated art to the public enterprise of vaudeville by making vaudeville appear to be quite homelike. Publicity for the Keith circuit, for example, emphasized that women and children would be protected in these vaudeville theaters: "Especially has he [Keith] aimed to interest and protect ladies and children, for whose comfort and enjoyment no expense is spared, every modern accommodation being provided for their benefit."[34] As part of this program, managers designed matinees and gatherings especially for women and children and hired "girl ushers" to provide them with "comforts and conveniences" (including booster seats for children).[35] Describing Keith's theater in Cleveland, Archie Bell observed that "the whole, while it is very, very large seems only to be an ordinary-sized house . . . so instead of feeling that you are in a vast auditorium, you have a comfortable feeling of being in the intimacy of the drawing room."[36]

To make theaters intimate and secure for women, managers also sought to eliminate masculine elements of the theater atmosphere. The female ushers, for example, attempted to end smoking in the theaters because "nothing is more annoying to most women than the smoke from cigar, cigarette or pipe," and the managers who hired these ushers held them up as improvements over the often reckless and untidy male ushers. The female ushers were emblems of the neat appearance and courteous behavior expected of all patrons and employees.[37] Discussions of women and children dominated the characterization of the female spectator, but managers addressed women as individual patrons as well. The female ushers, as they domesticated and demasculinized vaudeville theaters, also showed that women outside of family boundaries had a place in vaudeville. And some of Keith's advertisements recognized single women as patrons when they encouraged schoolgirls to attend vaudeville theaters in groups. Keith, for example, praised young women who organized a "theatre club, to go every Saturday afternoon."[38]

Keith's publicity primarily chronicled the circuit's education of the masses, the new image of the gallery, and the refinement of women in the audience. Unpublished sources, on the other hand, paint a different picture. The private recollections of Keith managers reveal that these campaigns were only partially successful. Along with discrediting much of Keith's public image, managers' unpublished reports reinforce the underlying anxieties in Keith publicity, including the tensions between a hierarchically fragmented audience and a mass of patrons and between undisciplined masculine spectators and polite feminine patrons. With one eye on Keith's "Sunday school" standards and another on profits, Keith managers recorded their battles against rambunctious patrons who disrupted their audience's decorum and disclosed their pride and sometimes shame in their audiences' shared pleasures.[39]

Since at least 1902, managers on the Keith circuit had been heeding theater operator Edward Renton's advice for the smooth running of vaudeville theaters: to assist booking agents and other managers in scheduling and monitoring acts, Renton encouraged managers to record any "objectionable matter . . . [that] had to be eliminated from an act" and their assessment of the audience's response to the performances.[40] Managers in the Keith circuit included this information in the weekly reports they sent to one another. In these reports managers were supposed to make "a conscientious effort truthfully to record the degree of favor with which each act was received by THE AUDIENCE," according to Renton.[41]

These reports should not be read as authentic accounts of the audience's values and responses, despite Renton's claims, but they should also not simply be dismissed as projections of the managers' personalities and anxieties onto their patrons.[42] These reports need to be taken seriously, in part, because managers had a strong financial incentive to interpret their patrons' tastes accurately. "It should be distinctly understood," wrote one manager in 1904, "that the criticisms are made largely upon what seems to be the opinion of the audience and does not represent the opinions of the writer. The people who pay the money should always be given first choice."[43] Another added in his review of Winona Winter: "Personally I could never see her, but she pleases the audience and it is they who pay to be satisfied."[44] When these managers identified their audiences' preferences correctly, they were able to put together popular bills and their theaters were more successful. These reports are also revealing historical documents because they often include managers' confessions of their mistakes in reading their audiences—disclosures that are indeed rare in published accounts. It is important to keep in mind that these reviews are managers' perceptions of the audience, not unmediated records of audience behavior, but also that these authors were highly motivated to offer the most accurate portrait possible and recorded adjustments to some of their traditional biases and expectations.[45]

Cultural Hierarchy and Mass Appeal

In their unpublished correspondence, managers focused on how disparate groups fit together in the audience. Did elite patrons set themselves apart from average vaudeville patrons, or did these groups blend together? How could managers break the gallery's distinctive hold over vaudeville? They most often perceived hierarchical divisions of class and gender between their customers, although at times they hoped for mass approval and the dissolution of social boundaries. Keith administrators, however, were much less ambivalent in their treatment of black patrons: they supported racial segregation, preferring to keep black customers outside of the often unpredictable and fluid mixture in their theaters.

In particular, Renton instructed theater managers to create a racially divided balcony, with the rear section reserved for African Americans, and to provide a "separate ticket window and stairs for the negro patrons."[46] Most popular in the urban centers of the Northeast, Keith's circuit participated in the increasing racial segregation in the North in the early twentieth century, despite civil rights laws prohibiting racial discrimination. An Illinois civil rights law, passed in 1885, outlawed racial discrimination in public accommodations, municipal services, and schools, and laws in New York and Pennsylvania also prohibited racial barriers in public facilities and theaters.[47] Regardless of these laws, however, racial discrimination intensified in northern cities, as restaurant, theater, and hotel proprietors discouraged the patronage of African Americans. Historian Allan Spear's description of an increasingly "biracial" Chicago in the early twentieth century applies as well to other northern cities in which vaudeville, particularly the Keith circuit, was growing in popularity.[48] Entertainment entrepreneurs regularly ignored the civil rights laws, convictions under the laws were difficult to win, and the penalties for violation were usually insignificant, sometimes as low as $5. In 1910 a Chicago jury sided with a theater that had denied an African American patron a seat on the main floor, and Chicago theaters regularly defied the state's antidiscrimination laws in their publicity, one theater proclaiming in 1913 that African Americans would not be allowed to sit on the main floor.[49]

It is not surprising, therefore, that the managers of Keith's houses tried to segregate African American customers in their theaters and were alarmed when these patrons demanded equal treatment. In 1914 black comedian Bert Williams's performances at Keith's Hippodrome in Cleveland drew negative comments from the manager: "A dark cloud hovered over Cleveland yesterday afternoon and last night. It hesitated and then entered the Hippodrome lobby. The cause was Bert Williams. The United States census shows that there are about three million dark skinned humans in this country, and after a close count yesterday I believe that four of them were absent. Naturally, most of them wanted to sit downstairs or in the boxes."[50] Similarly, in his evaluation of Cooper and Bailey, a team of black comedians and singers, manager Harry Daniels remarked in 1903: "With lawsuits on our hands and 'niggers' insisting on boxes and front orchestra seats, I think Mr. Albee will cut out coon acts in the future. We do not need them, and they draw an element here that we do not want to cater to. Had more trouble today on the opening and had to sell front seats to coons which drives away the regular patrons."[51] These reviews demonstrate not only managers' antipathy toward African American customers but also their frustration over these patrons' refusal to either stay away or remain in a segregated balcony.

African Americans battled against vaudeville's segregation policies, as well as discrimination in other entertainment venues. The popular African American newspaper, the *Chicago Defender*, urged African Americans to "sue every time they are refused in theaters."[52] In May 1911 Wallace Paldrow sued a motion picture theater in Lima, Ohio, after he was denied entrance. He subsequently won his lawsuit, based on an Ohio civil rights law, and the theater owner was fined.[53] Along with protesting their exclusion from theaters, African American patrons also objected to their segregation in theaters. *Crisis* reported that an African American man who had been barred from sitting on the first floor of a theater in Los Angeles won a lawsuit, receiving $50 for damages and costs.[54]

Black patrons had the reputation of being indecent spectators—too dirty and wild for Keith's vaudeville. In the 1916 film, *Two Knights of Vaudeville*, two black men, dressed in ill-fitting old suits, find tickets to a vaudeville show on the street. They put on fancy clothes (top hat and tails), pick up their dates, and take their seats in a fancy box in the vaudeville auditorium. The men then behave horribly, leaning over the edge of their box seats, ogling the white female singer (identified as Queenie Singer), and imitating the contortions of Mademoiselle Azora, the Bending Girl. The black women try to control their escorts but cannot prevent them from jumping up and down and fighting with each other. Finally, the men's dog sneaks into the theater, trips the juggler onstage, and joins its owners in their seats.[55] Animals and African Americans, particularly men, are represented as base elements that disrupt the order of vaudeville.

Considering these images of black patrons, it is somewhat surprising that managers' reports did not mention the misbehavior of African Americans in Keith's vaudeville theaters. In their private reports, Keith managers focused primarily on African Americans' access to their theaters, rarely describing any unruliness of African Americans in the theaters (beyond their refusal to sit in their assigned seats). Although African Americans may have participated in some of the gallery's antics, managers did not point to black audience members in particular. Perhaps black patrons who gained entrance to Keith's theaters were so invested in disproving their reputation for being indecent that they did not dare attract attention by displaying any raucous behavior. Also, perhaps African Americans were too isolated in these white-dominated theaters to express their tastes and demands as exuberantly as other groups did. Furthermore, African Americans' access seems to have been regulated so strictly that any tensions about black patrons' position in relation to white performers onstage (would they, for example, gawk at and insult white women onstage?) were safely subdued. Some legitimate performers were concerned about their association with animal acts and blackface acts onstage, often stipulating that they would not perform on a bill with blackface acts and complaining about being positioned next to an animal act. But the presence of black patrons in the audience does not seem to have been as threatening to these actors and actresses since they did not usually disclose anxiety about being linked to or contaminated by black spectators in Keith's houses.

Managers' attempts to segregate African Americans made race the most pronounced social division in Keith vaudeville theaters, but managers also perceived gender and class divisions among white audience members.[56] They seemed confident that men and women and members of different classes liked different acts and congregated in separate sections of their theaters. According to one manager, for example, a playlet by Henry Miller was "intensely dramatic in spots, the comedy being almost entirely eliminated. Our orchestra and box patrons can appreciate his work—it will be lost on the balcony and gallery."[57] In his discussion of the Patty Brothers' "head walking," the Detroit manager saw similar divisions in his theater: "Personally I do not believe that his head jumping appeals to anybody except the degenerates in the gallery. It is shocking to those of finer sensibilities and can only result in the mental and physical disability of the performer."[58]

Such a compartmentalization of social groups and tastes in the theater suited the smorgasbord of the vaudeville bill. As Robert Snyder concludes, "[V]audeville . . . was based on a simple idea: stage shows with something for everyone."[59] Managers frequently observed that parts of a bill or even sections of individual acts appealed to particular groups in the theater. The Pawtucket manager, for example, praised violinist Rae Eleanor Ball on April 10, 1916, because her music was "varied to suit all classes."[60] In 1920 the Philadelphia manager advised vocalist Daisy Nellis to diversify her act, which was suffering in vaudeville because it was "for lovers of high class music as she plays only classical numbers. . . . [A]t least one popular number would have helped."[61] Managers' depictions of different segments of the audience embracing or rejecting individual acts or parts of a single act on a vaudeville bill reinforced the dichotomy between high and low culture and its correlation with social class. They easily translated the variety of vaudeville programs into a hierarchy of high and low taste and class identity.

The nature of comedy was often at the heart of a manager's evaluation of an act's appeal to different classes in the audience. In his February 17, 1908, account of Caron and Herbert's athletic and comic act, the Philadelphia manager described the appeal of their low comedy to the gallery: "The comedy is particularly pleasing to the gallery. This finish where the comedian pretends to jump into the seascape curtain pulling it down disclosing the stage hands behind it got a big laugh."[62] Film and vaudeville historian Henry Jenkins chronicles the rise of a new style of humor that included gags or "bits" dissociated from narrative continuity and an emphasis on the emotional and physical "mechanics" of laughter rather than the intellectual appreciation of humor.[63] The new humor was based on physical comedy—pratfalls, broken dishes, and tussles onstage—as well the uncontrollable physical response to these gags, "a visceral reaction to crude shock, intense stimulation, and immediate sensation." According to Jenkins, the popularity of the new humor intensified debates about the value of high versus low humor—moral humor that inspired reflective laughter versus amoral humor that elicited uncontrollable laughter.[64] Managers attempted to suppress the unrestrained behavior of low comedians onstage and the uncontrolled response of low patrons to these antics. But managers' language also suggests that the rowdy responses they associated with low patrons often became the norm of vaudeville appreciation.

Consistent with their organization of theatrical spaces according to social class, managers often associated low comedy with the gallery patrons. When Brown, Harris, and Brown presented a "disjointed affair" of singing and comedy in Cleveland on April 9, 1906, "the balcony and gallery thought it immense," wrote the manager, but "[t]hose in the orchestra and boxes did not much care for it."[65] In his review of blackface comedians Coakley and McBride, Keith manager Charles Barnes identified rough, "blue" comedy with the gallery: "This is essentially a gallery act. The talk is coarse, even indecent at times. They received two curtain calls but almost all the applause came from the gallery and balcony."[66] In this case, the racial masquerade coded the act as low, appealing particularly to disreputable patrons. After his January 28, 1918, performance, Steve Freda found that very little of his act was left intact after the manager, Charles Lovenberg, listed his required cuts: "He is offensive to people of refined taste. . . . [Cut] songs 'hot time for the old men when the young men go to war' and the line in song 'broke her wicky, wacky woo'; omit last encore and don't invite audience to sing."[67]

On February 17, 1908, the Philadelphia manager wrote that Felix and Barry's act included "a lot of knock about and grotesque comedy which tickled the gallery."[68] If we take "tickle" literally for a moment, we can imagine the volatile audience/performer relationship managers were trying to control. Although Felix and Barry only metaphorically reached into the gallery and provoked patrons' involuntary laughter, many other vaudeville acts ridiculed, addressed, and threw objects at the audience. These routines were troubling to managers because they encouraged audience involvement, a violation of the standards of audience restraint and passivity that circuit administrators were trying to impose. In 1906 the Cleveland manager worried that the excesses of Louis Simon and Grace Gardner's act were particularly offensive to those in the orchestra seats: "While there is no doubt that the act created a great deal of laughter, I think it is a little bit rough for our orchestra patrons. In knocking the dinner off the table Mr. Simon succeeded in wetting nearly everyone in the first row of the orchestra seats. Food, sawdust, rice, etc. were thrown about in such a reckless manner that a man took an awful chance in sitting in the first five rows."[69] Managers also frowned on acts that staged disruptions in the audience, including a performer posing as a patron who interrupted the act in some way. The Woonsocket, Rhode Island, manager reflected on the implications of such tactics for the reputation of "up to date vaudeville" in 1914: "This business of [a] performer upon stage being interrupted by his partner running through audience, tussling with house attachés and clamoring for permission to go upon the stage is a bit of by-play that has long since served its usefulness as constituting real up to date vaudeville. It might appeal to some, but it grates harshly upon the finer sensibilities of a cultured and refined audience."[70]

The sanctity of the "fourth wall" was also violated by patrons who sought to alter the course of acts onstage. Managers described their attempts to regulate gallery patrons' behavior (including interruptions and negative responses) as a way of protecting the refined clientele. For example, when Princess Baratoff's Russian songs met with a cold reception on October 9, 1911, the "riffraff in the gallery" tried to drive her offstage, but they were "quickly suppressed . . . by the house officers."[71] For the most part, however, managers seemed exasperated—often helpless—in the face of the gallery patrons' behavior. In fact, managers' reports suggest that the gallery patrons' uproarious expressions of disapproval were commonplace. When Solomon, known as a "champion freak," appeared in Cleveland on February 19, 1906, he apparently aroused a strong reaction from the gallery: "The Monday afternoon audience landed on him before he was on stage five minutes. I am sorry the act is here. It was impossible to keep the boys in the gallery from guying him, and the people in the orchestra seats did not seem to enjoy it."[72] According to managers, gallery patrons were not only more vocal than people in other sections of the house in their negative responses but also more likely to interrupt or sing along than the orchestra or box patrons. In an attempt to distract and disrupt Emma Carus's "classical" singing, the "boys in the gallery whistled a low refrain to one of her songs, but instead of disconcerting her, it had quite the contrary effect and she encouraged it."[73]

Despite managers' disdain for gallery patrons' riotous behavior, they often described the most successful vaudeville acts as "riots," conveying the exuberance incited by an act as well as the ongoing influence of the low in vaudeville. On March 23, 1908, Eva Tanguay's performance, for example, was labeled "a riot!,"[74] and several years later, Nellie Nichols created similar excitement: "This young lady walked on and just grabbed the audience by the neck and held them as long as she pleased. She has played here before but never has been a riot. . . . [I]t may be that the audience had heard enough close conversation in the preceding act and that they were a little skeptical about what was going to follow: so they thought they would hold Miss Nichols for about thirty minutes and get their money's worth right then and there."[75] These accounts of "riots" correspond with other terms managers used to convey the success of acts. For example, Providence manager Lovenberg stated that W. P. Cahill "drew the first real blood of the afternoon."[76] Managers interpreted these riotous responses as mass approval, in which the familiar divisions between high and low dissolved. The violent language in these descriptions thus portrays highbrow patrons, who usually appeared to be reserved and haughty, as swept away in the pleasures most often associated with lowbrow patrons.

Managers seemed to distrust these riotous moments, and although they often stated that the patrons' tastes would determine the course of vaudeville, in a few cases they disregarded the pleasures of the "low" patrons in their audiences. Charles Barnes's evaluation of James A. Kiernan's 1906 act, *The Taming of the Beast*, reveals a rejection of gallery patrons' preferences: "The theme of the act is not a pleasant one and at times borders on the risqué. It deals with the son of a rich man infatu-

Publicity photograph of Eva Tanguay for her January 6, 1908, performance in Providence. Known for her wild personality, her sexually brazen performances, and her temper tantrums backstage, Tanguay was almost always a showstopper, although managers cringed when she ignored Keith's guidelines for moral, family entertainment. Courtesy of Special Collections, University of Iowa Library.

ated with an adventuress, who finally wins over the old man by her witchery. There is a lot of 'go' in it, but it appeals to the gallery rather than to the orchestra. . . . In fact the whole act should be toned down. Many laughs throughout, and the finish after rousing good song was satisfactory. . . . Never want to play this act again . . . as it does not appeal to the class of people who are our patrons."[77] Troubled about the act's apparent success (the "laughs throughout" and the "rousing good song"), this manager diminished the influence of the gallery by rejecting future engagements of *The Taming of the Beast.* Perhaps such rejections were tied to managers' embarrassment about their audiences' poor taste. Managers may have resembled the so-called respectable patrons who felt guilty when they enjoyed vulgar acts. Another Keith manager was displeased by the success of a slapstick routine, *Fun in a Boarding House.* "Of course, it gets many laughs," he admitted, "but when it is all over, people seem to be sore at themselves for having been amused at such a bunch of rot."[78] The "riots" of vaudeville were probably often shaded with denial and shame, as some managers and patrons attempted to distance themselves from the immediate physical and emotional pleasures of the slapstick acts and the sensual routines.

But how did highbrow acts, the alternative to these provocative stunts, fare in vaudeville? In her 1914 portrait of vaudeville, Caroline Caffin suggested one answer.[79] She observed that the vaudeville managers' central task was to meet the demands of the "contrasting elements" in vaudeville's "democratic" audience while avoiding the demon of highbrow entertainment, "for it is the first law of the cult of Vaudeville that 'Highbrow Stuff Never Pays.'"[80] Although "Highbrow Stuff" did often pay in vaudeville since legitimate performers usually profited greatly from their jumps into vaudeville and their acts at times helped vaudeville managers attract new patrons, Caffin is nevertheless correct to argue that the controversy over highbrow acts was tied to the contrasting elements in the vaudeville audience. Managers recruited highbrow acts such as grand opera vocalists and Shakespearean actors in their attempt to cater to the "best" and, in their public rhetoric at least, believed the multitude would follow. Their correspondence with other managers, however, reveals an uneven, often hostile, response to artistic acts.

When sophisticated acts failed, as they often did, managers blamed their downfall on their audiences' intractable ignorance and bad taste. The manager of the Bijou Theatre in Woonsocket, for example, explained that Loradoe's reproductions of "priceless art" in living statuary "received little in the way of applause [and was] a trifle too elevated perhaps for many. . . . After running two or three looms all day, or taking care of 3 or 4 spinning frames, many of them could not be expected to manifest any great degree of interest in the classic lore of ancient art. Some of them are still wondering as to who Preserpine [Persephone] and Galatea might have been. Many of us are undoubtedly somewhat 'rusty' in our Mythology, the beautiful legendary lore of ancient Greece, the figures of which have been so immortally perpetuated by the masters of the old, old school. But it is all a bit too 'high' for Woonsocket."[81] And the "high class act" of Ethel Walker's company was "over the [audience's] heads," according to the manager of Pawtucket's Scenic Theatre in 1918. He also complained that Walker's salary of $125 was too "much money for a classic act for the thick heads we get here."[82] The Woonsocket and Pawtucket managers' comments can, in part, be attributed to the difference between big-time theaters and small-time houses in secondary cities like Woonsocket and Pawtucket. The Union Hill, New Jersey, theater manager, for example, explained that Grayce Scott's condensed dramatic play was "too talky, lacks action, and needs stage management" but that "it might appeal to the high brows in some of the big cities where Miss Scott has some drawing power."[83]

Although Woonsocket patrons may have differed from their more "cosmopolitan" counterparts in Boston, New York City, and Philadelphia, even managers in big-time theaters sometimes characterized their audiences as uncouth and uneducated. Robert Larsen, manager of Keith's theater in Boston, wrote that the audience "listened politely" to G. Aldo Randegger, a "classic" Italian pianist, "but it was very evident that the greater majority of them were merely bored. When they come to Keith's they want vaudeville."[84] The Metropolitan Operatic Quartette, explained another reviewer, "will draw the lovers of grand opera but the hoi polloi of vaudeville will not appreciate it."[85]

Regular patrons may have been bored by concert pianists, but the new elite spectators often rejected the standard vaudeville fare. Actress Lily Langtry's 1906 engagement on the Keith circuit exemplifies managers' battles to convert these new customers to vaudeville. Describing Langtry's appearance in Philadelphia, manager Charles Barnes wrote: "[E]very word and gesture is of the highest culture and distinction. . . .

Cultural Hierarchy and Mass Appeal

[T]he advance sale of box and loge seats is flattering." He further explained that "this was distinctly a Langtry house today. 70% of the audience are women and probably 50% of these are comparatively new to vaudeville. For that reason there was not as much applause for the vaudeville acts as would otherwise have been expected."[86] Two months later, her appearance in Boston elicited similar comments from Keith's management. Explaining that the downfall of the Merkel Sisters was due to "the preponderance of Langtry patrons instead of the real vaudeville people," the theater manager added: "It must be remembered that this is Langtry's second week and that a large portion of the afternoon attendants are in solely to see her and care for nothing else."[87] Perhaps afraid of sullying their social status by attending vaudeville, Langtry's fans made sure they stood out from other patrons. It is not difficult to imagine these viewers applauding Langtry but turning away, bored and disgusted, from the Merkel Sisters, perhaps to whisper a few judgments to a friend or spouse, confident of their superiority over regular vaudeville patrons and the Merkel Sisters. But, as we will see, the division between "hoi polloi" and the "lovers of grand opera" was not always this clear in vaudeville.

The "thick heads" and "degenerates" in the audience surprised managers on several occasions when they applauded highbrow acts.[88] Although vaudeville publicity claimed that elite tastes and behavior were replacing the gallery's traditional antics, managers' accounts suggest that the gallery's refined preferences were, in fact, a shocking oddity. In 1921 the manager of the Scenic Theatre in Pawtucket recorded his reaction to Richard Kean and Company: "A high class act, all the scenes were very well done, to my surprise the act went very good, I was afraid it would go over the heads of the audience."[89] Of Ralph Smalley's cello solo on September 23, 1909, the Woonsocket manager wrote with similar amazement that "the music is all classical but caught even the gallery here."[90] Another manager reflected on his colleagues' errors in predicting the gallery's intellectual level. Noting the popularity of a sketch based on Charles Dickens's literature, the manager of Keith's Hippodrome in Cleveland confessed that "I think we often image [*sic*] that some things are 'over their heads,' when such is not the case."[91]

In fact, some evidence suggests that managers were more comfortable looking down on gallery patrons, scolding them as if they were undisciplined children, than celebrating their audience's apparently unified appreciation of highbrow acts. Their descriptions of these occasions often mentioned the familiar (and in some ways reassuring) dichotomy between highbrow and lowbrow patrons. In 1908 the Detroit manager explained that the Basque Quartette, although "singing all in French and [presenting] all operatic selections [was] a rich treat for our box patrons and . . . also holds the closest attention of the gallery and balcony."[92] This review diminishes the gallery patrons by referring to them as merely attentive, whereas it praises the elite patrons for savoring a "rich treat." Another manager, surprised to see the spectators in the lower-priced seats applaud Adelaide Norwood, remarked: "I didn't expect much from the afternoon crowd with our popular price balcony, but both balconies 'ate it alive.'"[93] According to managers, elite patrons' tastes were delicate, but lower-class customers' enjoyments were somewhat savage, even when they approved of acts directed at people in higher-priced seats. Finally, pleased and surprised by the diverse appeal of English actor Albert Chevalier, Charles Lovenberg still saw divisions in the audience's response and did not believe that most of the ordinary patrons could fully understand the singer's work: "Unquestionably a great artist and, while no doubt the great bulk of the audience probably do not appreciate him at his full value—especially at the salary received—I was pleased to note today that they are brainy enough to realize the greatness of the man's work."[94]

The descriptions of rough patrons who hungered for slapstick and the images of fragmented audiences were reminders of the failures of Keith's campaign for cultural ascendance. But such trends held their own rewards for managers. Managers could confidently place themselves above the gallery boys when these patrons clamored for messy food fights or a peek at lingerie, and audience members' apparently contrasting tastes suggested that cultural capital neatly matched economic capital. But as managers' weekly reports suggest, the expanded and sometimes blended vaudeville audience was often mysterious and incomprehensible. Often unable to interpret social status from the expression of cultural tastes, managers approached the illusive and unpredictable mass audience with some distrust and confusion.

Managers' candid descriptions of their patrons disclose tensions not only between spectators in the gallery and those in box seats but also between men and women. In fact, managers often cast the contrasts between high and low in gendered terms, with working-class men facing off against elite, polite women. Whether or not the gallery was filled exclusively with men or boys, managers most often referred to masculine patrons in the cheap seats, and they coded loud interruptions such as stamping feet and guying performers as masculine. Furthermore, descriptions of gender divisions in the appreciation of acts were also common in managers' weekly reports. The accounts of the reception of two vocalists reveal managers' perceptions of male and female tastes in vaudeville. The Boston manager commented that Camille d'Arville's appearance on May 15, 1905, attracted a "large number of young ladies in the audience this afternoon whom I have every reason to believe came to hear Miss d'Arville."[95] Approximately nine months later, the Cleveland manager noted a similar response to Therese Dorgeval: "She went as well as any vocalist that I have ever heard in this theatre. However, there was a rush for the smoking room as soon as she made her appearance, for we have a lot of 'wise' young men who visit this theatre every Monday afternoon, and they do not like vocalists."[96]

Whereas "boys" emerged as the perpetrators of gallery antics and fans of rough comedy, "ladies" appeared to be the censors of vaudeville acts. Describing a fire-eater's performance in Pawtucket on September 27, 1909, a manager wrote that he "eats hot wax, molten lead, [and] bites of electric light carbons." To assuage concerns about the acceptability of this behavior, he added simply: "Nothing offensive to women."[97] Just as managers invoked women's tastes as an indication of an act's acceptability, they also noted women's disapproval to prove that an act had overstepped Keith's limits. One manager criticized the Castanos' contortion act because "the woman is much too large for this sort of work," concluding that the act was "considered vulgar by many of the ladies in our audience."[98]

The female censor was a multilayered concept: she was not only a prim lady but also a naive child. What ladies and children shared, according to managers, was disinterest in prurient displays. "Women and children are not amused at a drunken ten minute dialogue on a darkened stage. To a man the sketch is not bad," explained Keith's manager in Philadelphia in 1903.[99] World's Trio was also deemed inappropriate for women and children and thus for vaudeville audiences in general: "[T]hese tough acts will not go with our audiences. . . . [W]ith the stage boxes filled with women and children they devoted much time to 'beer' . . . 'highballs' . . . and the worst of all sorts of slang."[100] Given women's association with children, it is not surprising that women's taste appears to be childlike in the managers' accounts. Keith's Philadelphia manager explained that he regarded Batty's Bears, an animal act, "as one of the most interesting of children's and women's animal features obtainable. . . . [T]he big cinnamon bear is harnessed to a wagon containing little black bears, and gets a big laugh from the women and children as it opens the act."[101] Keith's manager in Boston was also dismissive of women's childlike preferences when he explained that Kreisel's animal act "pleases the women and children at the matinees [but is] not of sufficient importance to interest the male patrons."[102]

Just as managers believed female patrons needed to be protected from suggestive material, they also portrayed women as being particularly impressionable and fearful in their weekly reports. The Great Lafayette's sketch had "quite a sensational finish which was startling enough to have a lot of women run up the aisle, out of their seats."[103] Harry Jordan noted on December 1, 1913, that the comedy team of Cressy and Dayne created "continuous and uproarious [laughter] and several times, women were threatened with hysteria."[104] In 1918 the Keith manager in Woonsocket noticed that a mind reader, Madame Ellis "was particularly convincing to women. . . . [F]rom the number of letters received tonight seems as if the women folks . . . fell for this 'hard.'"[105]

The connection between "ladies" and children upholds the definition of the female censor when she is positioned as the protector of her young charges (her maternal instincts enabling her to judge the morality of vaudeville acts), but the equation of women and children also contains some troubling inconsistencies. As a 1906 issue of *Keith News* noted, children were seen as uninhibited spectators: "If they like a thing their applause or laughter is unstinted and spontaneous."[106] This description of children's enthusiasm and unfettered applause resembles managers' comments about gallery patrons' exuberance, although such comments were more often rebukes than celebrations. Nevertheless, children provided one conduit between the behavior of "ladies" and the uproarious, masculine conduct of gallery patrons.

In fact, managers' reports and newspaper reviews also reveal that female vaudeville patrons were interested in more than censorship and children's clowns. Lillian Shaw, a singing comedienne who frequently drew the complaints of managers because of her forward style of comedy, encouraged women's rowdy responses by planting a woman in the audience who would answer her questions according to a prior plan. In Chicago, for example, she "asked the women in the audience if they should marry [and] a woman (a plant) cried no."[107] Press coverage frequently noted that women, more than men, in the audience responded favorably to Shaw's critique of marriage. One reviewer commented: "Her exposition of the woes of married life made every bachelor maid in the house congratulate herself." Another wrote that her song "If I Was Single Once Again" was "good for numerous laughs from the feminine portion of the audience."[108] Shaw herself described the appeal of one of her songs that depicted a terrible marriage: "There is one thing certain[:] . . . more women laugh at the song than men."[109] Such gendered responses to criticisms of marriage occurred in other acts as well. When Ethel Levey appeared at Keith's theater in Philadelphia in 1907, women in the audience were particularly enthusiastic because they knew she had recently won a divorce from her husband, comedian George M. Cohan. She received "prolonged advance applause," according to theater manager Charles Barnes, "probably owing to the fact that she has just been victorious in her divorce suit and all the women sympathized with her."[110]

One vaudeville playlet, *In 1999*, written by William C. DeMille (film director Cecil B. DeMille's brother), shows how women in vaudeville expressed their pleasure at seeing women take over the "men's" world onstage. DeMille's futuristic sketch presented women at the helm in the business world, social clubs, and the movies. Men, according to one manager, were portrayed as "effeminate and hysterical . . . doomed to remain in the home for housework and also to be the object of affection for the bold female of business."[111] Such a reversal of gender roles and hu-

*Lillian Shaw. Shaw's humorous criticisms of marriage seemed
to please women in the vaudeville audience more than men.
Courtesy of The Harvard Theatre Collection, The Houghton Library.*

miliation of men seemed particularly delightful to vaudeville's female patrons. In 1912 W. W. Prosser, manager of a vaudeville theater in Columbus, described women's enjoyment of DeMille's playlet: "The idea of social conventions, customs, etc. applying to the man instead of the woman is the nucleus from which are evolved any number of laughs. The acts seemed to find instant favor with both sexes, and the women were especially delighted."[112] Another manager agreed that the playlet struck "particularly the feminine portion of the house."[113]

Keith's family entertainment was based, in large part, on the containment of erotic performances and sexual pleasures among patrons, but managers viewed women, in particular, as chaste spectators. In one of the few reviews in which a manager acknowledged male sexual desire, the "female censor" emerged as the antithesis of the sensuous male. Princess Rajah's sexually expressive dances in 1909 allegedly drew different responses from men and women. According to the manager, she "performed the [Cleopatra] dance throughout without exhibiting anything in the way of a movement that I could see is to the slightest extent off color. . . . [S]ome of the women seem to be shocked to some extent but the men were apparently pleased."[114] Lovenberg, in addition, recognized that Dora Ronca's sensual movements attracted male patrons: "The first part of Miss Ronca's act fell decidedly but she managed to pull up at the finish with her 'Dixie' and patriotic music; not because any part of her playing was good but because of the roll of her eyes and gyrations of her body. From the standpoint of a musician Miss Ronca is exceptionally bad . . . but she catches the boys."[115]

Women also surprised managers by showing some erotic interest in particular acts. Juggler Paul Conchas's October 9, 1915, performance challenged the Boston manager's assumptions about the female censor's objections to sensual displays of the body: "The only thing I feared last week was that his feats were really too astounding to look at, especially for women, but all his work was strongly applauded today."[116] Although this manager claimed that Conchas's feats—perhaps juggling knives or cannon balls—were the source of his anxiety, he may also have been concerned about the display of the juggler's body since publicity photographs of jugglers sometimes highlighted their nude, muscular torsos.[117] Another incident, in which women enjoyed the reenactment of a boxing match, revealed a similar connection (somewhat erotic) between women and male athletics: "[D]uring the fight proper the audience became thoroughly worked up, a great many of the men and a lot of the women in the audience becoming very much interested and getting into the spirit of the thing by yelling and cheering, a most unusual demonstration for this house."[118] The audience reaction to this competition in vaudeville may have been unusual for various reasons, including the volume of yelling and cheering, but one of the manager's reasons for describing this response as uncharacteristic was undoubtedly the extent to which women joined in this male pleasure. Women not only were enjoying a male-oriented sport from which they were traditionally denied access but also were "worked up," a state of excitement usually designated as masculine. This was not the first time entertainment entrepreneurs had been caught off guard by women's attraction to male bodies and the physical competition of boxing. The 1897 film of a heavyweight championship bout, *The Corbett-Fitzsimmons Fight*, attracted large numbers of women. Although the film version did not replicate the viewing conditions of a live boxing match—traditionally a male-dominated event—it still suggested women's sexual titillation and sporting zeal.[119]

Managers did not openly address women's sexual pleasures as patrons, but they hinted that women's libidos were a factor in the popularity of one type of performer: the strong man. Eugene Sandow, a strong man of the early twentieth century who was famous for his weightlifting feats as well as his fig-leaf costume, reportedly appealed particularly to women in 1903. "His innovation of giving talks on physical culture at the afternoon performance," explained Keith's Detroit manager, "is a hit with the women folk."[120] This manager was careful to emphasize that Sandow's talks, not the display of his body, pleased female patrons, but the fact that he arranged a special afternoon session revealed that he recognized women's enthusiasm for Sandow onstage and offstage. Even when women in the audience were not specifically described as fans of strong men, managers' reviews of these performers point to some tensions surrounding female spectatorship. Al Treloar was an improvement over Sandow, according to one Keith manager in 1904, because he had "less affectation and appeals to the audience more as a manly man."[121] The muscle-bound Sandow may have been considered effeminate because of his posing onstage—a "feminine" display of the body. As Miriam Hansen has argued about Rudolph Valentino, when men become the object of a sexualized gaze, their masculinity is destabilized.[122] The strong men's dependence on a female, sexual gaze went against the grain of the usual relationship between a disrobing woman or a flirtatious soubrette and men in the audience as well as managers' predominant portrayal of the maternal, somewhat prudish, female patron.

These descriptions of the female censor suggest that women indeed gained influence in an audience that was becoming increasingly restrained physically and emotionally, as Richard Butsch has argued. But their participation should not be read as insignificant because women's responses seemed to weigh heavily in many managers' evaluations of acts. Managers listened to women's comments and watched their facial expressions for signs of disapproval. Concerned about a performer's frequent use of the word "hell," one manager wrote: "I noted the faces of the ladies around me and failed to discover one sign of disapproval."[123] As we saw earlier, managers tried to suppress gallery patrons, often overlooking or minimizing their preferences, but the examples of the female censors' influence suggest that the managers heeded what they perceived to be women's desires. Their recognition of women's sensibilities was, however, somewhat limited since they saw women in the audience as motherly and frail and were surprised by any evidence of their aggressiveness and sexuality. In this light, it is particularly important to remember the multiple ways women took power in vaudeville: through the codes of the female censor (set and reinforced by male managers) and through the appropriation of more masculine behaviors. Although accounts of women's uproarious (masculine) behavior appeared less frequently in managers' reports and in the published descriptions of vaudeville, this avenue of power for women reminds us that women did not simply pacify the vaudeville audience and that their role was not limited to exerting moral and aesthetic influence. Their pleasures and power in vaudeville were not wholly contained in the role of female censor prescribed for them by managers.

The 1901 Edison film, *Rubes in the Theatre*, illustrates many of the tensions surrounding class and gender in vaudeville audiences.[124] Two rubes with long, bushy hair and tattered clothes stand in the first row,

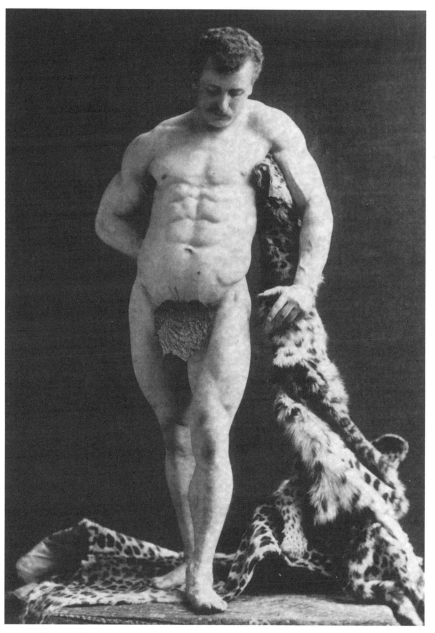

*Eugene Sandow. Although Sandow had a female following in vaudeville,
he was criticized by one vaudeville manager for his lack of manliness.
Courtesy of The Harvard Theatre Collection, The Houghton Library.*

and refined patrons stand beside them and in the row behind them. Waving his arms wildly as he eats an apple and shouts with laughter, one of the rubes is a model of coarse spectatorship. The well-dressed audience members point at him and, glancing knowingly at one another, acknowledge their superiority over the rubes. A woman in a high-collared white dress seems particularly shocked by the country bumpkins. Despite her embodiment of refined femininity, however, she is not a symbol of highbrow spectatorship. She laughs heartily at the rubes and is caught up in the crowd's swaying, clapping, and waving. The spectators fill the screen completely, adding to the impression of a crowd. The physical closeness and jostling among the patrons make them almost appear to be blending together. As the film presents the comic contrast between the rubes and the other patrons, it also illuminates the power of a crowd to level these distinctions. Coded as different and deviant spectators, the rubes nevertheless merge into the crowd.

With women cheering on boxing matches, "hoi polloi" paying attention to literature, and the box patrons occasionally immersed in "riots," vaudeville theaters were sites in which patrons could test new freedoms and cross social boundaries. Any white shopper or worker, parent or child who could afford the price of a ticket could enjoy an assortment of acts from the buffet of a vaudeville bill—from a comedy team's cross-fire act to a scene from a Shakespearean tragedy. The potential for experimentation in vaudeville and the congregation of a diverse audience (of white men and women from a variety of classes and ethnic groups) depended on the construction of spatial compartments with corresponding social groups and aesthetic tastes as well as administrators' claims that the pleasures of the mass were led by the "best" patrons. It was not, however, easy for managers to decipher the fledging mass audience they had so diligently worked to assemble. Often behaving as perplexed parents, these managers were frustrated at their inability to control the behavior of boys in the gallery, frequently bewildered by women's preferences for sports and nudity, and suspicious of an entire audience's enjoyment of Shakespeare. The source of managers' paternal anxieties, these confusions and rebellions were also the basis of vaudeville's excitement and popularity.

LADIES OF RANK

THE ELINORE SISTERS' ETHNIC COMEDY

Popular in vaudeville between 1894 and 1909, Kate and May Elinore portrayed contrasting Irish American characters, women divided by culture, class, and ethnic identity. The many misunderstandings between Kate Elinore's rough and rebellious immigrant women and May Elinore's refined (and usually American-born) women were the basis of the team's numerous comedy sketches. In their most popular sketch, *Dangerous Mrs. Delaney*, Kate Elinore's character (Mrs. Delaney) is newly rich but horribly unprepared for high society, whereas her daughter Rose, played by May, is eager to take her place among the upper crust of society. Rose eyes the mansion; her mother is loyal to her shanty. Kate Elinore portrayed immigrant clowns, and May Elinore, in contrast, presented feminine social climbers who attempted to suppress the clowns' erratic behavior with their lectures on manners and morals. Taken together, Kate Elinore's rank ladies and May Elinore's ladies of rank reveal the sometimes subtle but always pervasive subplots of ethnic, class, and gender hostility in an entertainment industry increasingly preoccupied with feminine respectability.

With their immigrant characters and plots of upward mobility, the Elinore Sisters fit squarely into the tradition of ethnic comedy in vaudeville. Between approximately 1880 and 1905, most vaudeville bills included one to three acts of such "broad and unsophisticated" ethnic comedy.[1] Historians of vaudeville have introduced us to most of the performers—usually male—who specialized in rambunctious ethnic comedy in vaudeville. Joe Weber and Lew Fields, well-known German (also identified as Dutch) comedians, spoke with thick accents and fought each other vigorously onstage. Thomas J. Ryan dressed in ragged clothes and wore a red wig and whiskers in his portrayal of an Irish man always ready to drink and fight, and Julian Rose succeeded in vaudeville with his comic monologues about a Jewish immigrant's mishaps.[2] In his famous act, *Levinksy at the Wedding*, he remarked: "On the invitation it says, 'your presence is requested.' Right away presents they ask for."[3]

Such ethnic comedy declined in vaudeville for several reasons. Various organizations, representing Irish and Jewish Americans, for example, began to protest against negative portrayals of members of their ethnic groups. Theater managers, in turn, began to censure acts they believed would raise the ire of these groups. "Look out and have him cut his comedy Irishman if your town is strongly A. O. H. [Ancient Order of the Hibernians]," wrote the Boston manager in his review of one comedian in 1903. Another warned his colleagues against booking an act with "Hebrew" comedy because "[s]omeday the Hebrews are going to make as big a kick as the Irish did against this kind of burlesque of their nationality."[4] Along with responding to external pressure to clean up ethnic comedy, Keith managers attempted to replace low, slapstick comedy with more subtle and sophisticated comedy to help make the reputation of vaudeville more respectable. Thus, not only did the Elinore Sisters' sketches feature comedy about upward mobility, but also their style of comedy was caught in vaudeville's own crusade for cultural ascendance.

A careful study of the Elinore Sisters' career offers new insights into the history of ethnic comedy in vaudeville. The prevailing emphasis on

Kate Elinore (left) and her younger sister, May. Kate was the comedian,
whereas May played the straight role and looked pretty.
Courtesy of the Billy Rose Theatre Collection, The New York Public Library
for the Performing Arts, Astor, Lenox and Tilden Foundations.

the stereotypes of uncouth immigrants as "ethnic boundary markers separating the bourgeois Americans from the ethnic characters on stage" must now make way for a fuller, more nuanced appraisal of these caricatures—an analysis sensitive to gender.[5] Previous scholars have focused largely on how ethnic comedy reflected American xenophobia around the turn of the century, arguing that the ethnic caricatures in

The Elinore Sisters' Ethnic Comedy

vaudeville not only provided a crude guide to the increasingly multicultural urban landscape but also allowed native-born Americans to find a secure place for themselves in this milieu—a place above the immigrant buffoons onstage.[6] An interpretive framework that includes gender complicates this analysis. First, it provides a window onto the controversies surrounding Kate Elinore's status as a rare female clown. Most of her publicity described her in some way as an exceptional woman who dared to join men in the arena of slapstick, and she built her strong, eccentric female characters on traditions of female impersonation. Second, attention to the gender of immigrant clowns and their foils also shows that the immigrant clowns were not entirely negative figures who soothed patrons' nativist fears of the strange, urban masses. As the Elinore Sisters' sketches and many other vaudeville acts reveal, the immigrant clowns represented the pride of members of ethnic and working-class groups in their battles with stifling female social climbers. Such "civilizing women" were laughed at in these sketches; their repressive rules often seemed ill founded, and their manners grandiose.[7]

This hostility to feminine authority onstage resonated in several overlapping contexts. Irish American women's position as leaders of their families' upward mobility and assimilation was a contentious issue in the Irish American community. Some Irish immigrants believed that the aspiration toward "lace curtain" respectability diminished traditional Irish culture, and others resented Irish women's power to carry out these campaigns for middle-class status. Whereas immigrant women from Ireland frequently worked as domestic servants (closely observing middle-class life in America), the second generation of Irish women in America often experienced greater upward mobility than Irish American men as they moved out of menial service jobs.[8] Literature, musical comedies, and vaudeville all reflected these trends by presenting Irish American women as economically and culturally ambitious, dragging their reluctant husbands and fathers with them.[9] Furthermore, as we have already seen, big-time vaudeville reinforced the notion that women were the primary agents of upward mobility since vaudeville managers advertised the many ways they had redecorated their theaters and reformed entertainment for women. The derision of the female foil (so erudite and orderly) and the celebration of the clown's rebellions in the Elinore Sisters' routines thus lay bare a simmering antagonism toward feminine influence in vaudeville and in the Irish American community.

Kate Elinore's role as a slapstick clown was indeed controversial because she countered a male tradition of ethnic comedy in vaudeville, but more broadly, her performance style raised questions about the definition of a woman's sense of humor. The debate over women's humor in the early twentieth century revolved around the question of whether the enjoyment of "low" comedy, such as slapstick routines in vaudeville, was contrary to women's nature. Constant Coquelin, for example, wrote in 1901 that "[t]he lighter, the more fantastic, the daintier the humorous fancy, the quicker it appeals to a woman."[10] Robert Burdette reiterated Coquelin's conclusions about women's refined humor in 1902: "[T]his sense in her is delicate, sympathetic, refined to the highest culture. True humor delights her, while buffoonery, if it be brutal, shocks her."[11] When women's humor was acknowledged, it was limited to subtle, intellectual, sensitive comedy.

One result of this definition of women's humor was that in male/female comedy teams in vaudeville, the woman's role was usually the "straight" role or the "feeder" for a comic male partner. A manager on the Keith circuit, for example, noted the reversal of traditional gender roles in Hines and Remington's comedy act: "Unusual inasmuch as the woman is not used as the 'feeder' but does most of the work and is really the life of the act."[12] Theater critic Robert Speare saw Kate Elinore as usurping the male comic role; he described the Elinore Sisters as an "absolutely novel woman act. . . . [T]he idea is that of the straight comedian and the rough comedian, only instead of its being two men now it is two women."[13] Vaudeville theater manager Charles Lovenberg referred to Kate Elinore in his assessment of Earl and Wilson's musical comedy act: "This act was a great surprise for in it was found a woman who is actually funny almost as much so as the comedienne of the Elinore sisters. She makes up as an eccentric country girl and has a very funny line of talk, and the novelty of the woman doing the comedy and the man, the straight work, is very acceptable."[14] The Elinore Sisters, with Kate Elinore as a brash comedian, were indeed an odd pair in vaudeville.

The Elinore Sisters' Ethnic Comedy

The commentary surrounding Kate Elinore focused on the exceptional nature of a grotesque female comedian.[15] A December 20, 1906, review noted that Kate Elinore "had determined to carve out a new pathway for herself, one which women had never before trodden. 'I'm going to do something different, something grotesque,' she said."[16] To this end, she wore mismatched costumes, spoke in a gruff voice, and highlighted awkward, often aggressive movements onstage. In 1909 one reporter was surprised by her "low" comedy. "She is one of those marvels Heaven seldom sends us—a truly funny woman," he explained. "She is a low comedienne who does not mind making herself look ugly or ridiculous in order to make her audience laugh."[17] In her 1914 history of vaudeville, Caroline Caffin remembered Kate Elinore's appearance: "Never was a woman less troubled with self-consciousness. Her face is one broad, expansive smile which seems to radiate from the top of her little nob [*sic*] of hair . . . and from every angle of her square built frame."[18] Another reviewer noted that "her make-up is a nightmare of the milliner's art. Her voice makes a fog horn sound like an echo."[19] Perhaps the most striking example of Kate Elinore's eccentric appearance was her costume for a performance on November 30, 1909: "gauze draperies spangled with small kitchen utensils."[20]

Kate Elinore contrasted the vanity and perky sexuality expected of female performers as she cultivated a grotesque style and appearance that conformed to the traditional stereotype of a working-class Irish woman. According to theater historian Paul Distler, vaudeville's Irish characters, male and female, were "a little loud [and] too free spirited for the basically Anglo-Saxon stock."[21] Frequently, actresses portrayed the Irish woman of motion pictures and the theater as a maid who disrupted her employers' middle-class home with her careless mistakes and adventurous spirit. A popular scene in several early-twentieth-century films involved a maid who wreaks havoc when she tries to light a fire in a stove. *The Finish of Bridget McKeen*, an Edison film produced in 1901, shows Bridget struggling to set a fire. After several bumbling attempts, she pours kerosene in the stove. The resulting explosion vaults her into the air in a large puff of smoke. The final shot focuses on her gravestone, reminding viewers of the chaotic, dangerous world of Irish maids. The epitaph reads: "Here lies the remains of Bridget McKeen

*Caricature of Kate Elinore by Marius de Zayas. Elinore chose
a grotesque comic style and absurd costumes over feminine beauty.
From Caroline Caffin's* Vaudeville *(1914).*

who started a fire with kerosene."[22] In addition, Irish vaudeville singer and comedian Maggie Cline was known for her forthright manner and large size. She joked onstage about her weight (allegedly around 200 pounds), and her domineering physical presence added punch to her popular renditions of songs about fighting Irish men, such as "Throw Him Down McCluskey" and "Down Went McGinty": "Maggie put them both over with the same type of hip-swinging walk. She needed all of thirty feet of stage for the combined song and gestures, the hitch of her belt fore and aft, the glance aloft at the galleries as she called on the Irish to help with the chorus, and the sweep around the house of her husky right arm as she illustrated the dramatic moment in the story of McCluskey."[23]

Tapping into the unruliness associated with working-class Irish women in her defiant stage performances, Kate Elinore drew on a tradition in Western culture in which the instability associated with women was also a source of rebelliousness in public displays and protests. In early modern Europe, women and men (often through cross-dressing) incorporated the association between women and the lower body—including reproduction and sexuality—into their social inversions and civil disruptions. "The lower ruled the higher within the woman," explains historian Natalie Zemon Davis, "and if she were given her way, she would want to rule over those above her outside."[24] Although many women argued that women were "*not* by nature more unruly, more disobedient and fickle than men" (emphasis in original), this connection was the source of popular imagery and activity that undermined gender hierarchy.[25] Kate Elinore clearly carried on this tradition, but her performances also point to the ways class and ethnicity shaped the uses of the unruly woman. In ethnic comedy in vaudeville, the definition of particular groups of women (immigrant women, working-class women) as sexually, physically, and verbally excessive provided a source of female comedians' rebellions against male authority, including their adoption of male comic styles of performance in vaudeville.

Kate Elinore's energy and rebelliousness must be considered within the plots of her sketches, particularly in relation to the orderly female characters presented by her sister, May. Filled with Kate Elinore's ranting and physical gags, the Elinore Sisters' sketches focus on a low Irish woman's repeated clashes with social authority and convention. In their sketches, as in many other vaudeville routines, the symbol of acculturation and propriety is an elite woman. In contrast to Kate Elinore's restless and rambunctious characters, the traditional female comic antagonist, exemplified by May Elinore's characters, is thus a civilizing woman.

To understand the tension between order and disorder as well as the struggle against feminine authority in the Elinore Sisters' acts, it is useful to turn first to the interpretative framework established by film and vaudeville historian Henry Jenkins. The contest between an unruly clown and a comic antagonist in the Elinore Sisters' sketches resembles the "anarchistic comedy" that Jenkins has identified in vaudeville and in Hollywood films of the late 1920s and 1930s. Anarchistic comedy depends on the juxtaposition of an expressive, out-of-control clown and a comic antagonist who symbolizes "civilization, all that is stifling or corrupt in the social order."[26] Expressing freedom and energy as they fight against the comic antagonists ("dupes, killjoys, and counterfeits"), the clowns offer the audience an escape from the restraint and control associated with civilization.[27] This identification with the clown corresponds to what sociologists have characterized as a release from the emotional constraints of mass society or a "quest for excitement."[28] Whereas the clown's outbursts address a desire for spontaneity and freedom, the audience's feelings toward the clown remain equivocal because clowns are usually outsiders of some kind—representatives of the "underculture." Jenkins thus concludes that viewers may identify with the clowns—seeking vicarious escape—but that they may also distance themselves from these grotesque characters.[29] In this light, Kate Elinore's characters were indeed more than negative stereotypes, repulsing middle-class viewers with their mismatched costumes and crude manners. Her chaotic characters also attracted vaudeville patrons because they offered moments of excitement and relief from civilizing restraints.

All of the Elinore Sisters' routines contained "anarchistic comedy." Their most popular vaudeville sketch was *Dangerous Mrs. Delaney,* of which there were two versions—one written in 1898 by George M. Cohan (a popular vaudeville performer as well as a sketch writer) and the other written in 1902 by Carroll Flemming and William Jerome. Mrs. Delaney, played by Kate Elinore, is a working-class, immigrant Irish woman who quickly vaults into high society after winning a large financial settlement in a lawsuit she filed because her husband was killed by falling into a city sewer. She disrupts elite social circles by spitting in public places, yelling insults at anyone who challenges her, and punching men at parties. Her daughter, on the other hand, has learned the proper etiquette for her family's social climb and attempts to reform her mother's behavior.[30] But Mrs. Delaney is explicitly valorized in the 1902 version of *Dangerous Mrs. Delaney*. Although her daughter has tried to convince her of the sophistication of her daughter's suitor, Mrs. Delaney is not fooled by his flowery language. She realizes that her daughter's boyfriend is simply trying to obtain the Delaney fortune and rescues her daughter from her fraudulent beau.

Mrs. Delaney fails not only to assimilate but also to attract men. She boasts, for example, that one man at a party said she was the "sweetest woman in cremation" (47). Along with her appearance and vocabulary, Mrs. Delaney's violent reactions are incongruous with respectable behavior. When a "little weasel of a man" requested that she "remove her mask," Mrs. Delaney explains, she "hit him so hard that I had to go to the hospital and have me fist cut out of his ribs" (47). In another instance, she describes a man's comments about her face: "I told him that I had shooting pains in my face he said I used too much powder. I said I thought of having it steamed he said if it was his he'd have it boiled" (82). Throughout these routines, Mrs. Delaney exchanges insults and punches with other characters, chasing away anyone who does not please her and even bringing in heavy artillery to win her battles.

In *The Irish 400* (written in 1897), Mrs. Murphy, played by Kate Elinore, embarrasses her daughter May with her bad manners, her allegiance to Ireland, and her "unfeminine" behavior. For example, after agreeing to join her daughter in a fashionable Turkish bath, Mrs. Murphy confounds her by asking for a glass of mixed ale. On their way home from the bath, May admonishes her mother for spitting on the floor of the streetcar. Mrs. Murphy then spits in the conductor's pocket, and they are kicked out of the car.[31] Later May recounts that her mother interrupted a concert by a famous Polish pianist, Ignacy Paderewski, to ask her, "Phwat county in Ireland did Paddy Roosky come from?" Throughout the sketch, May instructs, cajoles, and scolds her wild mother.[32]

Although these sketches focus on the relationship between mothers and daughters, others feature the struggle between employers and their maids. In *The Adventures of Bridget McGuire*, which toured on the Keith circuit in 1902, an Irish maid bosses her husband and fools his employer. Bridget McGuire, played by Kate Elinore, is a recently unemployed maid married to Judkins, a live-in butler of Mrs. Rapps. Judkins attempts to hide her in his employer's house, hoping to conceal his recent marriage because Mrs. Rapps has a "holy horror of . . . married servants," but Bridget's large appetites—for food and alcohol—soon upset the household. Mrs. Rapps discovers Bridget as she reaches for a decanter of whiskey. Bridget snaps, "That's not the first time whiskey has been the downfall of Ireland."[33]

The ensuing dialogue between Bridget and Mrs. Rapps exposes Bridget's vulgarities and Mrs. Rapps's pretensions. Mrs. Rapps mistakes Bridget for her wealthy, eccentric aunt and flatters her in hopes of winning an inheritance. When Mrs. Rapps offers Bridget some "refreshment," Bridget initially demurs, in a manner that she believes befits a wealthy matron: "No thank you I never drink anything." Nevertheless, she soon "grabs a glass" from her "hostess" and then begins to drink out of the decanter, politely explaining, "If you insist—I don't mind if I take a little drop" (115). Bridget continues drinking throughout the sketch and becomes more and more abusive toward Mrs. Rapps, revealing more of her "true" identity. Describing her belief in spiritualism to Bridget, Mrs. Rapps asks, "Are you afraid of spirits, Auntie?," and Bridget replies, "Not when I can get them by the neck," holding up the bottle of whiskey (116). Bridget's thirst is matched by her appetite for food. When Mrs. Rapps suggests a light lunch, Bridget says she might be able to force down a "few pounds . . . I mean mouthfuls" (117).

Since Mrs. Rapps believes that Bridget is her aunt, Bridget is able to gain power over Judkins, barking orders at him as if she were his boss. At one point, unsatisfied with Judkins's service, Bridget hits him with a roll, exclaiming, "He's a bum servant" (121). The confusion of identities empowers Bridget in two ways: not only is she in a temporary position of authority over Judkins, but also her charade reveals that Mrs. Rapps is a disingenuous groveler. Although Bridget continually errs in her imitation of a society woman, her mistakes intensify the impression of Mrs. Rapps's desperation. When Mrs. Rapps shows her to her room, Bridget remarks that the sofa is "simply supercilious," and later she chastises Mrs. Rapps for being "ordacious" (126). Despite Bridget's malapropisms, Mrs. Rapps strives to please and impress her, still believing she is her wealthy aunt. Furthermore, Bridget's common sense contrasts with Mrs. Rapps's religious beliefs. Bridget, for example, remarks that she always thought a spiritualist was called a "pocketpicker," remaining skeptical of Mrs. Rapps's spiritualism throughout the sketch (116). In these ways, the mistaken identity both reinforces Bridget's coarseness and gives her power over her husband and his employer.[34]

Bridget McGuire seems to be the butt of jokes when she fails to fit into high society, her rough ethnicity emerging despite her attempt to impersonate the rich aunt. But she also offers relief from and rebellion against the comic antagonist. Her energy, ethnic identity, and, at times, common sense are all championed over Mrs. Rapps's rigidity, superior airs, and femininity.[35] Indeed, all of Kate Elinore's maids and mothers (Mrs. Delaney and Mrs. Murphy) reveal that May Elinore's comic antagonists are flawed—stuffy, inauthentic, and domineering. These sketches thus portray the rough, immigrant clown as a hero, casting a positive light on ethnic pride and working-class allegiance. Furthermore, Kate Elinore's characters depict a woman's power to disrupt hierarchies, in contrast to the equation of femininity with repressive social authority in May Elinore's comic antagonists. As opposed to the civilizing woman, the female clown rejects the feminine role, often triumphing over the femininity, class status, and acculturation associated with the civilizing woman.

Kate Elinore's rejection of feminine performance codes and her characters' assaults on elite femininity provide new insights into the uses of ethnic stereotypes in women's comedy. Recent feminist accounts of women's comic performances hold that these performances are open to liberating feminist laughter as well as misogynist interpretations: comic women who violate gender codes call attention to the artificiality of femininity but are also open to attack for their deviation from the

norm. Critics, for example, have pointed to a long line of female characters—from Miss Piggy to Roseanne—who mock the ideal of femininity
by exposing the exuberance, anger, and power beneath the thin veneer
of feminine charm. These women, in turn, have often been the objects
of derisive laughter because of their feminine failures.[36]

Feminist interpretations of women's comic performances have thus
examined the ability of female comic spectacles to undermine gender
roles, but they have often overlooked other aspects of identity and
power, such as ethnicity. The dual readings of women's comic performances—one supporting and the other undermining gender hierarchies—do not, for example, capture the ways in which performers like
Kate Elinore used ethnic stereotypes to attack femininity. Most feminist
critics have been reluctant to acknowledge that female comic performers may articulate their rebellions against gender constraints through
other subordinations.[37] Here we need to explore historian Robert Allen's
argument that the cultural production of subordinate groups should
not merely be read "in terms of its resistance to the power of more dominant groups." Rather, "'resistant' practices might well be polyvalent,
not only directed against those conceived of as 'above,' but constructing
yet another object of subordination."[38]

Kate Elinore's attacks on male authority emerged through her imita-
tions of working-class, immigrant women. In this way, she relied on
class and ethnic hierarchies of women to challenge patriarchy. Although
Kate Elinore (as Mrs. Murphy, Mrs. Delaney, and Bridget McGuire)
treated femininity as a mask to be manipulated and discarded to impress
party guests or fool employers, she was nevertheless clear about what
did not constitute femininity: working-class Irish American women.
Kate Elinore's comic performances were therefore not so much a critique of femininity as an expression of the exclusivity of femininity. Her
caricatures, including rough Irish maids trying to imitate or please
"ladies of rank," actually reinforced the ranking of working-class immigrant women beneath femininity.

The masculinity of Kate Elinore's characters, and even of Kate Elinore herself, was based in large part on the traditions of female impersonation associated with two character types on the stage: the Irish
maid and the "old maid." Kate Elinore drew on both caricatures in her

The Elinore Sisters' Ethnic Comedy

roles. The male performers so often associated with these characters made these women's masculinity part of the comedy onstage. Between 1890 and 1907, the comedy team of Daly and Devere presented an act titled *Bridget's Word Goes* or *The Janitress* in which Daly dressed as an Irish maid—"a most capacious female, pugnacious to a degree and anxious to air her opinions on any and all subjects."[39] The most famous transvestite Irish maids were, however, presented by the Russell Brothers, who began their stage career in the 1870s, approximately twenty years before the Elinore Sisters began performing. Earning their greatest success playing Irish maids in the sketch *The Irish Servant Girls,* the Russell Brothers struck each other with mops and brooms and emphasized their characters' wantonness by raising their skirts periodically. By 1907, Irish "watchdog" groups such as the Ancient Order of Hibernians attacked the Russell Brothers' "misrepresentation" of Irish women, and some Irish organizations began to disrupt the Russell Brothers' stage performances.[40] Since their career overlapped the last half of the Russell Brothers' career, the Elinore Sisters were often compared to this team. In the late 1890s, for example, one reviewer remarked that Kate Elinore's "violent method and her rawboned mimicry are as individual and likable as those of the Russell Brothers."[41] Another reviewer described Kate Elinore as a direct descendant of the transvestite Russell Brothers: "There was a day when the Russell duo laid out any audience that ever appeared, but they shall have to give way to Kate Elinore."[42]

Although the stock character of the Irish maid is most important for understanding the roots of Kate Elinore's portrayals of rough Irish women, particularly Bridget McGuire, her characterizations also rely on the traditional presentations of the "old maid" in vaudeville and early film. Both the "old maid" and the Irish maid lacked femininity and insulted middle-class men and women with their aggression and vigor. Despite her previous marriage, Mrs. Delaney resembles the classic "old maid"—an unattractive man hunter. Although the words to the opening song of the first version of *Dangerous Mrs. Delaney* portray a delicate, desirable woman, it is easy to imagine how Kate Elinore's appearance and movements would have provided sharp contrasts to the lyrics:

Who'll have a chance at something tasty
Not too hasty, slim of wasty [*sic*]. . . .
Gentlemen you have a perfect treat on
Something you can afford to be sweet on.
Chance your luck. Show your pluck.
I'm throwing myself away. (45)

This caricature of the "old maid" as a woman who desperately throws herself at men was popular in vaudeville as well as early-twentieth-century films. Such films as *The Disappointed Old Maid* (1903), *The Old Maid and the Burglar* (1903), and *The Old Maid and the Fortune Teller* (1904) feature sexually aggressive women who are rejected by men and rebuked for their ugliness. The "old maid's" lack of femininity was underlined by the men who sometimes performed this role in vaudeville and in many films. Gilbert Saroni, the most famous of the "old maid" female impersonators, starred in vaudeville and in the films *The Old Maid Having Her Picture Taken* (1901) and *The Old Maid and the Horsecar* (1901). As in *Dangerous Mrs. Delaney*, many of the comic gags in these films focus on the "old maid's" face, which causes mirrors to shatter, cameras to explode, and, most important, men to recoil in horror.[43]

Kate Elinore's physically and verbally antagonistic comedy seemed masculine to observers, just as male performers often seemed most suited to the portrayal of rough Irish maids and "old maids." It is not surprising, therefore, to find Kate Elinore at the center of speculations about her true sex and accusations that she was a transvestite. Several observers, for example, challenged the portrait of Kate Elinore as an exceptional female performer by arguing that she was, in fact, a man. "It's quite a common thing with us to have the daily papers insist that I am a man for reasons all their own," explained Kate Elinore in one article, "and many is the letter received asking us to settle a dispute or wager."[44] In one case, the comedian's dresser announced that she had won $5 for settling a bet about the mystery of Kate Elinore's sex by verifying that she changed clothes in the ladies' room. But the dresser confessed that she was still unsure about whether or not Kate Elinore was a woman. In another article, Kate Elinore described how her "masculine" voice—a voice she allegedly cultivated to replace her "singing" voice—incited debates about her sex. She recalled walking home from a performance and overhearing one man challenge another: "I tell you the big one is a man and no mistake and I'll bet you anything you like on it." Much like her popular stage characters would have done, Kate Elinore interrupted the men and announced (in a "guttural" tone), "Excuse me sir, but you are a liar."[45] Her gruff manner and voice left the men even more confused about her gender. In 1913 Kate Elinore's association with female impersonation was strengthened when she replaced George Monroe, a female impersonator, in the leading role of *All Aboard*, a musical revue by Lew Fields. After Monroe left the show suddenly, "[s]ome one thought of me," explained Kate Elinore; "I stepped into George's part, also into his clothes."[46]

The inquiries about Kate Elinore's sex demonstrate that her slapstick portrayals of immigrant women and flirtatious widows were clearly part of traditions of male performance in vaudeville. Not only did Kate Elinore play the male comic role in relation to her sister's straight role, but also she portrayed stock characters associated with female imper-sonation. In this light, the accusation that Kate Elinore was a man may have been an attempt to erase her rejection of the norms for women's performances. Indeed, the myth of Kate Elinore's hidden manhood re-placed a rebellious woman with a traditional male clown.

This rumor of female impersonation corresponds to several histori-ans' claims that female impersonators in vaudeville were a misogynist response to women's power.[47] Creating a convincing illusion of femi-ninity through their expensive wardrobes, makeup, and manners, the "prima donna" female impersonators—beautiful, glamorous, and fash-ionable—indicated male control over the female image and role as they presented the ideal "woman as ornament."[48] Julian Eltinge, one of the most popular female impersonators in vaudeville, was known for his gowns and expert makeup (his publicity magazine offered beauty se-crets to women). Pointing to Eltinge's authority over femininity, one critic explained that "it takes a man after all to show women the path to beauty. Julian Eltinge has so developed female impersonation that today he is the glass of fashion for the thousands of women in search of beauty secrets."[49] Male performers' impersonation of Irish maids and "old maids" and the myths about Kate Elinore's cross-dressing also helped bolster male authority, but far from creating the feminine ideal (as the prima donna or "glamour" impersonators did), these manly maids expressed the antithesis of femininity.[50] The men who impersonated Irish maids and "old maids" marked particular women as undesirable as they ridiculed sexually aggressive women.

The suspicion that she was a cross-dresser not only softened Kate Elinore's intrusion into the male-dominated field of ethnic comedy but also intensified her ethnic caricature by implying that working-class Irish women were not really women. The confusion over gender in the publicity surrounding Kate Elinore thus exaggerated the manliness of working-class Irish women, reinforcing the class and ethnic limits of femininity.[51]

Kate Elinore was indeed unusual because she occupied the traditional male role in these sketches and drew on the transvestite traditions associated with the portrayal of Irish maids. Nevertheless, the Elinore Sisters' sketches also include many of the traditional elements of vaudeville's ethnic comedy. Although Kate Elinore challenged gender conventions in vaudeville, May Elinore exemplified the feminine role in vaudeville's ethnic comedy—the civilizing woman. The comedy of many vaudeville routines with immigrant characters depends on the fact that a woman is the clown's antagonist, serving as a representation of bourgeois values. For example, in *The Mill Owner's Daughter*, a vaudeville sketch written by M. S. Robinson and H. S. Gibson in 1902, an Irish man and his daughter signify different degrees of assimilation into high society. The authors describe the father as "an uneducated Irishman, who has acquired wealth, but not Polish [*sic*]," whereas his daughter "has been educated and has acquired Polish."[52] And the male/female comedy team of Favor and Sinclair presented a sketch called *The Maguires* in which an Irish plumber clashes with his upwardly mobile daughter.[53]

It is revealing to compare Kate and May Elinore to one of the most popular male/female comedy teams in vaudeville, Thomas J. Ryan and Mary Richfield, because Richfield, like May Elinore, played the classic civilizing woman in the long-running Mag Haggerty sketches in vaudeville. Written by Will Cressy, one of vaudeville's most prolific sketch writers, and performed by Ryan and Richfield, the Mag Haggerty sketches focus on an Irish hod carrier who must mingle in high society after his daughter Mag marries a millionaire. This successful series spanned approximately ten years and includes at least four different sketches: *Mag Haggerty's Father*, probably first performed during the 1901–2 vaudeville season; *Mag Haggerty's Father's Daughter*, produced in 1904; *Mag Haggerty's Reception*, written in 1905 and presented in 1906; and *Mag Haggerty, M.D.*, which toured in 1909.[54]

In *Mag Haggerty's Reception*, Mag Haggerty reminds her father that he will be meeting a "lady of title! of rank!" at an upcoming party. Mike Haggerty responds, "Yis, a rank lady."[55] In *The Irish 400*, the Elinore Sisters' 1897 sketch, Mamie (played by May Elinore) tries to convince her mother (played by Kate Elinore) that her suitor is respectable by telling her that he "comes from a family of rank." Her mother retorts, "[T]he rankest I ever saw."[56] As the resemblance between these jokes suggests, both the Mag Haggerty sketches and the Elinore Sisters' routines focus on questions of rank in immigrant Irish families, highlighting in particular the efforts of ladies of rank to reform the rank characters around them.

In the Mag Haggerty sketches, the woman represents the successful bridging of class and ethnic boundaries, and the man embodies the gulf between bourgeois society and working-class, ethnic life. Tussling with Mag's servants, performing Irish jigs, and confusing Mag by using malapropisms, Mike Haggerty is the source of disorder in these routines. But Mag, through her campaign to uplift her father and impress her elite companions with her highbrow tastes, is also the target of ridicule. In *Mag Haggerty's Father's Daughter*, Mag is unsuccessful in her attempt to move her father from his shanty to her new home on "Cintral Park West." Mike insists that he will "not be a Gintleman" (2). Mike is often the butt of jokes when he is baffled by bourgeois manners and the mysteries of modern technology, such as the telephone. For example, he does not understand the telephone his daughter has installed in his "shanty." He says the voice on the line has "wrinkles in it," and searching in vain for the voice's "body," he asks, "Where the divil is that feller?" (18). But the telephone later becomes a source of Mike's superiority. As Mag leaves, she reminds her father that he can "call [her] up at anytime." He responds, "I'll be more apt to call you down" (20). Mike seems justified in "calling her down" since Mag often looks ridiculous when she puts on airs. For example, she decides to change her name to "Margurite" instead of Mag and calls her father her "paternal parent" in an attempt to appear "refined" (4).

In *Mag Haggerty's Reception*, Mag tries to teach Mike the proper manners for an upcoming party, which he refers to as a "deception" (12). When Mag tells him to say "I'm glad to meet you" to guests even when he isn't "glad," Mike exclaims, "I tould you I had the name of this thing right! DE-ception" (14).[57] Later in the sketch, when Mag is teaching Mike to read, the student, in some ways, knows more than the tutor. Mag tries to get him to identify three letters—A, P, A—and Mike becomes enraged, knocking over the chalkboard, because these letters are the abbreviation for the anti-immigration American Protective Association. Although Mag insists that they are simply letters of the alphabet, Mike concludes that "[t]hey amount to a whole lot—if you tie them together right" (11–12). The plots of these sketches allow Mike Haggerty to preserve his pride and masculinity at the expense of the civilizing woman.

Taken together, the comedy teams of the Elinore Sisters and Ryan and Richfield emphasize the dual images of Irish women—as civilizers and rebels—and show how the contrasts between masculine and feminine behavior framed both teams' comedy. Featuring an exceptional female clown who was often accused of being a man, the Elinore Sisters' sketches demonstrate, in particular, that the juxtaposition of masculinity and femininity reinforced the battles between the clown and the comic antagonist even when a sister act deviated from the more traditional male/female combination. The Mag Haggerty sketches and the Elinore Sisters' acts show that the ethnic clown was often valorized, whereas the femininity and acculturation represented by the civilizing woman were degraded. But the Elinore Sisters, as opposed to Ryan and Richfield, drew on the tradition of the masculine, working-class Irish woman to bring chaos and exuberance into the immigrant families in these sketches. Unlike Mike Haggerty, Kate Elinore's characters do not simply outwit, embarrass, and escape a suffocating feminine authority. Instead, they present an alternative version of female power that contrasts the civilizing woman's attempts to control her family through moral influence, instruction, and repression. Kate Elinore's powers lie in her physical exertions, unlike the physical reserve associated with the civilizing woman, and in the expression of her own desires, unlike the civilizing woman's emotional containment. As we saw earlier, women in Keith's audiences at times adopted an aggressive style in their responses to boxing matches as well as depictions of humorous gender reversals onstage. When these women responded to vaudeville by releasing rather than reserving physical and emotional energy, they followed Kate Elinore as a model of power and an alternative to the civilizing woman.

These attacks on civilizing women resonated with hostility toward female authority, particularly women's drive for class ascension, throughout American culture around the turn of the century. The upwardly mobile and uptight civilizing woman—the symbol of order in these vaudeville sketches—was a key factor in class tensions in the Irish American community as well as vaudeville's drive for respectability.

One of the central conflicts in the Irish American community around the turn of the century was between the newly established middle-class or "lace curtain" Irish and the working-class Irish.[58] By 1880, the number of American-born Irish exceeded the number of Irish immigrants, and this new generation improved its economic status. According to the 1900 census, for example, American-born Irish were succeeding disproportionately in white-collar occupations such as clerical work and bookkeeping. But as historian Timothy Meagher explains, the status of the new generation of middle-class Irish Americans was ambivalent: "No longer the newest of the new immigrants or the poorest of the poor, they were also not accepted by America's native stock elite."[59]

Irish American women were pivotal in the path to upward mobility, often leading their families from "poverty to comfort, from shanty to lace curtain."[60] In fact, Irish immigrant women and their daughters had more opportunities than men in their communities to observe and emulate middle-class American life.[61] Usually arriving in America when they were young and single, Irish women flocked to domestic service, where they gained an "intimate glimpse of what middle-class America was really like."[62] The second generation of Irish women in America had more success in the economic marketplace than their brothers, husbands, and fathers as they moved into white-collar jobs like clerical work, sales, and teaching. American-born Irish women, for example, accounted for almost half of the teachers in Worcester, Massachusetts, by 1910.[63] Although women usually were not employed after marriage, their decisions in planning family purchases, regulating their husbands' spending, and monitoring their families' savings were keys to upward mobility.[64]

Popular literature and drama at the turn of the century reflected this phenomenon by portraying women as civilizers who attempted to control their husbands' drinking and lift their families into the middle class through hard work and thrift. For example, Finley Peter Dunne's turn-of-the-century newspaper sketches focused on struggles for social mobility among the Irish in Chicago. In the Donahue family's debates over such status symbols as a piano that were often featured in Dunne's sketches, Mrs. Donahue and her daughter Molly were social climbers, whereas Mr. Donahue resisted their pretensions.[65] In addition, Edward Harrigan's popular musical comedies, such as *Cordelia's Aspirations* (1883), frequently focused on an Irish woman's attempts to assimilate into elite American society. Cordelia, for example, carefully saves money to move her family to Madison Avenue (from Mulligan's Alley), but her husband is unhappy away from the camaraderie of his old neighbors. At the end of the play, he sings "I'll Wear the Trousers, Oh" as an indication that he is not going to put up with his wife's demands any longer and then flees to Mulligan's Alley.[66]

As these examples suggest, men often resented Irish women's power and their attempts to reform men. "The resentment stemmed not just from being the object of an uplifting campaign," concludes historian Hasia Diner, "but that women carried on that campaign."[67] Many men were uneasy about Irish women's drive to acquire education, white-collar jobs, and bourgeois manners. Some expressed concern that Irish women would marry outside of the Catholic church or decide not to marry at all because they believed Irish men were too uncouth to be proper husbands. Although such fears proved to be unfounded (most first- and second-generation Irish women married Irish men), they disclose tensions in the Irish American community about women's authority and aspirations for upward mobility.[68] Ambivalence about middle-class status and acculturation was thus tied to fears of women's influence over men as well as their independence from men.

Just as women were identified with upward mobility in the Irish American community, the image of an ideal female spectator—moral, chaste, and highbrow—was the linchpin of the Keith circuit's campaign for increased respectability. But the eclectic vaudeville audience was not united behind Keith and Albee's uplift of the industry; nor were managers wholly convinced of the need to exorcise all rowdy, vulgar comedy—material defined as insulting to middle-class women's fine tastes. In fact, managers continued to offer entertainment that focused on resistance to female authority—entertainment such as the Elinore Sisters' sketches and the Mag Haggerty series, which featured immigrant clowns as heroes and showcased slapstick comedy. The manager of the Bijou Theatre in Woonsocket, Rhode Island, for example, revealed his distaste for low comedy in his description of Gwynne and Gosette's sketch in 1916: "There were moments during the action of the piece when many persons laughed, seeming amused at the 'comedy'? Personally I was at a loss to discern any. If setting upon a pan of moist dough and upon arising having the mass adhere to one's anatomy constitutes comedy, then I'll take tragedy."[69]

Many acts that had ethnic comedy and slapstick gags succeeded in vaudeville by taking advantage of the divisions in the audience: they played to the gallery's adventurous spirit, while ignoring the patrons in the higher-priced seats in boxes and on the orchestra floor. One Keith manager reported in 1904 that the ethnic comedy in an Irish cross-fire routine was a "good gallery act . . . very lively talking act but the orchestra and box patronage here will never be able to 'see' acts of this style. They don't understand them at all."[70] Not surprisingly, Will Cressy, author of the Mag Haggerty sketches, was known for writing for the gallery. On February 3, 1908, the manager of Keith's theater in Philadelphia remarked on the performance of a Cressy sketch: "Will Cressy knows what the gallery wants and gives it to them. This sketch is a little rough in spots and at times just escapes being objectionable."[71] Such discussions of the appropriate character of comedy in vaudeville reveal concerns over the gallery's competition with patrons in higher-priced seats for influence over the course of vaudeville. These battles in the audience and between administrators and the audience were reinforced by the conflicts presented in the Mag Haggerty routines and the sketches of the Elinore Sisters. Mike Haggerty's and Mrs. Delaney's rebellions against their daughters paralleled the gallery's resistance to the ascendance of the civilizing woman in vaudeville.

Although most historians have focused on vaudeville's unequivocal appeal to middle-class women, managers' unpublished comments about low comedy and the enduring popularity of the Elinore Sisters as well as the Mag Haggerty sketches demonstrate that vaudeville administrators approached the ideal female spectator and their impression of middle-class feminine tastes in contradictory ways. They tried to uphold their vision of feminine standards, but at the same time, they championed working-class masculinity onstage and rewarded female performers who challenged the characterization of women as primarily reserved, delicate, and family oriented.[72] Participating in this dialogue about women's "lace curtain" aspirations and the moral authority of female patrons in vaudeville, the Elinore Sisters' sketches addressed far more than nativist anxieties about the containment of immigrant masses. The ethnic humor in these routines derided exaggerated ethnic traits while also celebrating the ethnic characters' ability to outwit and escape civilizing women—the ladies of rank. Gender polarities shaped these comic scenarios of immigrant life, just as ethnic stereotypes fueled Kate Elinore's gender transgressions. Her fistfights, insults, and sexual adventure challenged the traditional division of labor in male/female comedy teams, mocked the definition of feminine influence so central to vaudeville's advancement, and underscored the degree to which resistance to upward mobility and Americanization was infused with resentment over shifting gender relations. For brief moments at least, the rank ladies ruled.

A HAS BEEN OLD-LADY STAR

JULIA ARTHUR IN VAUDEVILLE

"Vaudeville is certainly to be elevated and receive a fitting crown by your advent into it," wrote agent Jule Delmar to Julia Arthur, an actress associated with the legitimate stage and Shakespearean productions.[1] Delmar's note applauded Arthur's decision to perform on the Keith vaudeville circuit in 1923, a career move that had become popular among legitimate performers by the early twentieth century. British actress Mrs. Patrick Campbell entered vaudeville in 1910, earning $2,500 a week,[2] and French stage star Sarah Bernhardt first toured vaudeville in 1912, drawing a salary of $7,000 per week. American actress Ethel Barrymore played on the Keith circuit in 1912, followed by Julia Arthur in 1917 and 1923. When examined as part of the industrial history of vaudeville, these engagements point to vaudeville's program of cultural uplift. But contrary to Delmar's praise of Arthur, legitimate actresses were not simply crowns symbolizing vaudeville's refinement. Rather, ongoing ambivalence about cultural uplift among vaudeville administrators and patrons created an environment that was often hostile to these legitimate performers. Julia Arthur's career reveals that legitimate actresses faced challenges to their reputations as artists and moral women when they turned to vaudeville.

Despite the positive publicity surrounding these actresses' vaudeville tours, theater managers were often weary of such performers, whom they saw as simply washed-up actresses out to make a fast buck. Henrietta Crosman, an American actress who had performed for Augustin Daly, Charles Frohman, and A. M. Palmer and who had starred as Rosalind in an extended run of *As You Like It*, appeared in vaudeville in 1916 at the age of fifty-five. The manager of Keith's theater in Providence, Charles Lovenberg, explained his doubts about legitimate actresses in vaudeville when he reviewed her act: "The business done at the box office Monday afternoon and evening demonstrates to me once more that the people do not want these 'has been old-lady stars.' . . . I am quite sure that the putting up of the names of these old ladies has the decided effect of keeping people out of the theatre rather than to draw them in. I think they have some following but that is more than offset by the people who don't want to see them. I have had this experience now several times, notably with Mrs. Leslie Carter, Mrs. Langtry, Olga Nethersoll [*sic*] and Fritzi Scheff, and I believe I am thoroughly cured."[3] Theater critics often joined in the attack on these women, charging that by appearing in vaudeville, they were bringing themselves down to the level of female performers who walked the tightrope or pranced around with trained animals. And these older actresses, often married and sometimes divorced, also faced criticism that they lacked family love and loyalty when they sold themselves to the vaudeville public. But these critics did not have the last word. The actresses defended themselves as ladies, deliberately distancing themselves from acrobats, blackface performers, and animal acts while promoting their artistic sensitivity and downplaying any pecuniary benefits of cheap amusements like vaudeville. The controversies surrounding these women in vaudeville thus involved questions of women's proper social roles as well as the parameters of high and low culture.

Julia Arthur's career illustrates the constellation of tensions that accompanied many actresses' vaudeville tours. Born on May 3, 1869, as Ida Lewis, she was the fifth of sixteen children of Thomas J. and Hannah Lewis. Reportedly influenced by her mother's study of Shakespeare, Arthur began her theatrical career at the age of fourteen when she joined the repertory company of Daniel E. Bandmann. In 1891 she earned acclaim from the theatrical community for her role in *The Black Masque*, an adaptation of Edgar Allan Poe's *Masque of the Red Death*. Following this role, Arthur joined A. M. Palmer's stock company, the preeminent company in America. Her prestige grew when Sir Henry Irving invited her to be a member of his Lyceum Company in London in 1895. During the next two years, she toured with Irving in London and America, performing several Shakespearean roles—Lady Anne in *Richard III* and Imogen in *Cymbeline*—that were enthusiastically received. After organizing her own company, she produced and starred in a dramatic adaptation of Frances Hodgson Burnett's novel, *A Lady of Quality*, which proved to be one of Arthur's most popular plays. Arthur married Benjamin P. Cheney, a wealthy businessman, in the midst of her successful run in *A Lady of Quality* on February 3, 1898.

In 1899 she discussed plans to perform the role of Hamlet, but when critics attacked her proposed female Hamlet as a comic stunt appropriate to vaudeville (even though Arthur had not mentioned vaudeville in her scheme), she abandoned the idea and retired from the stage altogether in 1900. She returned fourteen years later, performing first in benefits for the Red Cross and the European Actors' Relief Fund, then in *The Eternal Magdalene* (1915–16) and *Seremonda* (1916–17), and next in sketches in vaudeville during the 1917–18 and 1923–24 seasons. In 1923 she finally fulfilled her goal of playing Hamlet when she toured vaudeville with a scene from the Shakespearean tragedy. Although legitimate performers' vaudeville engagements were common by 1917, Arthur's vaudeville tours, particularly her appearance as Hamlet, troubled the managers of vaudeville houses and seemed to either aggravate or bore vaudeville patrons. The controversy surrounding Arthur's employment in vaudeville, along with other actresses' dips into vaudeville, focused on several key questions: Was it appropriate for an aging, married woman to pursue fame and money in a theatrical career? Was art lost in the hectic, comic world of vaudeville?

The relationship between vaudeville and legitimate performers was complex and contentious because it was framed by unresolved conflicts

Julia Arthur in Vaudeville

over feminization and upward mobility. Since players from the legitimate stage often turned to vaudeville when their careers were slumping (when they had passed middle age or several of their plays had flopped), they brought tarnished reputations to vaudeville. And despite the industry's claims of refinement, a vaudeville engagement could exacerbate a performer's decline.[4] Theater historian Leigh Woods has identified this dynamic in Sarah Bernhardt's vaudeville tours. Bernhardt first entered vaudeville in 1912, accepting Martin Beck's offer of $7,000 per week, and later she played in American vaudeville again in 1917 and 1918. She performed the final acts of her famous plays, including *Lucrece Borgia, La Tosca, The Lady of the Camellias,* and *Théodora.* Touted as the "world's greatest actress," Bernhardt was supposed to lend legitimacy to vaudeville with her opulent gowns, extravagant sets, and "foreignness," including French dialogue. But she was in her late sixties when she first appeared in vaudeville and had health problems, which had led to the amputation of her right leg and a kidney operation. On her final vaudeville tours, Bernhardt's value declined significantly. Her salary dropped (she was offered $2,500 per week for a 1920 tour that never materialized), and she no longer had the clout to control the types of acts that appeared on her bill (she waived her requirement that she not appear on vaudeville bills with blackface acts). At this point, vaudeville patrons probably paid to see her because they were curious about her increasing frailty. Bernhardt's vaudeville tours thus indicated the industry's equivocal approach to refinement as well as her declining prestige: "The refinement she signaled in vaudeville," explains Woods, "proved to be as fragile as she was."[5]

Legitimate actresses and actors faced the difficult challenge of adapting to vaudeville standards and pleasing a vaudeville audience. In their private reports, vaudeville theater managers recorded their audiences' rejection of or indifference to these legitimate stars, assessed these performers' short-term value to vaudeville, and described sketches that failed to fit into vaudeville's particular style. The manager of Keith's theater in Cincinnati captured some of the problems of legitimate acts in vaudeville in his review of Julius Steger's 1912 offering: "If tears and weeping are wanted in a vaudeville show this is the greatest act the vaudeville world has ever seen. But no comedy act on earth can res-

Julia Arthur in Vaudeville

urrect an audience from the atmosphere of depression which this act leaves."[6] In 1904 another manager found that Miss Annie Irish's dramatic act (a re-creation of a woman's imaginary conversation with friends) was "drawn out too long and borders on the tiresome."[7]

One explanation for such negative evaluations is that these acts did not meet audiences' expectations for fast and funny performances. As film and vaudeville historian Henry Jenkins argues, vaudeville not only had distinct standards but also reshaped legitimate acts to these standards when they moved into vaudeville: "Far from remaking vaudeville into a more respectable form, these actors were remade by vaudeville."[8] Although it is difficult to make generalizations about such a diverse field as vaudeville, it is possible to outline some differences between dramatic realism and the "vaudeville aesthetic."[9] Vaudeville demanded affective immediacy (performers tried to draw an outward response from the audience very quickly) as opposed to the more reserved, intellectual response desired in the legitimate theater. On the vaudeville stage, the elevation of spectacle over narrative and the direct performer/audience relationship contrasted with legitimate drama's emphasis on extended plot and character development and the indirect (or largely unacknowledged) relationship between performers and the audience. Also, players retained creative control in vaudeville acts, often writing their own routines, initiating innovations, and maintaining their own sets, whereas directors were gaining power over productions in the legitimate theater. Dramatic actors had to condense and add "ginger" to their classic plays in vaudeville, and their personalities moved to center stage in their productions.[10]

Managers' private records clearly reveal just how difficult this transformation was. Lovenberg lambasted Elita Proctor Otis's sketch "because it is only good about ten minutes out of 27" and snapped, "[T]hat will be about all for that."[11] In his discussion of Grayce Scott's sketch, a condensed version of her play *Divorcons*, one Keith manager said: "I have never yet encountered a vaudeville act made over from a successful play that seemed to land. In my opinion the act is too talky, lacks action and needs stage management."[12] The manager of Keith's Hippodrome in Cleveland wrote: "I suppose that if I was a student of drama I would call this a dramatic gem. From a vaudeville standpoint I think

Julia Arthur in Vaudeville

the act is a little slow. . . . There is no action and the plot resolves itself into a dialogue. . . . [N]ot quite suited for the second largest theater in the world."[13]

Although legitimate acts often "fell down" in relation to surrounding vaudeville turns, they frequently had value for vaudeville managers because of the name recognition of the stars. Samuel K. Hodgdon, manager of Keith's theater in Boston, recommended Sadie Martinot because of her name, not because of her sketch, to other managers on the Keith circuit: "From the Philadelphia criticism of the act I knew that it was artistic, but quiet and with very little comedy, but I needed a name to head the bill. . . . The houses were fair yesterday, and I attribute it largely to her. So far as the sketch itself is concerned it is not suited to vaudeville."[14] Actress Annie Yeamans received a similar evaluation. In 1905 one manager wrote that her "act does not amount to anything, merely the drawing power of her name," and another manager agreed that Yeamans's act was "thoroughly all right to place once."[15] Managers also admitted that they prized comic opera star Pauline Hall primarily for her broad name recognition. "Of course we don't expect any great things from Miss Hall, on the stage," explained Lovenberg. "We pay her money to draw the people in and this being her first time here I think she will do it. . . . I wouldn't care to repeat."[16] Actresses' names were thus at the center of vaudeville's extensive publicity machine, which could often produce enough hype to draw a crowd even though the managers complained that actresses could not sustain this mass appeal beyond a single booking. The flashy marketing of these names and bodies proved to be a troubling framework for actresses' vaudeville engagements.

Whereas managers privately debated the value of legitimate actresses in vaudeville, assessing their acts in relation to vaudeville's standards and considering their ability to draw crowds, public discussions of these women's vaudeville engagements struck a different chord, focusing on whether or not these actresses lost their femininity and artistry when they appeared in vaudeville. Stories about these women's independence and authority in vaudeville often pointed to their excesses: they frequently appeared to be greedy and deceitful in their pursuit of fame. These public discussions (and scandals) thus reveal the tenuous balancing act between feminine respectability and the pursuit of money, power, and popularity in theatrical careers, particularly vaudeville.

The vaudeville aesthetic—namely, the centrality of a single performer in an act—and the large salaries offered by vaudeville administrators often gave women more authority in vaudeville than they had in the legitimate theater. They gained control over their productions and were able to reject undesirable roles offered them on the legitimate stage because they could turn to a vaudeville tour of their own design. "I am grateful to vaudeville for the independence it has brought me," declared dramatic actress Ethel Barrymore. "Now when a manager tells me I must play in something that is palpably weak I can refuse."[17] Barrymore also assumed the role of actress-director in vaudeville by controlling the rehearsals for her vaudeville productions. Similarly, Virginia Harned, an actress who had worked for Daniel Frohman and performed with and married actor E. H. Sothern, found creative freedom and financial control in vaudeville. She wrote her own vaudeville sketches, performed in the leading roles, and handled her own vaudeville bookings.

Actresses also attracted attention for the authority they exerted over vaudeville managers. These women often made it clear that they thought the regular working conditions and rules of vaudeville did not apply to them. They laughed at managers' attempts to control them and scorned traditional vaudevillians. In his report on Harned, the manager of Keith's theater in Boston commented that she made her own rules on his circuit:

> Miss Harned seems to consider her dip into vaudeville as a sort of excursion, not as a serious business proposition. She made things most unpleasant for us at the afternoon performance by sending word when called, ten minutes before she was to go on, that she could not be ready for a half hour. Of course, we could not stop to argue, but simply had to make the best of it. . . . Personally, I do not consider Miss Harned's sketch worthy of her, and this seems to be the general verdict amoung [*sic*] our patrons. Like other ventures of this kind, Miss Harned will do for once, but wouldn't be worth anything near her present salary for a repeat.[18]

Julia Arthur in Vaudeville

Along with ignoring schedules, Harned wielded authority by demanding a list of valuable goods, including expensive vases, for her vaudeville tour. Harned's requirements were not an isolated case. Julia Arthur "broke a vaudeville record for sumptuous traveling" when she rode in a private railway car with her personal secretary, manager, and maid, and Mrs. Patrick Campbell not only received a high salary (reportedly $35,000 for fourteen weeks) but also obtained a private stateroom in a Pullman car for her travel, a maid, and accommodations for her poodle.[19] A vaudeville press agent also noted that Campbell had to have a "deadly quiet stage while she rehearses." He explained further: "As far as possible we try to carry out the wishes of people like Mrs. Campbell."[20] The strict demands and disdain for vaudeville administrators of these actresses often made them appear to be shrews and snobs in the publicity for their vaudeville appearances.

These women's elite reputations—based on their identification with the arts—did little to detract from the accusations of their avarice and waste during their vaudeville tours. In fact, these performers seemed to be mired in the commercialism of vaudeville. Legitimate performers tried to justify their vaudeville engagements by praising the uplifted vaudeville audience, the hardworking vaudeville performers, and the improved conditions backstage. The bottom line, however, was money. Discussing her vaudeville appearance, British actress Jessie Millward stated that the "audiences are decidedly high-class and sympathetic."[21] But Millward confessed that the sophisticated audiences were not vaudeville's main attraction: "And the salaries—well, frankly that is vaudeville's chief charm."[22] Similarly, in 1910 Mrs. Patrick Campbell professed her fondness for the fine vaudeville audience but then admitted that her high salary was the primary inducement for her to leave Great Britain to go "vaudevilling" in the United States. "There's but one truth," she declared: "I was stony broke. So I came over here."[23]

The discussion of women's high salaries in vaudeville and the fashionable goods they purchased with their paychecks confirmed what many observers had already concluded: women onstage were vain and frivolous, not truly artistic or professional.[24] In this way, the commercialism of vaudeville seemed to be a heavier burden for actresses than for actors. "We stood for pretty actresses advertising tooth powders and face powders and corsets and cigars," concluded "the Matinee Girl," the author of a regular column in the *New York Dramatic Mirror*, "but when it comes to the men of the profession, who are supposed to be intelligent, and whom we have grown to respect for their good work, lending themselves to silly advertising . . . [it is] bad taste."[25] When Drina De Wolfe, a young actress, was interviewed in 1903, she emphasized the dangers of wealth to an actress's reputation: "The atmosphere of frivolous musical comedies still follows me, and even now I am known largely because of what the newspapers have said of my gowns, my jewels, my automobile, and my alleged private car. . . . But I am so tired of hearing of the luxury in which I am supposed to live, that I would willingly give up every comfort I have . . . if people would only believe that I am seriously in love with my art."[26] The riches that actresses earned and displayed pointed to their economic independence but also debased their moral and artistic standing. Actresses were silly; actors were artistic and smart.

It is not surprising that women faced more of a stigma in vaudeville than men because actresses in general had a lower social status than actors. Historians have noted that the reputations of actresses were suspect because of their associations with illicit sexuality. Nineteenth-century actresses, according to theater historian Claudia Johnson, challenged the feminine ideals of modesty and chastity as they traveled across the country independently, worked in sexually integrated environments, and encountered sexual activity (such as prostitution) in theaters.[27] In fact, the correlation between actresses and sexual exchanges was so strong that actresses in Victorian Britain were erroneously identified as prostitutes. Theater historian Tracy Davis explains that the association between actresses and prostitutes endured for many reasons: not only were theaters often located in areas known for sexual commerce and actresses commonly read through codes of pornography, but perhaps most important, actresses and prostitutes "both were objects of desire whose company was purchased through commercial exchange."[28]

The issue of sexual commodification (and illegal sexual commerce) thus intensified when legitimate actresses moved into vaudeville since this industry was linked to the advertisement of body and name. Vaudeville emphasized three issues that undermined actresses' reputations: financial extravagance, mass appeal, and the focus on physical spectacle. These actresses seemed to be selling their bodies and their names—neither of which depended on artistry—to the mass audience of vaudeville. Virginia Harned's 1908 vaudeville tour demonstrates the prevalence of these elements. Critics demeaned her vaudeville production because it focused on physical display. One review concluded that "the idea seems to be to give Miss Harned an opportunity to appear in clothing designed to emphasize her figure."[29] Another critic commented that her "expensive ermine cloak [was the] most interesting part of the sketch."[30] Finally, in her sketch *The Idol of the Hour*, which she wrote herself, Harned introduced the tension between mass appeal and femininity. "I don't care about that remote, impersonal thing—the public. I want only to be a woman, to be taken care of," declares Harned's character in the playlet. Vaudeville's ongoing emphasis on a mass audience, despite its proclamations of uplift, suggested that actresses were wantonly offering themselves to the public.

The controversy surrounding legitimate actresses' vaudeville appearances also featured questions about the proper spheres of activity for women, particularly aging women. The pressures of aging and domesticity had a greater impact on women's careers in the theater than on men's, ending women's careers sooner than most men's and rendering them vulnerable to charges of disrepute for pursuing stage careers instead of remaining within the confines of family life. Theater historian Benjamin McArthur notes that a central difference between actors and actresses in the early twentieth century was their average age. Few actresses remained onstage past age thirty-five, and according to his analysis of the 1900 census, almost half of all working actresses were under twenty-five, nearly twice the proportion of young actors.[31] In addition, actresses, unlike actors, faced the question of whether or not to remain onstage after marriage. Sensational accounts of married women who performed onstage often charged that these working women were undermining stable, moral family life because they craved the thrills and grandeur of the theater.

Julia Arthur's vaudeville engagements provide a detailed look at the ways the shifts from the legitimate stage to vaudeville involved debates about women's public place as well as their economic and sexual power. Arthur's most controversial vaudeville engagement was her appearance as Hamlet in 1923. The debates surrounding cross-dressing and crossing from the legitimate stage to vaudeville, however, were not new to her. In 1899 she announced for the first time that she would play Hamlet, and although she never mentioned any plans for a vaudeville tour as Hamlet, her intended transvestism was interpreted as an act of cultural descent best suited for vaudeville. Although her plan to play Hamlet in 1899 was not realized, the publicity surrounding her announcement revealed links between high and low culture and gender roles.

Arthur's performance of the role of Hamlet in 1923 was part of a tradition of legitimate actresses interpreting this Shakespearean character. In 1776 Sarah Siddons was the first actress known to play the part of Hamlet, a role she repeated many times in her lifetime. The second half of the nineteenth century saw a wave of female Hamlets: Charlotte Cushman in 1851, Julia Seaman in 1879, and Anna Dickinson in 1884. Millicent Bandmann-Palmer reportedly played Hamlet over 1,000 times in the late nineteenth century, and Sarah Bernhardt launched a successful tour as Hamlet in 1899. Many of these women, including Bernhardt and Bandmann-Palmer, seem to have taken this role because they were actor-managers who had the authority to claim the best part in the play. The manager of her own company beginning in 1892, Bandmann-Palmer was known for having a "stern grip on a young company and a tight rein on the finances."[32]

Many female Hamlets were quite popular, and some received positive responses from theater critics. Marjorie Garber explains that "[t]he modern sense of this cross-dressed portrayal as a stunt or a trick, a dog walking on its hind legs, seems to be a matter of cultural relativism."[33] This was not the case, however, for Julia Arthur's transvestite excursions into vaudeville. In fact, her experiences as Hamlet reveal not only that a cross-cast Hamlet was interpreted as a stunt at the turn of the century but also that when a female Hamlet literally performed alongside a "dog walking on its hind legs" in vaudeville, the cross-dressing became more controversial and more embarrassing for the performer.[34]

Following a mediocre season in legitimate drama in 1898–99, Arthur announced in the summer of 1899—the theatrical off-season—that she would undertake the role of Hamlet. Her plan was met with skepticism and mockery partly because of the events of the previous season, in which Arthur had announced her marriage to millionaire Benjamin Cheney, lost a lawsuit to a theater manager, and earned mixed reviews for her Shakespearean roles.

In 1899 Arthur was completing her second season in her most popular play, *A Lady of Quality*, in which she portrayed Clorinda Wildairs, the daughter of a rough country squire in eighteenth-century England. The play begins with Wildairs in male dress, fencing and drinking at a party, but she soon renounces breeches and embarks on several romances with men. Although Sir John Oxon, a libertine, takes advantage of her, the heroine manages to rise above the shame to marry a nobleman. After he dies and she becomes a wealthy widow, she marries another nobleman, the Duke of Ormonde. In the most remarkable scene from the play, Wildairs kills Oxon with a riding whip and hides him under the couch in a room where she later receives party guests. The play was somewhat controversial for its indictment of the sexual double standard and for Wildairs's indeterminate moral status.[35] In addition, although most reviewers praised Arthur's performance, they found the play artistically flawed. A Boston critic, for example, stated that *A Lady of Quality* "is not a drama that ranks high even in days of mediocre stage literature. . . . [L]eaving out the breeches, the murder and the corpse under the sofa, the play would not be likely to be endorsed by box office receipts."[36] In other words, this play relied on stunts—namely, cross-dressing in "breeches" and violence.[37]

Arthur reported her discomfort with her popularity, explaining that she was torn between the financial success of *A Lady of Quality* and her goal of artistic integrity: "From the day I first stepped upon the stage, I resolved that when I grew rich enough to have my own way, I should devote my best efforts toward interpreting the one great master of drama—Shakespeare," recalled Arthur.[38] But the astounding success of *A Lady of Quality* made Arthur reluctant to leave this role until a backstage encounter allegedly brought her artistic aspirations back to the surface: "I was about to respond to my seventh recall . . . when someone stepped up to me, saying, 'Surely, Miss Arthur, you have reached the summit of your ambition. . . .' No sooner were the words uttered than

Julia Arthur in Vaudeville

Julia Arthur as Clorinda Wildairs in A Lady of Quality, *her most popular play, circa 1897. Whether in Wildairs's black satin breeches or Hamlet's sultry ebon hose, Arthur found that cross-dressing created a profitable buzz in the press. Courtesy of The Harvard Theatre Collection, The Houghton Library.*

all the glittering triumphs seemed a vain and empty recompense after the years and years of struggle."[39]

Although Arthur carefully cast this backstage meeting as the turning point in her struggle between art and popularity, other observers pointed to a different cause: her marriage to railroad magnate Benjamin Cheney. Now that Arthur was financially secure and attached to a new male authority figure (a husband, not a manager), her relationship with the public and her profession was in flux. Would she be free to pursue art? Or would she, in fact, retire from the stage altogether? One critic described her new status: "Miss Arthur is no longer a struggling artist at the beck and call of managers. She has become, through her recent marriage, a woman of wealth and social prestige. At first it was rumored that she had resolved to renounce the glamour of the stage for the quiet delights of a domestic life, and then, when the announcement of her appearance this season set these rumors at rest, it was whispered that she would devote herself to an exclusively Shakespearean repertoire."[40] Soon after her marriage, Arthur spoke out against the speculation that she would retire, defending her decision to stay on the stage in large part as a commitment to art. As one journalist explained, "The persons circulating these rumors forgot, however, that Miss Arthur's most prominent characteristic has been her love for her art."[41] Marrying a millionaire apparently recast Arthur's choices: retire to domesticity or perform only Shakespeare.

Arthur initially chose Shakespeare. In 1898 she began to augment her appearances in her popular play with roles in classical works such as *As You Like It, Romeo and Juliet, Pygmalion and Galatea,* and *Mercedes.* When these plays garnered only a lukewarm reception, Arthur returned to *A Lady of Quality,* but soon she fell ill and discontinued the production. In December 1898 Theodore Moss, manager of Wallack's Theatre, sued Arthur, alleging that her illness was merely an excuse for her to break her contract. When Moss won the case against Arthur in January 1899, his lawyer declared, "The truth is that Miss Arthur concluded that she would rise to greater heights in a Shakespearean role than in her part in *A Lady of Quality.*"[42] Arthur, apparently bitter over the financial failures of *As You Like It* and *Mercedes,* lashed out at the New York City public, charging that it favored ragtime plays and May

Irwin. A rotund comedienne in musical comedy and vaudeville who specialized in coon songs (syncopated tunes with racial dialect), Irwin had
competed directly with *A Lady of Quality* with her musical comedy *The
Swell Miss Fitzwell*. In 1897 Irwin's farce played at the Bijou Theatre in
New York City at the same time that Arthur's play was at Wallack's
Theatre in the same city. Arthur described her rival as an exaggeration
of the elements Arthur was trying to escape when she abandoned *A
Lady of Quality*. The very idea of Irwin in classical drama struck many,
including Irwin herself, as humorous. She joked about the possibility of
her playing classic theatrical roles like Camille or Juliet. "Imagine me,
the wan-faced, delicate little flowerlike Cammy, with a hectic flush and
a springlike cough," she suggested humorously. "Where could I sing my
coon songs?" Concerning the role of Juliet, the hefty Irwin quipped,
"But where would be found a balcony strong enough?"[43] One way for
Arthur to resolve these dilemmas over art, popularity, and domesticity
was to define herself as clearly in opposition to the jolly and often grotesque May Irwin.

When Arthur proclaimed her intention to play Hamlet in the 1899–
1900 season, her struggles over high and low culture intensified. Critics viewed Arthur's proposed Hamlet as a further indication of her mis-
interpretation of Shakespeare and a morally suspect exploitation of her
body. These charges fed the broader impression that Arthur's announcement was a "stunt." According to critics, a stunt was both a
physical spectacle that detracts from or disrupts a dramatic narrative
and a story or scandal concocted by performers to heighten their fame.

The *New York Journal* joked that, in preparation for her Hamlet role,
Arthur had "ordered a ton of the finest melancholy and a pair of black
silk tights."[44] Discussing Arthur's costume fitting for the part, one reporter announced that her cross-dressing would be wholly convincing
("My informant tells me that he never saw a handsomer young man in
his life than Miss Arthur makes in this costume") but also emphasized
the eroticism of Arthur's Hamlet ("The tights which will incase her
shapely limbs will be of darker purple").[45] This focus on Arthur's sexual
attractiveness troubled other critics who seemed more concerned with
preserving the artistry of legitimate drama. In September 1899 *Broadway Magazine* denounced Arthur's plans to play Hamlet as well as the

Julia Arthur in Romeo and Juliet, *1899. After earning mixed reviews and little money for her portrayal of Shakespearean heroines, Arthur announced her intention to play Hamlet. Courtesy of The Harvard Theatre Collection, The Houghton Library.*

public's desire to see her legs: "The public seems to be more interested in the probable appearance of the legs . . . than in the manner of the character presentation. At best Hamlet is about as enlivening as a soggy blanket in a rainstorm, but when played by a woman it is simply a theatrical monstrosity."[46]

Along with focusing on the unseemly but titillating physical spectacle of a female Hamlet, critics also pointed to Arthur's questionable motives for playing Hamlet—fame and money, not "art." Many critics concluded that Arthur's announcement of her Hamlet production was a hoax—a story invented by a press agent to "set people talking about his star."[47] In addition, several critics interpreted her plans to play Hamlet as an opportunistic imitation of Sarah Bernhardt's Hamlet: "It is generally thought that Miss Arthur has been influenced in arriving at this determination [to play Hamlet] by the pecuniary if not altogether artistic success scored by Sarah Bernhardt."[48] Another critic asserted that "Bernhardt's genius has now cleared the way, and now every actress who has been told she looks 'cute' in men's garb is free to look Hamletward."[49]

Arthur never hinted that she would perform in *Hamlet* anywhere other than on the legitimate stage. On July 22, 1899, the *Dramatic News* reported that she had booked the Broadway Theatre for *Hamlet*.[50] Nevertheless, critics raised the specter of the circus, comic opera, musical comedy, and vaudeville as they interpreted a cross-dressed Hamlet as cultural descent. "A female Hamlet somehow reminds one of a side show and freaks," concluded an Indiana reporter in July 1899, and another critic pondered, "If the divine Sarah [Bernhardt] were to abandon the stage for the high wire there would be a rush for balancing poles among the 'leading ladies' in America."[51] Another observer conjured up visions of vaudeville and musical comedy performers, including May Irwin (apparently a leading symbol of cultural decay), as transvestite Shakespearean stars: "May Irwin is preparing to discard wing dances and coon songs and emerge as Sir John Falstaff. . . . [A] not unimaginable result may be to see Othello put on stage by Julia Marlowe as the Moor, Lulu Glaser as Iago."[52] Marlowe, an esteemed Shakespearean actress, and Glaser, a comedian popular in vaudeville and comic opera, were a particularly incongruous pair to this critic. Lulu

Glaser as Iago; May Irwin as Falstaff; Sarah Bernhardt on the high wire—these images suggest that observers denigrated Arthur's Hamlet by identifying it with low culture. For them, the combination of artists like Arthur and Bernhardt with cheap amusements was shockingly ridiculous.

The comparison between Arthur and Irwin mirrored other accounts of legitimate theater that tried to elevate the legitimate stage as art and legitimate players as artists in relation to debased "others," such as vaudeville and performers identified with vaudeville. These contrasts were necessary because vaudeville's brash commercialism, emphasis on spectacle, and dependence on the name recognition of "stars" appeared to be spreading to loftier branches of the theater. For example, in their quest for artistic status, actors and actresses attempted to repudiate the commercialism connected with theater, reached for the prestige of fine arts such as music and literature, and sought greater distance from circuses and vaudeville. In 1896 one reporter noted that "it will not do to say that the line cannot be drawn, and that the term 'actress' is a generic term comprehending all women who make their appearance on the stage. To be a speechless ornament in tights is not to be an actress."[53] Supporting such claims of hierarchical divisions among performers, the *New York Mirror* (later the *Dramatic Mirror*), founded in 1879, hoped to lift the acting profession by offering an alternative treatment of theater to that of the *New York Clipper*. The editors of the *Mirror* complained that the *Clipper's* discussions of theater alongside "prize fights and baseball games . . . dragged actors down to the level of the circus."[54] Like the circus, vaudeville was a sideshow in contrast to legitimate theater.

The debate over an endowed theater in the early twentieth century also reveals that the reputation of legitimate theater depended on the exorcism of elements of "low" culture, such as commercialism and stardom. In the summer of 1901, *Theatre* published a series of articles supporting the establishment of an endowed theater, part of more widespread criticism of the Theatrical Syndicate (or the "trust"), a union of six theatrical managers established in 1896. Essentially a booking office, the syndicate gained a monopoly over the routes of productions for the legitimate stage. Many actors disdained the syndicate because it "symbolized the theatre's arrival as a big business"; commercial interests seemed to have overtaken artistic concerns.[55] As opposed to the trust, an endowed theater, according to the writers in the forum in *Theatre*, would firmly establish acting as an art by removing it from greed, the fads of public taste, and the star system. "Imagine a theatre in which all the plays produced should be of a high literary standard, should be all unobjectionable morally; should be played by the best actors and actresses, the part being distributed according to fitness and not according to favoritism," wrote A. M. Palmer, theater manager and the head of successful dramatic companies.[56] Two months later, the prominent actor Wilton Lackaye compared the idea of an endowed theater to the successes of the Metropolitan Opera House and the Boston Symphony Orchestra, and like other commentators, he saw an endowed theater as a way to curb the star system. "There will be no more creation of 'stars' by methods which hitherto were left to the patent medicine man or the tooth-paste promoter," asserted Lackaye, adding that "the divorcée, the pugilist and the bridge jumper will be relegated to the side shows, where they belong and will no longer defile those boards honored by the genius of Sophocles, of Shakespeare, or Molière."[57] Vaudeville seemed to be just the place for these frauds and freaks.

Although Lackaye did not specifically refer to vaudeville in his discussion of the dangers of the "tooth-paste promoter," the link between vaudeville and advertising was already established in many journalistic accounts. Writing in the *New York Dramatic Mirror*, "the Matinee Girl" explained that legitimate performers turned to vaudeville because of financial need: "We are all in vaudeville because there is more money in it. The hungry artist chokes down that which is in him and paints a soap advertisement because it means ready cash."[58] The legitimate performer who appeared in vaudeville was thus associated with advertising and stardom, two aspects of commercialism that many critics hoped to banish from legitimate theater to the "low" of vaudeville.

Critics also emphasized that the legitimate theater should eliminate sexual spectacles and other visual attractions of the stage. Albert L. Parkes, for example, criticized the sensory rather than intellectual attractions of legitimate productions: "The new type of manager has found it more profitable to dazzle the eye with scenic and mechanical stage realisms than to appeal to the brain by presenting plays that demand a high order of cultivated talent for their proper interpretation."[59] His analysis corresponds to other critics' claims that the legitimate theater was losing its superiority over vaudeville as it increasingly emphasized visual impact and performers' names and personalities. These qualities—dangerous to artistic goals—were supposed to be isolated in the industries (like vaudeville) that were most open about their commercial, as opposed to artistic, aspirations.

Arthur, perhaps swayed by the expectation that the wife of a millionaire would embrace domesticity and discouraged by the criticism of her Hamlet announcement, abandoned the stage altogether in 1900, putting questions of popularity, artistry, and ambition to rest—but only temporarily.[60] In 1914 she returned to the legitimate stage, and just two years later, she began the first of her two vaudeville tours. Why did she turn to vaudeville at this point in her career after rejecting it in 1899, despite many critics' expectation that her plans to play Hamlet would take her there? Vaudeville's reputation had improved since the 1890s, and there was more public acceptance of married women's employment in 1914, but the prestige of vaudeville and the morality of married women onstage were still somewhat contentious issues. As we will see, Julia Arthur hardly escaped criticism in her postretirement vaudeville tours.

To understand Arthur's vaudeville engagements in 1917 and 1923, we need to begin with a consideration of her return to the stage in 1914 because at this point critics addressed themes that framed her later vaudeville tours: Should Arthur, as a married woman, seek employment? Should she undertake roles in classical drama? With her return to the stage, Arthur joined a debate about the combination of marriage and employment that reached a crescendo in the 1920s. Not only did women's employment increase, but married women in particular were more likely to be in the work force. The percentage of women in the work force who were married rose to 23 percent by 1920.[61] More married women entered the labor force in the 1920s: whereas 9 percent of wives were in the labor force in 1920, 12 percent of married women were employed in 1930. But the labor market was still hostile to wives. Historian Nancy Cott explains that despite the rising number of employed married women, "[g]ainful employment outside the home was a fact for only a small proportion of married women."[62] When the National Education Association surveyed 1,532 cities in the mid-1920s, for example, it found that 60 percent of the school boards discriminated against married women in hiring teachers.[63]

It is not surprising, then, that married women's motivations for employment were an explosive topic during this period. "The high level of attention given to women who intended to pursue career and marriage," explains Nancy Cott, "attested to how extraordinarily iconoclastic that combination was."[64] There were two central arguments for married women's paid employment in the 1920s, one focused on middle- and upper-class educated women and the other on working-class wives. The first emphasized that wives preferred to work outside of the home, that marriage (seen as egalitarian and companionate) was a key to women's fulfillment, and that employment could enhance a wife's or mother's family life. The second argument centered on the oppressive economic needs driving working-class women into employment rather than these women's desires. Reformers at the Women's Bureau of the Department of Labor, for example, argued that women entered the labor market because of family loyalty, often in response to "abnormal" circumstances such as the incapacity of a male breadwinner. Neither of the most popular arguments for married women's employment questioned the necessity of marriage for women or the subordination of women in marriage. Julia Arthur's career shows that a married woman's return to employment demanded careful justifications that did not usurp husbands or deprecate marriage.

Theater critics often put married actresses on the defensive by suggesting that the glamour of the stage lured them away from their responsibilities at home. Most actresses, whether they returned to the stage or not, asserted their commitment to home. One journalist asked actress Mrs. Leslie Carter, "Is the call of the home of less moment than the lure of the Land of Make Believe, and is home life irksome compared to that of the stage?"[65] Carter answered, "I certainly expect to be happier leading a domestic existence than ever I have been on the stage."[66] But Carter's answer was not entirely convincing. Many observers were suspicious of actresses' claims of domestic bliss because these performers often ended their retirements (with a flourish in the press) to return to the stage. They seemed to be rejecting the home, as boredom and drudgery, in favor of the pleasures of the theater.

Like Carter, most actresses stated their commitment to home when they retired from the stage and even used domestic duties as a rationale for resuming stage careers. Arthur explained her 1914 return to the theater in a variety of ways, almost always portraying herself as serving others—European nations at war or her husband. She claimed that she felt compelled to help in war work and that she needed to make money to support her husband's failing finances. Arthur worked for charity when she first returned to the stage in 1914. Reporting on her performance to raise money for the European Actors' Relief Fund, Harleigh Schultz concluded that Arthur gave up the "life of a society maiden . . . for charity's sake."[67] When she appeared in plays unconnected to the war effort during the 1915–16 and 1916–17 seasons and could no longer emphasize her service to country, commentary on her career turned to her desire to perform and her sacrifice for her husband's financial needs. One article in 1917, for example, depicted Arthur's departure from and return to the stage as equivalent sacrifices to matrimony. Enumerating the thrills of stage work that Arthur did not, according to the author, desire, this writer pointed to Arthur's self-abnegation: "She left it for the love of a man. She returned to it for the love of the same man—her husband. . . . Not because her heart hankers for old time applause, not because she wants excitement or change, nor yearns for spotlights and grease paint, nor even to earn luxuries, beautiful gowns and jewels for herself is Miss Arthur now appearing on the stage as a wage-earning wife."[68] These constructions of her return to the stage continued throughout her vaudeville tour in 1923. One 1923 article stated that Arthur joined the Keith circuit "to recoup the family fortunes."[69] Such depictions of actresses as reluctant stars, turning to the stage out of family loyalty, not personal ambition, had long been popular. Biographers, for example, portrayed famous nineteenth-century actress Fanny Kemble as a "dutiful daughter" who relinquished her intention to be a writer and took a dramatic part to augment her father's crumbling finances.[70]

In discussing her return to the stage, Arthur also used art to soften any suggestions of financial need or personal ambition. In one interview, she downplayed her husband's financial crisis, claiming that he was simply short of "ready money" and that she was not in fact "compelled" to rescue him financially. At the conclusion of the interview, she revealed that her long-standing commitment to art had propelled her back to the stage: "I love the work of appealing to the public across the footlights. I love the literary element."[71] On December 22, 1916, in *Variety*, Arthur remarked: "Once again on the stage, nothing could lure me back to private life. There seems much to do for an earnest worker and one who really loves the art for its own sake."[72] Carefully filtering her ambition through art, Arthur, in this case, avoided the question of the financial benefits of her return. Art served as a dominating muse demanding obedience from reluctant women, a higher ideal to which performers sacrificed themselves, and an alternative to the commercialism and popularity associated with entertainment industries like vaudeville.

Several accounts of Arthur's return noted Cheney's opposition to his wife's career goals but emphasized their tranquil resolution of this conflict. Newspaper reports explained that Cheney had kept his wife out of professional life for many years, despite her desire for the stage, yet most accounts also praised Cheney for his change of heart and characterized their marriage as happy.[73] Arthur explained in one interview that "I have longed for the chance [to return] for years in spite of our delightful home life but Mr. Cheney would not consent. He threw up his hands at the idea."[74] Arthur did not protest the notion that she could not resume her career without his permission, and Cheney's control of his wife's career seemed compatible with a peaceful home life. Overall, the discussion of the various reasons for Arthur's return to the stage deemphasized Arthur's own drive for success and reasserted the beneficence of her husband's authority, even when he blocked his wife's career.

Critics, fans, and family members expected Arthur to appear in classical drama when she resumed her career. Arthur's mother-in-law wrote in 1915: "We all enjoyed your appearance on the stage again and think you did finely. We all hope to see you in Shakespearean plays again."[75] Instead, her most famous roles prior to her vaudeville tours were in plays that critics often found to be alarmingly similar to vaudeville—sensational, titillating, and crude. Her most famous plays between 1915 and 1917 were *The Eternal Magdalene* and *Seremonda*. A play advocating that prostitutes should be reformed rather than banished, *The Eternal Magdalene* was "cheap melodrama" and "crass comedy."[76] The comments in one review sounded remarkably like the criticisms of vaudeville spectacles: "She deserved also a part that should give her ampler opportunity than pictorial posing in grave attitude, the speaking of sonorous speeches undistinguished in imagery or word."[77] If the phrase "grave attitude" were omitted—or replaced by "erotic"—this sentence could easily be an indictment of vaudeville's frivolity and immorality—spectacles and monologues lacking any uplifting narrative.

Similarly, many critics agreed that *Seremonda*, despite its claims of uplift, was also cheap entertainment. This romantic play chronicles the return of a husband, long thought dead, on the eve of his wife's marriage to a new lover. Some critics praised the author's (William Lindsay's) verse as "poetic glow" but found the scenery sloppy and the characterizations shallow. Furthermore, many looked cynically upon Arthur's claims of theatrical uplift. Salita Solano, for example, commented that "[w]henever the public overwearies of scented girl-and-music shows, crook plays and little studies in obstetrics, a playwright is certain to bob up with a poetic drama, crying, 'Look to my standard and I will lead you away from life's crudenesses into a realm where tilting bouts are held for the privilege of wearing a lady's glove.' Then, granting he shouts loudly enough and that the name of the play's star has been sufficiently advertised on tooth paste tubes and non clutch corsets, the public will sigh in resignation and go in small numbers for the first three weeks only."[78] Although he explained the failure of *Seremonda* as the result of public taste for "girl-and-music shows," Solano suggested that these shows and *Seremonda* shared a reliance on commercialism and stars. In this light, Arthur's turn to vaudeville seemed quite natural since many critics believed she was already there.

After gaining a mediocre reception for *The Eternal Magdalene* and *Seremonda*, Arthur took her first dip into vaudeville during the 1917–18 season with *Liberty Aflame*, in which she recited a patriotic speech dressed as the Statue of Liberty. Her patriotism proved to be somewhat controversial in the context of vaudeville. On the one hand, many critics suggested that Arthur used patriotism rather than a skillful act to win approval in vaudeville. One reviewer explained: "Her monologue was long on patriotism and short on merit: about ninety-nine percent of the former and one percent of the latter. The monologue was rhetorical and bombastic and the success it achieved was secured, of course, through its patriotic appeal."[79] On the other hand, some claimed that the serious topics covered by Arthur, including the sinking of the *Lusitania*, were not appropriate to the rollicking, comic style of vaudeville. "While it is true that this tragedy was more horrible than human tongue can describe," wrote one critic, "it seems entirely out of place to endeavor to imitate the tone of the dying victims on the vaudeville stage."[80] Both perspectives on *Liberty Aflame* saw Arthur as a poor fit in vaudeville, but Arthur's apparent patriotism nevertheless shielded her from suggestions of her own immorality and greed, issues that emerged in her later vaudeville tours.

For her next vaudeville offering, Arthur resurrected her earlier plan to portray Hamlet, and like the critics in 1899, observers in 1923 repeatedly called her Hamlet a stunt; she was an actress offering a sensational act (such as a physical spectacle or a freakish feat) and exploiting her name recognition to garner a large salary. A critic for the *Baltimore Evening Sun* argued that although Arthur was an "experienced artist" and a "Shakespearean student," her role as Hamlet was "frankly a vaudeville stunt."[81] He believed that all female Hamlets were "devoid of verisimilitude and truth" and that Arthur's production was simply "a bit of opportunism."[82]

The accusation that Arthur's Hamlet was an opportunistic stunt suggests that she was involved in deceitful self-promotion, a rumor that often circulated around actresses' lucrative vaudeville tours. Although such derogatory comments drew on the popular stereotype of actresses as vain and conniving, they also captured the way many performers worked to advertise their acts and themselves. Like other performers, Arthur tried to generate flattering publicity and avoid criticism; she was even willing to play a few tricks to get the results she wanted. Arthur, in particular, seems to have been painfully aware that many critics and fans were concerned about her age. In a February 5, 1923, letter to Arthur, Anna Marie Jungman addressed the issue of Arthur's age: "You may not realize how this new interest has wiped away the years. On the stage I thought you looked years younger; but when I saw you in your dressing room I knew you did."[83] Other observers were not so charitable. Stating that he could not say any "nice things about Julia Arthur's venture into vaudeville," one critic reminded readers of her advanced age by referring to her career on the legitimate stage "before our day and generation": "Our mother has pleasant recollections of her charms as the heroine of 'A Lady of Quality.'"[84] To deflect negative attention from her age, Arthur took the bold step of using pictures of herself as Hamlet taken twenty-four years earlier as the official publicity photographs for her 1923 tour. In this light, Jungman was right: her publicity photos literally "wiped away the years." The photograph on the cover of the *New York Star* in 1923, for example, features a young Julia Arthur with the same costume and furniture as in her portrait as Hamlet in *The Julia Arthur Book*, published in 1899. In these photographs, Arthur is sultry in her revealing Hamlet garb. Some show Arthur with her legs bare except for shoes with leather straps that wind up her calves to her knees, whereas in others she wears dark stockings. But in almost all photos, her legs are central, and only her upper thighs are concealed by a short skirt. In one of these photographs, Arthur is sitting on a bench with her legs positioned assertively, her knees slightly apart; the toe of one extended foot rests delicately on a pillow. She is pensive and erotic, slightly defiant yet vulnerable.

Along with trying to mask her age, Arthur promoted her vaudeville tour by emphasizing the uplift of vaudeville that had allegedly taken place during her retirement: "Before I left the stage . . . it was known as the 'varieties.' Vaudeville as it exists today was not known. . . . The audiences in vaudeville theaters are the greatest surprise of my present experience. They are of a much higher average of perception and intelligence than I expected; not that I held them meanly, but as I have explained, modern vaudeville has developed during the time I was absent from the stage."[85] Her comments are important because they show that vaudeville's history was a resource Arthur could use to preserve her own reputation. But as we have seen, the ascendance of vaudeville was not as clear-cut as Arthur's snapshot indicates. The ambivalent reputation of vaudeville haunted her tours.

In fact, rather than firmly establishing vaudeville's Shakespearean stature, Arthur's tour on the Keith circuit exposed the persistent doubts

Julia Arthur as Hamlet, 1923. This photo was probably taken in 1899,
when Arthur first announced her plans to play Hamlet, but she used it to promote
her vaudeville tour twenty-four years later, at the age of fifty-three,
when she was trying to deflect attention from her age.
Courtesy of The Harvard Theatre Collection, The Houghton Library.

about vaudeville's place in the cultural hierarchy: Was art transforming vaudeville, or was vaudeville degrading the dramatic arts? Arthur seems to have been aware of the particular demands of vaudeville patrons and the aesthetic traditions of vaudeville when she planned her act. She chose the scene in which Hamlet murders Polonius behind the queen's curtain—a scene that resembled Arthur's earlier portrayal of Clorinda Wildairs, another androgynous murderer, in *A Lady of Quality*. This scene seemed to be an ideal compromise between the rowdy and the respectable in vaudeville. First, the murder scene gratified vaudeville's fascination with women's criminal involvement in sex scandals. Many women accused of murder and attempted murder cashed in on their fame by making vaudeville tours. Billed as the Shooting Stars, for example, chorus girls Lillie Graham and Ethel Conrad were headliners at Hammerstein's Victoria Theatre after they shot Graham's lover.[86] "Every pawnshop gun sold to a woman," recalled one veteran vaudevillian, "practically carried the guarantee of a week's booking."[87] If, as many critics noted, Arthur's femininity was readily apparent onstage, despite her Hamlet costume, the scene would have suggested a woman's criminal act. The scene allowed Arthur to capitalize on this fad without being directly linked to women who had actually been arrested for crimes. After all, she was only playing a role. Second, the scene appeared to be a good choice because it provided bloody action to grab the attention of vaudeville patrons yet removed Arthur from the violence by concealing the murder behind a drape. The scene also gave Arthur the opportunity to demonstrate her oratory skills and express some of the pathos of Hamlet. Perhaps she could succeed in vaudeville while keeping her artistic reputation and self-respect intact.

Despite her careful choice of scene and her crafty publicity, Arthur's vaudeville tour was not a success. A few critics praised her for improving vaudeville along with its brutish patrons, and some audiences seemed quietly moved by the act. One critic saw Arthur's act as a victory over vaudeville's usual base tendencies, but even he could hardly describe an enthusiastic reception of her act. "[T]he mere idea of dragging a vaudeville audience from their easy laughter and chuckling nonchalance by interpolating Shakespeare would terrify the stoutest heart. . . . However, Miss Arthur achieved her aim. She was accorded extreme

Julia Arthur in Vaudeville

attention."[88] In a letter to Arthur on March 21, 1923, Horace Ellis, after identifying himself as a man with "University connections," championed Arthur's Hamlet as a "renewal of stage interests in dramatics of the highest sort," concluding that "the approval which the mixed audience gave your beautiful offering vanquished all doubts as to the willingness of the general public to applaud such efforts as any true Shakespearean actress may essay today."[89]

In these few accounts, the mass vaudeville audience seems to join together in appreciation of Arthur's highbrow offering. But most reviewers did not paint such a reassuring picture. Arthur's standards did not seem to be unequivocally high culture as she catered to the low patrons and competed with the incessant pratfalls and belly laughs of vaudeville. It was, in fact, difficult to credit Arthur with uplifting vaudeville since she had become "vaudevillized" in many ways. She circulated erotic photographs of herself and reminded many observers of other ambitious women who had built vaudeville careers on personal scandals. Bland Johnson, for example, explained that Arthur would be "among dramatic actresses culled from winners of seashore beauty contests and former wives of film stars who won more notoriety than alimony from their erstwhile lords."[90] Other critics, in addition, were dismayed that vaudeville seemed to alter Arthur's acting style. Her act, according to one reviewer, was "too high and vehement in pitch," probably because "she had to snatch her audience."[91] Another explained that "[t]he essential characteristic of a variety program is a snappy, breezy quality in music, song and dance, a quality that relentlessly forces poetry into jingle and the classic aria into a tune."[92] For most critics, Arthur's tour was not evidence of the actress's power to reform vaudeville patrons; instead, it indicated that vaudeville not only survived but also devoured high culture.

Despite her attempts to approximate an attention-getting vaudeville style, many reviews noted that Arthur seemed to be lost on the eclectic vaudeville bills. According to one critic, the sketch failed because her Hamlet was "cut off from the supporting body of the play and thrust up beside Vincent Lopez's jazz orchestra. . . . This Hamlet must remain a stunt, not a thing of art."[93] A letter from a theater patron to Arthur on February 8, 1923, also reveals the concern that a mixed vaudeville bill contaminated legitimate acts: "To me it was nothing short of a miracle that in spite of the rest of the programme, you were able to give the performance you did." This patron was particularly critical of Edward Albee's failure to uplift the surrounding parts of the program. "The right type of man," the author charged, "would surely have arranged that the rest of the programme should have been lifted to a different level in order to do full justice to what you were about to achieve."[94]

Arthur's authority in vaudeville was further undermined by the recalcitrant vaudeville patrons who were not shy about expressing their preference for more traditional vaudeville fare. Newspaper reviews of her tour reveal that Arthur's characterization of the vaudeville audience as newly uplifted was more hopeful than realistic. "It is only fair to say that the actress ... was received on Monday afternoon with tremendous enthusiasm—after the scene was finished," quipped one Baltimore reporter; "during the progress of the episode the spectators coughed so frequently and loudly that it was often difficult to hear what the player was saying. ... Why is it, however, that no one coughs during the slapstick acts?"[95]

Julia Arthur's career, therefore, demonstrated the increasingly permeable boundaries between high and low culture, but not in the way most cultural elites had hoped. To most critics, the vaudeville tours late in her career were less an indication of vaudeville's new resemblance to high culture (which Arthur and the leaders of the Keith circuit claimed) than an indication of vaudeville's infectious spread to high culture. Arthur's appearances in legitimate drama prior to turning to vaudeville were denigrated as cheap spectacles that capitalized on titillating scandals, and Arthur's vaudeville offerings seemed to be engulfed by the surrounding slapstick and somersaults. Although vaudeville publicity portrayed Arthur as a moral artist, critics interpreted her vaudeville tour as the maneuvering of a desperate and deceptive woman. Arthur was neither and both. Seemingly dedicated to the elevation of vaudeville and committed to her domestic responsibilities, Arthur was also a professionally ambitious woman who demonstrated an almost Barnum-esque zeal for self-promotion. On the one hand, she justified her vaudeville tours with claims of family loyalty and artistic callings; on the other hand, she advertised herself as a sexual commodity. When they performed in vaudeville, an industry striving for cultural authority but not yet free from the power of the gallery gods, dramatic actresses like Julia Arthur often needed such split images and defensive rhetoric to succeed in vaudeville while also staving off its corrosive powers.

THE CORKING GIRLS

WHITE WOMEN'S RACIAL MASQUERADES
IN VAUDEVILLE

The leaders of the Keith circuit frequently congratulated themselves on just how far vaudeville had come since its inception.[1] Current vaudeville proudly courted women, they said, whereas past popular entertainment catered to men. Current vaudeville was clean, even educational, whereas past amusements were vulgar. But despite being proud of their movement away from these embarrassing antecedents, vaudeville promoters seemed to long for the amusements that were the roots of vaudeville. A nostalgia for past entertainment was evident in the special "old-timers'" bills that appeared periodically on the Keith circuit. On December 11, 1911, for example, the Keith vaudeville theater in Providence offered "Ye Olde Timers' Week," which featured, among others, Fox and Ward, two blackface comedians who first performed together in the 1860s, and George Primrose, a minstrel performer who had also appeared in variety shows.[2] This bill was a tribute to the past pleasures of vaudeville, including the physical exuberance, ribaldry, and masculine, working-class pride associated with such nineteenth-century amusements as the minstrel show. And although most recollections of vaudeville's past focused on ties to the rough, working-class history of the variety show, this bill demonstrates that vaudeville's traditional masculinity (a source of disdain and desire) was rooted in the racialized context of the minstrel show as well.

Minstrel show traditions were not simply replicated in vaudeville; their meanings shifted—sometimes dramatically, at other times subtly—when white women adopted racial masquerades in vaudeville. Women were not among the old-timers who represented the minstrel show in "Ye Olde Timers' Week" largely because they were excluded from antebellum minstrel shows, but women became involved in minstrel show traditions in many types of vaudeville acts around the turn of the century. White women, often in blackface, led groups of young black performers in "pickaninny acts"; white female vaudevillians sang popular coon songs; and many white chorus girls put on blackface in "girl acts," productions with large choruses as well as elaborate changes of scenery and costumes.[3]

Through racial dialect and blackface, these white women gained comic license and adopted an uninhibited physical style, as men in the minstrel show had, and white women's racial masks also invoked a sentimental vision of the past, similar to the minstrel show's nostalgia. In these ways, their experience extended two threads of minstrel show ideology. As Michael Rogin explains, "In minstrel ideology, blackface wildness invoked Africa, while blackface nostalgia conjured up the lost plantation."[4] But these women's wildness and their longing for the past differed from the minstrel show meanings because they were shaped by the particular gender and racial politics of vaudeville and by the social and culture trends at the turn of the century. White women's racial sentimentality usually emerged through the largely fictional image of the "mammy"—dependable, nurturing, and devoted to her white owner. They presented the figure of the mammy through their songs about the pastoral South, their appearances with black children in their routines, and their large, maternal bodies onstage. Although the mammy of the plantation (also known as "Old Auntie") had been a minor character in the antebellum minstrel show (often depicted in songs as a faithful caretaker), the mammy became a widespread figure in popular culture and politics by the turn of the century, after the minstrel show's popularity had waned.[5] She was "someone who loved unconditionally with forgiveness for the past, who was worthy of admiration and adoration and who at the same time offered strength and shelter from the realities of the adult, modern world."[6] Within vaudeville, the sentimental mammy suggested some dissatisfaction with the industry's progress but did not invoke masculine rebelliousness as the antidote to vaudeville's modern femininity.

White women's adoption of a childlike wildness through racial masquerades also differed somewhat from white men's energetic excursions in the minstrel show. Racial masquerade was one route to success and celebrity in vaudeville for women who were not conventionally attractive (particularly women who were fat), and these performers' rough and sexual racial style led to controversies about women usurping men's comic roles as well as discussions about women rejecting the role of erotic object onstage. Racial disguises provided the raw material both for white women's upward mobility and for a feminine subtext of vaudeville's past.

White women's racial masquerades often seemed old-fashioned in vaudeville because they evoked the minstrel show. Originating around 1830, the minstrel show peaked in popularity between 1846 and 1854. In the antebellum minstrel show, white male performers put on blackface to offer comic commentary on a variety of topics (including women's rights and slavery); make fun of immigrants, Native Americans, and African Americans; and undermine many experts and authority figures. The ridicule of African Americans was one part of this diverse entertainment form. Songs and dialogues in the minstrel show sometimes focused on grotesque portrayals of the northern black dandy (Zip Coon) and the happy, errant slave (Jim Crow). Although the minstrel show underwent many transformations in the nineteenth century, the basic structure included three distinct parts. In the first section of the show, a pompous interlocutor was situated in the center of a semicircle of performers in blackface (burnt cork or greasepaint), with two unruly end men, named Tambo and Bones, deflating the interlocutor with their comic barbs. The second part of the show featured variety acts, and the final segment was a one-act skit, often representing plantation life.

The blackface mask of the minstrel show was also a medium of misogyny. Overwhelmingly male dominated, particularly in the antebellum period, the minstrel show made independent women the butt of jokes and attacked "civilizing female morality."[7] It often included songs that ridiculed women's rights; for example:

When woman's rights is stirred a bit
De first reform she bitches on
Is how she can wid least delay
Just draw a pair ob britches on.[8]

The minstrel show also featured a stock low-comedy character: the grotesque black woman or the "funny ole gal." In contrast to male performers' creation of the "plantation yellow girl" (an attractive, well-dressed mulatto), female impersonators made the "funny ole gal" decidedly unattractive by wearing mismatched clothes and speaking in a shrill voice. The character's large arms and legs and often "oversized" shoes drew attention to her underlying masculinity.[9]

Historians have paid most attention to the minstrel show's racism, arguing that by presenting sentimental images of contented slaves in the South and rebellious, incompetent free blacks, the minstrel show primarily supported slavery during the period in which slavery was increasingly challenged and provided a justification for white control of blacks.[10] Recently, however, scholars have focused more broadly on how putting on blackface stirred up controversy about social issues beyond, but often linked to, race. Some have argued that the minstrel show helped white working-class northern men (the primary audience for this entertainment) unite together above blacks, gave them tools to challenge their subordinate status, and offered some routes of escape through fantasy. Through the image of the libidinous, carefree black, the minstrel show provided an outlet for spectators' longings for a preindustrial, rural past—a way to counter the discipline and dislocation of urban, industrial life. As David Roediger explains, "A mythical Black South came to fill the role of an imagined haven standing against the deadening aspects of progress for popular Northern minstrel audiences."[11]

The racial borrowings and masks of the minstrel show lived on in American culture long after the professional minstrel show declined in the late nineteenth century. Vaudeville and musical comedies became the primary sites of blackface entertainment, but the minstrel show also shaped the development of Hollywood films.[12] Rogin argues that, through their blackface masks, Jewish performers in films such as *The Jazz Singer* (1927) literally displaced African Americans on the screen and constructed new American identities, proving that the malleability of ethnicity was based on the immutability of race in America. Black-face, as Rogin explains, often conveyed a longing for a connection to the worlds of immigrant community and family that were tossed aside for a place in American modernity: "Blackface . . . was the transitional object whose emotional linkage to a world left behind facilitated movement forward and away."[13] These recent discussions of the pervasiveness of racial masquerade in twentieth-century American culture have largely bypassed vaudeville as well as white female performers, focusing instead on men in Hollywood or on white female authors.[14] But white women's performances in vaudeville, the minstrel show's direct descendant, are an important chapter in the story of racial disguise as a link between new and old identities, between modern culture and tradition, between the brutalities of racial hierarchies in America and the "white-washed" histories of racial unity.[15]

Whereas the minstrel show largely responded to the national debate over slavery, vaudeville's racialized performances emerged in the midst of political struggles over integration and black migration following Reconstruction. The migration of African Americans from rural areas and the South created significant African American populations in northern cities.[16] As the number of urban blacks increased and African American communities became more visible in these cities, segregation and discrimination intensified. Big-time vaudeville, with its segregated seating and the prominence of racial stereotyping in its productions, was one of the many institutions restricting African Americans' freedoms following Reconstruction.

White women's use of blackface first needs to be understood in relation to the racial rules in vaudeville, including the performance styles assigned to white and black performers as well as the emphasis on racial hierarchy in the theaters. Vaudeville managers allowed white players to take on a range of racial disguises, but they discouraged black performers from trying to look or act white. In contrast to white women who had the privilege of playing with blackness and with less physically inhibited, more sexual selves, black women struggled to be taken seriously, in many cases trying to break into the white ranks of leading ladies and highbrow artists.

Vaudeville managers wanted black performers' racial identities to be readily apparent and attempted to keep black performers locked into "low" categories, such as uninhibited dancing and slapstick comedy, whereas many white players could present highbrow acts. Charles Lovenberg's comments about concert singer Rosa Lee Tyler in 1903 dramatically reveal these pressures on black performers: "Like most of these people when they attempt classical singing, she falls decidedly short. Seems beyond the Negro race to do this. Her voice is metallic and screechy and her make-up is decidedly bad as she powders up considerably in order to disguise the fact that she is a Negro, but I shall endeavor to have her discontinue."[17] Four years later, Lovenberg also criticized singer Margaret Scott for trying to alter her appearance: "Miss Scott—for a colored woman—has a very good voice and has had some instructions. If she didn't paint her hair red and try to make up like a white woman the act would be considerably better."[18] Black performers who did not offer comedy were sharply criticized by managers. A theater manager from Indianapolis explained that "[a]udiences in this town are not prepared to accept negro acts unless they are comedy."[19] Lovenberg, in addition, denounced other attempts by black performers to broaden their acts beyond comedy. The Golden Gate Quintette, a singing group, tried to capitalize on its success by branching out into "white" styles, according to Lovenberg: "Like most colored entertainers, after they get a little bit of standing, they want to do the 'neat' work more suited to white people and in that way, lose the darkey [sic] personality. At the points where they did comedy work it was exceedingly well-accepted."[20] He was also disturbed when the leading black performers in the musical act *The Sunny South* wore "white people's clothes."[21]

Striving to keep racial identities clear onstage, managers were particularly concerned about avoiding even the appearance of interracial

romance. Even white performers had to avoid the suggestion of interracial attractions. When one member of a white comedy team decided
to use blackface but the other appeared without blackface, one Keith
manager complained in 1907: "I do not think that any audience wants to
see a white man making love to a negro."[22] Some performers, in addition, were controversial because they suggested an interracial relationship between performer and audience that was too intimate. In his description of black storyteller Honey Johnson, Keith's manager in
Philadelphia found that "this fellow is a fair singer, but his talk was a little rough and he tried to get confidential with the audience: as a result
they froze up on him. This town is too far South to stand for confidential talks from colored man, and consequently I cut out the talk."[23]

Despite managers' attempts to separate the races, there were instances of racial confusion and crossover in vaudeville. Keith's administrators, for example, carefully noted instances in which black performers could have passed for white. Commenting on Bailey and Brown's act
in 1907, the manager of Keith's theater in Philadelphia was particularly
concerned about the racial identity of a light-skinned woman in the act:
"She is nearly as white as you make them, and if she were not accompanied by the colored man in the act, no one would know it."[24]

Performers like Aida Overton Walker and Bert Williams, whose
racial identity was not in doubt, still raised questions about crossing
racial boundaries by attracting both white and black fans. Walker's appearance at Keith's theater in Providence prompted manager Charles
Lovenberg to speculate on her popularity with both white and black patrons: "Did not go with very much applause. . . . [I]t may be due to race
prejudice. The fact remains that she is a very big drawing card, attracting white people as well as people of her own race."[25] The racial politics
of Walker's act, however, went well beyond her ability to attract an interracial audience. She was most famous for her version of the cakewalk,
a dance in which performers strutted with their backs arched and their
heads thrown back.[26] Historians have traced the origin of the cakewalk
to a plantation dance in which slaves mocked their white masters' dance
styles.[27] At the height of the cakewalk craze around 1900, black performers were often recruited to teach the dance to elite whites. Tom
Fletcher reportedly coached Mr. and Mrs. William K. Vanderbilt in the

cakewalk, and newspapers noted in 1903 that Aida Walker taught the dance to white society women.[28] These examples from Walker's career illustrate that, despite the attempts by Keith vaudeville managers to uphold segregation of the races, racial borrowings and a cross-racial following were core elements of her act.

Bert Williams, a West Indian, began performing with George Walker in 1893 in a minstrel show, and together they developed a singing and comedy act for vaudeville. They also produced and starred in black musical comedies, such as *In Dahomey* (1903). Compelled to perform in the "straitjacket" of blackface and racial dialect, Williams also faced the color line of the popular stage in other ways.[29] When Williams embarked on a long-term contract with Florenz Ziegfeld to perform in the *Follies*, Williams and Ziegfeld agreed that Williams would not perform onstage with white women from the cast, and Ziegfeld promised Williams he would not have to travel in the South with the *Follies*. Williams also endured secondary accommodations (shabby dressing rooms and segregated lodging) even though he was a star.[30] Keith managers acknowledged Williams's popularity, although they often seemed more resigned to it than enthusiastic about it. "I guess this is the rule everywhere," observed the manager of the Hippodrome in Cleveland. "There's no getting away from the fact that Williams is a big card here." Also attesting to Williams's success, a theater manager in Cincinnati commented on the racial composition of his audience: "It is useless to describe Mr. Williams as he simply walked away with everything. . . . [T]his is a very strong southern town, and our gallery looked like a thunderstorm."[31]

Managers' discussions of the racial rules thus point to their resistance to performers' experiments outside of these racial boundaries in vaudeville, not the absolute nature of racial segregation in vaudeville. Nonetheless, managers clearly accepted white women's challenges to vaudeville's ideal womanhood far more readily than they tolerated black performers' attempts to cross the racial lines in vaudeville. Vaudeville permitted some play with both race and gender identities, but not to the same degree. White women's increasing use of racial masquerades indicates a freedom in performance choices that black performers were often denied.[32]

As the managers' comments reveal, vaudeville administrators restricted racial interaction onstage; black performers were not supposed to give the impression of being white even when they were onstage with other black actors, particularly if there was a romantic theme to the performance. Nevertheless, black and white performers could appear onstage together in vaudeville if white dominance was part of the structure of the performance and if sexuality was sufficiently subdued. Pickaninny acts were one such attempt to mix races and sexes onstage.[33] In these routines, white women led choruses of energetic young black performers in song-and-dance routines. The black performers were molded into the caricature of the pickaninny, a stereotype of black children as wild, stupid, and unkempt. Film historian Donald Bogle describes the pickaninny character as a "harmless, little screwball creation whose eyes popped, [and] whose hair stood on end with the least excitement," pointing to Topsy from the literary and stage versions of *Uncle Tom's Cabin* as the quintessential pickaninny.[34] One of the pickaninnies in Josephine Gassman's vaudeville act received praise for what one observer considered his main accomplishments—"puckering his lips and rolling his eyes in approved stage 'coon style.'"[35] The pickaninny image also circulated well beyond the stage and literature. In 1884 the N. K. Fairbank Company introduced the cartoon images of two pickaninnies, the Gold Dust Twins (Goldy and Dusty), to promote its brand of soap. The company even hired black children to hand out product samples and pamphlets at the 1904 St. Louis World's Fair.[36]

The musical fare in pickaninny acts consisted of the popular coon songs of this period. Coon songs combined syncopated rhythms with racist lyrics and often racial dialect. They built on the outlandish and ignorant Zip Coon character from the minstrel show as well as the servile and incompetent Jim Crow type. But coon songs made African Americans seem more threatening and sinister than the minstrel show caricatures.[37] They often portrayed aggressive and overly sexual black men who carried razors as weapons and had many volatile, short-lived romantic liaisons, thus linking black men to violent, sexual threats to the social order.[38] Another group of coon songs sentimentalized "Dixie" in part by presenting the figure of the mammy—maternal, servile, and contented—working in harmony with her white masters on the plantation. Both types of songs were significant to white women's racial masquerades.

Aside from including the common caricature of the pickaninny and the typical coon songs, these acts varied greatly in content. Some of the white women, praised for their beauty and their gorgeous gowns, seemed to stand far apart from their pickaninny choruses, guiding them but not sharing in their antics. When Ethel Whiteside appeared in a southern act with her pickaninnies, reviewers noted that "[s]he makes a pretty stage appearance in a red gown and she led the little fellows through the act in a way that compelled the audience to give the act a big reception."[39] Indeed, many managers on the Keith circuit believed that the less leading women did onstage, the better the act. Critics agreed that Mayme Remington's main contribution to her act was "managing" the skillful pickaninnies. One wrote that her act, "outside of her good looks, lay in her ability to get good work from her five colored helpers, who are a lively lot."[40] Another explained: "She doesn't do much herself, except wear dazzling costumes and manage the act. . . . The 'pics' are dark-skinned dominoes of dance."[41]

In other cases, however, white women put on blackface and seemed to attempt to duplicate the exuberance and wild activity of the pickaninnies. Josephine Gassman, a white woman who had performed as Little Eva in a stage version of *Uncle Tom's Cabin*, blackened her face and put on a dark woolly wig as she danced along with her chorus in her vaudeville act. The cover of the sheet music for her song, "Mammy's Carolina Twins," shows Gassman lifting the hem of her baggy dress over one shoulder while one of her pickaninnies, a young girl, does the same. Her style troubled some managers. In 1903 the manager of one of Keith's New York City theaters complained that Gassman's appearance was "almost discusting [*sic*] to a refined taste, and before she had worked four minutes she was sweaty, slimey [*sic*] and slopping, owing probably to her blackface makeup. We have buried the act in the show and docked her salary $25."[42] Even as late as 1920, a Keith manager who seemed to be particularly strict in the cuts for his Boston theater asked Gassman to "modify the wiggle" in one of her numbers.[43] Similarly, circuit administrators criticized other white women who did not appear to be sufficiently "above" the black performers in their acts. Leona Thurber, in particular, overstepped the boundaries of vaudeville propriety, and one theater manager advised his coworkers that she belonged as the "leading woman in a burlesque show."[44] Part of the explanation for these attacks on Thurber's respectability was that her "pickaninnies" were, according to several reviews, nearly "full grown."[45] It seems that Thurber's act did not involve a white woman with maternal control over black children; rather, it revealed the troubling image of sexually mature black men singing and dancing with a white woman—a combination that vaudeville managers tried to avoid.

As these reviews suggest, pickaninny acts were sometimes problematic on the Keith circuit. Managers and critics saw them as particularly coarse relics of the past, affronts to vaudeville's feminization. The manager of Keith's theater in Boston wrote about Mayme Remington's act in 1907: "It looks very much to me as though the rage for coon acts of this kind is about over, although Miss Remington's picks do some extremely clever work, work that in the old days would have brought down the house."[46] Another vaudeville manager, John Finn, found that Remington's act was "inartistic and appeals to nearly everybody but the cultured."[47]

Nevertheless, publicity about some of the pickaninny acts emphasized the respectability of the white women as well as their maternal authority over the young black performers. One critic described Thurber as a teacher and philanthropist, noting that she spent time offstage educating the children who performed in her act. "Poor little kids," said Thurber in an interview; "they have no one who cares particularly for them, and I want to help them all I can."[48] A report on Gassman described her in a similar way: "[S]he wrapped her pretty, plump, dimpled shoulders in an old shawl and cuddled down in a chair in her dressing room. . . . Then the trio of little pickaninnies whom she uses in her act cuddled down with her."[49] But these women's control was hardly secure onstage or offstage, and the relationships between the black performers and their leading white women was hardly harmonious. In one case in which the women's loss of authority was unequivocal, manager Charles Lovenberg reported that "Miss Remington's act was handicapped by the absence of her most important pickaninny who she said ran away from her on Sunday night."[50] And Remington stated in an interview

Cover of the sheet music for "Mammy's Carolina Twins," featuring
Josephine Gassman and her "pickaninnies," 1899. Some managers called
her style of dancing and her use of blackface disgusting.
Courtesy of Brown University Library.

that her "greatest difficulty" was retaining the youthful performers after they had become successful.[51]

Although their authority was not absolute, the white leaders of the pickaninny acts exploited the racial hierarchy of vaudeville to become leaders of a troupe of performers. In fact, racial disguise was often a key component of female performers' escape from subordinate roles in choruses. The publicity surrounding Lulu and Mabel Nichols, a sister act, emphasized that blackface had lifted them out of the anonymity of the chorus line. A 1907 article, "How a Sister Act Gained Fame and Local Color," reported that a director had pulled the Nichols sisters out of the chorus of the comic opera *The King's Jester* to present a blackface specialty. Lulu and Mabel recalled that they had been chosen because "we were Southern born and knew the ways of the mammies."[52] Significantly, blackface was identified as "a lucrative road to individual success," and the Nichols Sisters gained a reputation as ambitious risk takers for giving up their beauty and vanity.[53] One photograph shows them in floppy straw hats eating watermelon; in another they stand side by side in rather plain, ill-fitting dresses with their heads lolling down. In each shot, their skin is very dark, their eyes and mouths exaggerated with white makeup.[54] Rather than receiving marriage proposals from fans, the Nichols Sisters regularly faced accusations that they were men, largely because they borrowed the conventions of the traditional, male-dominated minstrel show. "At every performance we can hear someone in the front say: 'Oh, that one's a man. They can't fool me; I've seen too many minstrel shows.'"[55]

The leaders of pickaninny acts usually did not encounter such gender confusion because they were most often cast in a maternal light. The songs in these women's acts often featured the mammy image, thus reinforcing the newspaper descriptions of them as maternal. Gassman, for example, sang "Mammy's Little Pumpkin Colored Coons" (1897) and "Mammy's Carolina Twins" (1899), which depicted a mammy putting her "picks" to sleep in the tranquil South: "In an Ivy covered cottage / Whar de honey suckle's creeping, / Lives Aunt Jennie and her Carolina Twins."[56] These descriptions of white women in pickaninny acts and the themes of some of their songs made these women seem nurturing and domestic in contrast to other descriptions of them (in managers' reports, for example) as dangerous to vaudeville's reputation because of their sometimes sexually charged links with the unruly black performers.

The white women leading pickaninny choruses became, in many ways, mammies onstage, relying on the race relations that trapped the black mammy but reversing the racial and pseudofamilial roles by becoming the surrogate mothers of black children. The concept of the female slave running the plantation household had little correlation to the actual circumstances of slave women. Historians have found only a few examples of female slaves who worked as the "right hand" of white mistresses before the Civil War. But the stereotype of the mammy as contented, industrious, and, above all, loyal to her white owners was a powerful justification for slavery in the antebellum period as well as a defense of Jim Crow segregation around the turn of the century, the period in which the image of the mammy reached its greatest popularity. The mammy was prevalent in popular culture, academic histories, and civic culture during this period. The mammy caricature was well known to vaudeville performers, managers, and fans. Billy Blackburn, for example, included the mammy character in her routine, in which she presented southern stories and songs and changed to blackface in view of the audience, "making up as an old southern mammy."[57] Citizens also proposed memorials to the mammy, and one group of white southerners even sought support for a "Black Mammy Memorial Institute," which would train black students in the "arts and industries that made the 'old Black Mammy' valuable and worthy."[58] Taken together, these phenomena comprised a "cult" of the mammy around the turn of the century, according to Patricia Morton.[59]

The growth of the popularity of mammy imagery coincided with the emergence of sentimental portraits of the southern past that ironically arose along with the New South movement. As southerners were increasingly embracing industrialization and northern mores around the turn of the century, they were also drawn to romantic portraits of a distinctive southern past that erased racial conflict. Such homage to a fictive southern history emerged, for example, in the Confederate Lost Cause movement, which attempted to redeem the Confederate tradition, and in the hundreds of popular songs that presented the South as an escape from the northern city.[60]

The mammy was a complex figure. Overweight and maternal, she symbolized the benign relations between black women and white men — an alternative to the sexual depravity suggested by the portrait of the female slave as a Jezebel or an "octoroon concubine," a hypersexual woman who seduced white men.[61] As Catherine Clinton has noted, however, popular descriptions of the mammy often had a sexual under-tone. When southern men repeatedly referred to being "suckled at black breasts," they suggested erotic elements of the maternal mammy.[62] Thus, although the mammy was considered unattractive (she was fat, had very dark skin, and wore plain clothes, often including a scarf on her head), she was not entirely asexual. Along with sexual suggestions, a tension between power and subservience existed in the symbol of the mammy. She was depicted as "white identified," happy to be a slave, and devoted to her white family.[63] But the mammy also held power in the plantation house; industrious and capable, she was a rare image of blacks with power. The mammy stood alone as a positive portrait of black authority, but this representation was softened by the mammy's largely maternal influence. In these ways, the image of the mammy was a centerpiece of whites' "emasculation of slavery," according to Clinton. Slave men seemed weak in the shadow of the mammy. And the mammy deviated from "true womanhood in the sense of fragility, passivity and dependency" since she was strong and robust.[64] In D. W. Griffith's *Birth of a Nation* (1915), the mammy actually assaults black soldiers in de-fense of her white master's home.[65]

Mammies were thus domestic caregivers with hints of sexuality, happy-go-lucky servants who often ruled the white households as well as their own, and masculine black women who suggested the feminiza-tion of their black brothers, husbands, and fathers. This multilayered mammy imagery framed the identities of the white women who moved out of choruses and took leading roles in vaudeville through racial mas-querades. Although their power in these acts sometimes seemed bold (even masculine), it was softened by the nurturing aura surrounding them in their songs and publicity. And although their authority over the youthful black performers was often described as maternal, their acts were sometimes charged with an illicit sexual exchange between black male performers and white women.

The combination of an uninhibited, masculine comic style and the suggestions of a maternal mammy (a nexus of authority and subservience) was also evident in the career of May Irwin, a popular coon singer who was primarily known for her musical comedy career but who also appeared in vaudeville. In 1875, at the age of twelve, Irwin began to perform with her sister Flo in variety shows throughout the Midwest, and later she appeared in Tony Pastor's variety theater on Fourteenth Street in New York City. In the 1880s she moved into legitimate theater under the direction of Augustin Daly, playing primarily the comic role of servant. She later formed her own company and starred in a series of musical comedies that showcased her coon songs. In 1895 she played the lead role in *The Widow Jones*, which featured her rendition of "The Bully Song" (1895), a coon song by Charles Trevathan. Irwin also sang coon songs in her periodic vaudeville engagements, including a major tour during the 1907–8 season.[66] Unlike many other white women who used blackface, Irwin constructed her racial masquerade primarily through the dialect and lyrics of her popular coon songs. It is impossible to document the content of all of her vaudeville acts, but it is clear that Irwin regularly performed her hit songs from the 1890s, including "When You Ain't Got No Money" (1896), and that "The Bully Song" was a standard feature of her act.[67] Even when she came back to the vaudeville stage in 1925 after a period of retirement, she sang the old favorite. She reportedly teased the audience: "I could tell you I'd sing my old song 'The Bully' but that I haven't got the music. But that would be a stall. I have got it, and it's right down there (the orchestra pit), and I am going to sing it."[68] Some publicity also indicated that she often had a black boy come onstage during her performances of "The Bully Song," and she appeared on the cover of the sheet music for another coon song, "Honey on My Lips" (1896), with a black child.[69]

As the racial politics of vaudeville granted some white women authority over a chorus of black children, racial masquerades emboldened some white comediennes by setting them apart from svelte, perky chorus girls. Much of the discussion of May Irwin, for example, focused on the fact that she was larger, more forceful, and funnier than the average female performer. As one critic explained, May Irwin's "gladiator shoulders . . . tread of a goliath and . . . nervous energy of a locomotive" con-

May Irwin with "the new bully," 1897. A black child reportedly joined Irwin on the vaudeville stage when she sang her trademark coon song "The Bully Song." Courtesy of the Theatre Arts Collection, Harry Ransom Humanities Research Center, The University of Texas at Austin.

trasted with the characteristics of the "slim, sweet maid."[70] And critics acknowledged that Irwin's comic success, based partly on racial masquerade, was pioneering for white women. One report on Irwin declared that she had, "although there are some . . . who say no woman can possess it, a very keen sense of humor."[71] Another critic remarked that "[i]t is not easy for a woman to be funny and retain the sympathy and respect of her audiences."[72]

Irwin's physical power and controversial comedy were based on two interlocking elements: the subtext of black masculinity in her popular songs and her large size. Some of Irwin's coon songs allowed her to adopt the persona of a combative black man. "The Bully Song," for example, details the exploits of an aggressive black man who ultimately reasserts his authority over a competing bully. The vengeful bully finally kills his rival ("I lit upon that bully just like a sparrow hawk / And dat nigger was just a dyin' to take a walk"), and displays his sexual prowess. He boasts that after Miss Pansy Blossom dances with him, she says, "Law, Mr. Johnson, how high you make me feel."[73] Other songs attributed to Irwin around the turn of the century follow a similar pattern. In "Crappy Dan de Spo'tin' Man," Irwin also sings as a black man who is always gambling and ready for a fight, "for Crappy Dan has allus got his gun."[74] Filled with bravado, these songs emphasize the physically threatening black male body, an image reinforced by Irwin's corpulence onstage.

Irwin's large size also contributed to her physically and sexually imposing comic style. Her humor was defined as "broad," and her dances onstage were part of her jokes. According to one critic, her coon songs were "naughty," particularly "I'm Afraid to Go Home in the Dark," which was about a man who stays out all night because of his fear of the dark.[75] One reviewer commented that the "grotesque gait" she used in her cakewalks "never fails to secure a laugh when she ambles down the footlights."[76] Another noted that her act included a "funny, bulky substitute for a dance."[77] And her size was not simply part of the joke of her awkward rendition of the cakewalk; Irwin made it a topic of her comic banter as well. Although she did not apologize for her size in her interviews (one reporter, in fact, noted that Irwin was "afraid of getting thin"), she did make fun of her size onstage. For example, she referred to herself as a "hippotomatic" and the "jumbo of farce," joking that "[a] cigarette firm wants to use my picture on their cigarettes. They must be contemplating enlarging their packages."[78]

As Irwin's career suggests, racial masquerade was one avenue to vaudeville success (and to the infiltration of male roles) for women who were not conventionally attractive. Irwin, in particular, resembled other large white women who were associated with coon songs of the 1890s — namely, Fay Templeton and Marie Dressler.[79] One article tied these women to the original "raucous" coon songs as opposed to the "neat coon songs" of the early twentieth century. The women who sang the new coon songs were more likely to be glamorous and dignified on-stage, in contrast to Irwin and her comrades, who "made wild gestures and threw their voices at the appreciative gallery."[80]

What explains the affinity between fat white women and the rough coon song? In some cases, as we have seen, racial masquerades launched women out of mundane careers by making them unusually ugly, whereas publicity for their acts affirmed their white beauty beneath the masks. In other cases, unattractive female performers adopted racial masquer-ades, although sometimes reluctantly, to achieve fame in vaudeville. What these two groups of women shared was the use of racial mas-querade to create or augment an unconventional appearance that then became the currency of their comedy. Fay Templeton toured in vaude-ville dressed as a black washerwoman, regularly performed the cake-walk, and sang some coon songs, such as "I Want You, Ma Honey," which Irwin had also sang. Her publicity often focused on her size. In one interview, she described her "bout with the Demon Flesh," includ-ing one successful diet, the oddly racialized watermelon treatment.[81] But the most famous example of the link between size, beauty, and blackface for women in vaudeville is Sophie Tucker, a singer who per-formed for several years in blackface and was identified in 1906 as the "World Renowned Coon Shouter."[82] Early in her career, a manager de-clared, "This one's so big and ugly the crowd out front will razz her. Better get some cork and black her up."[83] Tucker reportedly was ashamed of using blackface and was glad to finally perform without it after her luggage with her traditional costumes did not arrive for an en-gagement in 1908.[84]

White Women's Racial Masquerades

For these women, blackface provided an immediate cue to the audience about how to read their acts: it marked them as comic objects. These women's racial masquerades and their fat made them clowns onstage; primarily removed from the position of erotic objects, these performers gained some comic and sexual freedoms. As Robert Allen has observed in his analysis of American burlesque, female performers who were "low Others" through their association with prostitution, the lower body, or the working classes gained comic license largely because they were cordoned off from bourgeois society. Unruly female performers were tolerated "so long as their transgressive power was channeled and diffused through their construction of grotesque figures."[85] In 1913 a Keith manager captured these dynamics at work in Marie Dressler's comedy: "One hesitates to contemplate what would become of Miss Dressler's vocation if she ever lost her weight. She is just the same big, boisterous gross clown of yore and always bordering so dangerously near the suggestive, if not getting altogether over the line. Nevertheless, she stirred up a riot of laughter and applause."[86]

Racial masquerades and fat indeed combined to make white women "other" in vaudeville, giving them space for rebellious and sexually aggressive performances but also making them the butt of jokes onstage. These women, however, were not wholly rejected as sexually repugnant; in fact, their performances could raise questions about the narrow parameters of feminine beauty and even suggest some of the drawbacks of being a sex object. One writer, for example, bemoaned the ignorance of male spectators who had neglected to send Irwin mash notes. "What is the matter with you boys?," the author asked. "Do you want a sweet smile over the footlights? Well, when May smiles, she smiles good and plenty."[87] Another critic admitted that Irwin was doing her "utmost . . . to surreptitiously hint that a sylph is not the only desirable idea of theatrical womanhood."[88] The white woman in blackface could also challenge the understanding that women wanted to be erotic objects onstage. Gertrude Fay and Hattie Coley, who performed in blackface with their partners Frank Fay and Clarence Coley, did not receive "Johnnie notes, for how is Johnnie to know they are pretty? This is a great comfort the girls say. Maybe it is."[89] These women—from May Irwin to Hattie Coley—were certainly ridiculed for failing to emulate the chorus girl, but they also suggested that freedoms and pleasures existed outside of this model of womanhood.[90]

Although May Irwin's racial masquerades and her large body suggested an imposing black masculinity, her persona also contained an alternative subtext—the mammy. Irwin's mammyesque qualities softened her authority, but these traits did not wholly neutralize her gender transgressions (since the mammy herself was often seen as inappropriately masculine). A few of Irwin's coon songs featured a mammy (for example, Irwin sang the 1899 song "Mammy's Carolina Twins"), and her publicity sometimes mentioned that black female maids and mammies were the inspiration for her coon songs and dances. One newspaper report stated that Charles Trevathan, the author of many of Irwin's coon songs (including "The Bully"), was "brought up on a plantation, with the rich melody of the negro 'mammy' songs ringing in his ears."[91] In addition, Irwin recalled that she learned the cakewalk after bribing her way into a dance put on by black employees at a hotel. She first saw "young waiters and prim little chambermaids" perform the cakewalk, but then a "bouncy Ethiopian with avoirdupois going beyond the reach of obesity pills" became impatient with the tame display and showed them a cakewalk with more grotesque gyrations. This became Irwin's model for her cakewalk.[92] Irwin was also photographed frequently with her black maid, Sarah, who in at least one picture was shown listening to Irwin singing a coon song.[93] These accounts reveal white performers' "theft" of black culture, a regular feature of the minstrel show tradition as well as musical and dance styles (such as ragtime) in vaudeville, but they also attempt to erase the exploitation of these racial borrowings by depicting the black woman as a contented, faithful servant—in some cases, identified directly with a mythical plantation.

Irwin herself had many of the mammy's traits. Her fat body was linked to her good humor, a trait that was also associated with the easygoing mammy and with maternity, a key component of the mammy image. Certainly the shimmy of Irwin's cakewalk would have called attention to Irwin's large breasts.[94] Press descriptions of Irwin's private life reinforced the maternity that her fat body suggested by pointing repeatedly to her domestic skills. She was a good cook, cared for an ill parent, nurtured her two sons, and liked to do her own housework even though she had skilled servants.[95] One article proclaimed that Irwin was the "model housewife."[96]

Along with the mammy image, the nostalgia in Irwin's acts emerged in songs featuring a gentle, emotional black male narrator who longed for his lover in a bucolic southern setting. "Louisiana Lize" (1899), "Magdaline My Southern Queen" (1900), and "Ma Mississippi Belle" (1903) present idyllic southern scenes—in which the narrators doze beside rivers and enjoy the southern breeze—that are linked to a woman's beauty and love.[97] Although it is not clear whether or not Irwin sang these songs during her vaudeville tours, she was pictured on the covers of the sheet music of these songs, and they were identified as her hits. As such, they may have been familiar to vaudeville audiences, adding another dimension to her image. These three songs were written by Robert Cole, James Weldon Johnson, and Johnson's brother, J. Rosamond Johnson, three black artists who combined romance and sentimentality with the ragtime coon song. Using milder dialect in their works than other composers did, Cole and the Johnson brothers tried to work against the stereotypes of African Americans as crude and animalistic. They usually wrote love songs with characters who were compassionate and sensitive in an attempt to undermine the notion that the "Negro was deficient in the finer sentiments."[98] In this group of Irwin's coon songs, the feminine black male narrator (docile and expressive) contrasts with the rough, aggressive black men of "The Bully Song" and "Crappy Dan de Spo'tin' Man."

The multiple racial caricatures in Irwin's act reveal the ways gender intersects with race in the representation of African Americans: the mammy and the feminized black men signified racial inferiority, in part, through their varying degrees of deviation from gender ideals, whereas the black brute was a disruptive, antagonistic force (particularly threatening to white womanhood) that suggested the need for white repression of African Americans. Similar to the widespread representation of African Americans in popular culture, Irwin's act features only one positive image of African American power—the mammy. Furthermore, Irwin's songs, with their contrasting portraits of black masculinity, exemplify the contradictory representation of black men in American popular culture. They embody supermasculinity and primitive sexuality but also have often been emasculated in popular representations. For example, early-twentieth-century films such as D. W. Griffith's *Birth of a Nation* depicted black men as uncontrollably sexual and violent, particularly toward white women, whereas early film versions of Harriet Beecher Stowe's 1852 novel *Uncle Tom's Cabin* presented Uncle Tom as merciful, affectionate, and submissive—as feminine.[99] Individual black male stars have also been framed in these contrasting ways. Paul Robeson, a singer and actor in films and on Broadway from the 1920s through the 1950s, was often portrayed as a strong, erotic, and brutal character. But he was also photographed and filmed in ways that feminized him by making him a spectacle of "passive beauty."[100] In the 1933 film *Emperor Jones*, Robeson played Brutus Jones, a southern black man who becomes the leader of a Caribbean Island but ultimately loses control as he becomes uncivilized.[101] In other cases, Robeson's body was photographed in the tradition of the white female body—docile and still—rather than in the tradition of the white male body in action.

Considering Irwin's tributes to the plantation South, recurring use of mammy imagery, and identification with the "old-fashioned" coon songs of the 1890s, it is not surprising that she was a nostalgic figure during her 1907–8 vaudeville tour. Critics observed that she was no longer in top form, noting her age (mid-forties) and her physical bulk. One reviewer described her as an "obese elderly lady, who hasn't seen her own shoe tips in years," and another commented that she "is growing fat . . . and at her entrance looks like a sister team. . . . Time was when May Irwin was 'coon-shouter-in-chief to the American public,' but since then she has lost a good deal of her unction and others have usurped her place."[102] In one review, the author compared her to a grandmother, noting that her coquettish behavior was now unseemly: "There was a time when May could with propriety indulge these playful . . . eccentricities, but it was away back in 1872."[103] She even found herself defending coon songs, declaring, "I don't believe the coon song has outlived its usefulness."[104]

Irwin, therefore, evoked a version of vaudeville's past that contrasted with much vaudeville publicity. Although her routines included an aggressive, masculine persona, facilitated in part by racial masquerade, Irwin largely pointed to a feminine past (with images of the mammy and gentle black men in a leisurely southern setting) rather than the rugged masculine past so often described by vaudeville promoters. Racial masquerades thus shaped an alternative vision of vaudeville's past as feminine and provided contrasts with one of vaudeville's most powerful images of modernity: the chorus girl.

During her vaudeville tours, Irwin faced questions about whether coon songs were outdated, and theater managers criticized many blackface acts for having "but little to recommend [them] in this day of modern vaudeville."[105] Such criticisms escalated through the 1910s. In 1918 one vaudeville manager declared, "Blackface comedy is antiquated."[106] And by 1920, a few managers even ordered performers to omit the words "nigger" and "coon" from their acts.[107] But although coon songs and pickaninny acts were declining in popularity, racial masquerade continued to shadow up-to-date vaudeville; in a new style of act that required slim, young, and orderly chorus girls, characters in blackface harkened back to the minstrel show and the mammy. These new acts emphasized the detailed organization of the scenes, the sexual allure of the women, and male control of the productions, but racial masquerades introduced elements of unruly womanhood (as they had in pickaninny acts and among coon shouters) that contrasted with the machinelike precision and patriarchal hierarchy of these productions.

Ned Wayburn, a fan of minstrel shows as a child and a coon singer in his early professional years, used his schooling in racial disguise in directing several girl acts in vaudeville. In 1896 Wayburn sang coon songs in a vaudeville act, and in Peoria in the same year, he performed with a "pickaninny."[108] Known for his coon songs and his ragtime piano playing, Wayburn was even identified in a 1896 program as a "Negro monologist."[109] He also performed on the Keith circuit as a blackface "rag-time pianist and monologuist."[110] He crossed paths with May Irwin when he became the piano player for her coon songs and the stage manager for her production of the musical comedy *The Swell Miss Fitzwell* (1897–98). One vaudeville program also listed Wayburn as Irwin's "ragtime pianist," and one of Irwin's songs, "She's a Thoroughbred," was written by Wayburn for the musical comedy *Kate Kip, Buyer* (1898).[111]

Between 1901 and 1905, Oscar and William Hammerstein and Marc

Klaw and A. L. Erlanger commissioned Wayburn to produce feature acts for the summer theatrical seasons. Following these engagements, Wayburn's acts often toured on the Keith circuit. From 1906 to 1909, Wayburn used his own production company to market his acts to the major vaudeville chains, bypassing Klaw and Erlanger and the Hammersteins. Vaudeville proved to be a valuable training ground for Wayburn. After working with choruses in vaudeville, he went on to direct productions of the *Ziegfeld Follies* and Broadway shows.[112]

Several of Wayburn's early vaudeville productions relied heavily on minstrel show traditions. His *Minstrel Misses* (1903) featured white women in blackface, and *Ned Wayburn's Girls of 1904* included coon songs and a scene in which the chorus girls, probably in blackface, danced to Theodore Morse's "Dixie."[113] Wayburn was not alone in producing shows with chorus girls in blackface. Tim McMahon and his wife, Irene Chapelle, who performed together in a comedy act, also staged two prominent girl acts that used blackface: *The Watermelon Girls* (1906–7) and *The Pullman Porter Maids* (1908).[114] Wayburn's later vaudeville productions, such as *The Rain-dears* (1906) and *The Side Show* (1907), did not emphasize racial masquerades, and only one of his later full-length productions, the *Ziegfeld Follies of 1922*, included a minstrel show routine. As his reliance on minstrel show imagery decreased, his focus on the strict management of chorus girls and the establishment of drill-like precision onstage increased.[115]

Hailed as a pioneer, along with Florenz Ziegfeld, in the glorification of the "American girl," Wayburn became a leader in the management and promotion of girl acts.[116] It is important to clarify here that vaudeville producers were not the first to expand on the minstrel show by adding larger casts and plush scenery. Following the Civil War, the minstrel show became larger, more expensive, and more refined, and by 1871, eleven all-female minstrel companies had emerged, their primary appeal being the display of women's bodies. Despite these all-female troupes, it was still unusual for male companies to include women.[117] The minstrel show's turn toward spectacle resembles transformations in other late-nineteenth-century entertainment forms as well as advertising and department stores. The Barnum and Bailey Circus expanded to three rings and three stages, putting more emphasis on "scale, variety and sheer splendor."[118] According to historian William Leach, several late-nineteenth-century inventions, such as the electric sign, the painted billboard, and the show window, helped create increasingly colorful and complex visual images to "show goods off day and night through all possible means."[119] Just as department stores improved the display of products in their windows and advertisers turned toward visual images and away from words, vaudeville promoted spectacles onstage.

Although Wayburn did not invent the union of sexual spectacle with the minstrel show, his productions are important because they were part of the escalation of girl acts in vaudeville. These acts, in particular, reveal the centrality of a particular type of chorus girl to the consumer culture that was gaining prominence in and around vaudeville. Jesse Lasky, Joseph Hart, and B. A. Rolfe became, like Wayburn, entrepreneurial giants in vaudeville in the early twentieth century as they produced a rising number of girl acts, most of which achieved headliner status. At Keith's theater in Providence, Lasky, for example, presented a total of twenty-three acts, including seventeen headliners, between 1903 and 1914. These acts were famous for the financial extravagance of the dramatic sets and costumes as well as the precision and beauty of the choruses. Keith's publicity for these girl acts emphasized the wealth behind the scenes: describing an upcoming production by Lasky (*At the Waldorf*), an article in *Keith News* held that "[t]here is no need to tell you how magnificently [it] is staged, for Mr. Lasky has the reputation for spending more money on costumes and scenery for his vaudeville acts than any other producer."[120] Praising Lasky's production of *The Redheads* in 1913, *Keith News* concluded that "it cost as much to produce this one forty-five minute act as it would to stage a two-act musical comedy of an elaborate nature, for which the public would be charged $2."[121] Just as the advertising highlighted the cost of producing such lavish girl acts, the performances themselves frequently showcased the lives of the rich. *At the Waldorf* revolved around the theft of a diamond necklace at an upscale hotel, and *At the Country Club*, another Lasky production, featured club members chatting, dancing, and singing around a posh country club's fireplace. Through such financial extravagance and the depiction of elite characters onstage, these acts exemplified a version of the elevation of vaudeville that contrasted with Keith's focus on vaudeville's ascendance to art. It was consumption more than artistic appreciation that marked up-to-date vaudeville.

Central to these lavish displays of goods and fashions was the attractive chorus girl. The female characters in these acts were, for the most part, active in their pursuit of leisure, romance, and consumption. Sporty and sensual, they were not dirty, fat, or domineering. Beginning with the *Follies of 1907*, Florenz Ziegfeld presented musical shows with sensual women in large choruses and many different sets and costumes in a single show. The Ziegfeld girl was perky and independent but not aggressive, with a "manageable . . . wholesome" sexuality.[122] What place did blackface have in Wayburn's similar ranks of cute chorus girls or in his scenes of modern consumption? The minstrel show traditions in his acts allowed past pleasures to interrupt his experiments with the glorification of the chorus girl (as a cog in a large chorus-machine) and the world of consumerism to which she was so central. As he pushed vaudeville ahead with extravagant acts, he used blackface as a connection to his own past as well as vaudeville's.

The Minstrel Misses, the headliner act for bills on the Keith circuit in the fall of 1903, shows how Wayburn blended his own background in the messy, rowdy minstrel show with his vision of fashionable, orderly choruses in vaudeville. According to newspaper reviews of *The Minstrel Misses*, the act began with a minstrel show parade in which the seventeen chorus girls, dressed in matching plaid suits, marched in unison while carrying musical instruments. The women then moved to the rear of the stage, where they applied blackface in full view of the audience. The next section of the act featured the women seated in a circle, with the "end women" feeding the interlocutor jokes.[123] Next, the women changed into new costumes, which included red bandannas on their heads, to sing a few final songs. As the following description of *The Minstrel Misses* indicates, the elaborate scenery and the onstage application of blackface were pivotal in the act: "[T]he stage is draped in purple hangings and the seventeen girls make their entrance not yet 'made up' as minstrels, but with white faces and all costumed with long coats of fantastic designs and color and high hats. Each is playing an instrument, and after a spirited parade they retire to little tables at the rear of the stage and proceed to 'make up' as darkies, in full view of the audience. . . . After the transformation is complete, no one would recognize in the grinning colored minstrels the seventeen demure white damsels that had previously made their entrance."[124]

The women's blacking-up scene, which attracted a great deal of attention in the press, was a common element of many blackface performances. It resembled earlier minstrel show traditions and was repeated later in American culture in many motion picture musicals that also featured blackface (such as *The Jazz Singer* [1927]).[125] Publicity for minstrel shows often drew attention to the act of making up by including photographs of performers before and after they applied their mask; one minstrel performer was renowned for putting on his makeup and taking it off in mere seconds.[126] Such advertising highlighted the authentic whiteness of performers: minstrel performers were only playing with blackness. Similarly, in her autobiography, Sophie Tucker revealed her motivation for removing one of her gloves at the end of her blackface act: it was a "good stunt at the end of my act to peel off a glove and wave to the crowd to show I was a white girl."[127] These scenes seemed to reveal the secrets of blackface, including the performer's identity, by exposing the labor usually undertaken backstage. But as Michael Rogin points out in his analysis of these scenes in Hollywood musicals, they also left the myth of self-creation intact. These images of performers blacking up upheld the American ideal of individual autonomy in identity formation, a freedom denied to many American citizens because of race. "What looks like uncovering origins and exposing how the magic works is the deepest mystification of all," explains Rogin, "for it attributes the ability to change identity to the individual construction of the self."[128]

The specific scene of blacking up marked the transition from order to disorder in *The Minstrel Misses* and crystallized tensions about Wayburn's patriarchal authority over the chorus girls. After the initial parade, which featured "business like" marching, the chorus girls turned to the long makeup tables. Descriptions of this process emphasized that it was hectic and messy. "The girls now engage in a mad race for first honors in reaching the minstrel goal," wrote one critic.[129] One photograph shows the women hunched over the table with their hands flail-

The Minstrel Misses, 1903.
Courtesy of the Billy Rose Theatre Collection, The New York Public Library
for the Performing Arts, Astor, Lenox and Tilden Foundations.

ing about their faces; spectators saw the women "grab" the woolly wigs
and "dive" into their gloves.[130] When they emerged in blackface, the
comic banter, described by one reviewer as a "cackle," began quickly, led
by "end woman" Bertie Herron. Publicity emphasized Herron's exuberance; the cover of a pamphlet advertising the act features Herron in
blackface bursting through a sheet of paper, smiling widely with her
eyebrows raised in surprise. Later in her career, when she was appearing with Bonnie Gaylord in an act called the Corking Girls, Herron
poked fun at the *Ziegfeld Follies*, perhaps to emphasize how different her
act was from the usual corps of chorus girls. In 1914 the manager of
Keith's Hippodrome in Cleveland noted that Herron's material, much of
which was apparently drawn from *The Minstrel Misses*, was quite "raw."
In this act, Herron remarked that "she could not go with Ziegfeld because she had a scar on her knee."[131] It is difficult to understand the full
meaning of the joke without knowing more about the Corking Girls'
act, but it does seem clear that Herron set herself apart from the
Ziegfeld girl's sexual objectification (her notoriously short skirt) and
called attention instead to her own ruggedness.

White Women's Racial Masquerades

Although blackface seemed to set the Minstrel Misses free onstage, it also conveyed their subordination to Wayburn. Wayburn, for example, pointed to the blacking-up scene as evidence of his will and authority, not just the Misses' comic license onstage. The director proudly recalled that he had gone against conventional wisdom when he insisted on showing the blacking up onstage: "[I]t was proposed to me that I should have a specialty played while the girls were making up off the stage. I wouldn't listen to this, and I'm glad I didn't now."[132] The publicity for the act included photographs of Wayburn directing the chorus girls while they were dressed in their racial disguises. One such shot had the revealing caption, "Training the Misses." The article accompanying the photograph featured Wayburn's description of his philosophy for putting on girl acts: he did not recruit stars to be in his acts, and he preferred chorus girls who did not have any formal training in music or dance because he taught them these skills himself, molding them to "work together in unison."[133] The racial masquerades reinforced the chorus girls' subordination to Wayburn, transforming the women into the director's pets and property. Other connotations of blackface also suggest the objectification of the Misses. As Susan Gubar explains, blackface, often referred to as "chocolate" or "mahogany," "links the performer to commodity objects."[134]

The discussion of blacking up thus captured broader tensions between order and disorder, which, in the context of this girl act, appeared to be a struggle between the control of the male director and the chaos of the blacked-up Minstrel Misses. The blackface was part of a balance between the chorus girls' temporary "vim" and the "precision" of Wayburn's overall structure of the act.[135] This balance was indeed precarious at the start of the Minstrel Misses' tour on the Keith circuit. When the Minstrel Misses first appeared on the circuit, the act was not immediately successful. Managers commented that they did not receive much applause, despite the novelty of the act, and one manager even noted that they were "dead ones" on his bill.[136] Most revealing, however, was theater manager M. J. Keating's observation that the act "needs more ginger infused to it."[137] Although suggestions for a solution to the act's lackluster premiere may have pointed to the need for more energetic performances by the many women in the act, they also primarily called on Wayburn's expertise, thus emphasizing his control over the women. One manager noted that Wayburn was "studying the act closely" and had stayed late making changes in the act.[138] Wayburn's tinkering was apparently successful since his Misses played a full season on the Keith circuit.

Besides transforming the Minstrel Misses into wild women onstage, their racial disguises introduced the figure of the mammy. The Minstrel Misses' songs included such sentimental tunes as "Climbing Up de Golden Stairs" (1884) and "Oh Dem Golden Slippers."[139] In addition, the Misses sang "The Good Old Songs Our Mammy Sung," and their costumes, including bandannas on their heads, invoked the mammy image. But they lacked other qualities of the mammy: they resembled trim flappers, not rotund grandmothers, and unlike some of May Irwin's routines and the pickaninny acts, no children were onstage to reinforce the hints of maternity in the Minstrel Misses' costumes.

Wayburn's acts show that low culture—vaudeville's disreputable antecedent—continued to be a resource for women's rebellious comic performances, even though his productions fortified male control and the manageable chorus girl. Blackface was one element of this negotiation, but as his later acts reveal, it was not the only way to mix grotesque womanhood with orderly spectacle. In his 1907 *Side Show*, for example, he borrowed from the circus to put a twist on the feminine spectacles of his girl acts. Wayburn devised a sensational finish in which a dozen chorus girls, in specially designed rubber suits, were inflated to become fat women. Charles Lovenberg found the "blowing up of the girls" to be a "scream."[140]

Following his early years in vaudeville, Wayburn's public discussions of his choreography increasingly focused on the precision and synchronicity of his choruses. "It is system, system, system with me. I believe in numbers and straight lines," declared Wayburn in 1913.[141] In particular, he developed strict categories and regimes for training chorus girls. In a 1916 article, "Show Girls Yesterday and Today," Wayburn explained that chorus girls used to be big, between five feet eight inches and five feet ten inches tall and often weighing more than 160 pounds, and somewhat scandalous since they frequently auditioned for parts in tights. His showgirls, in contrast, had an "inborn air of refinement about them. . . . They come gowned in the simplest of neat, stylish clothes."[142] He divided the women who came to his New York City employment agency into four categories, depending on their height, weight, and athletic ability. But all categories of chorus girls had to possess "regularity" (rather than beauty) since "the calf, ankle, waist-line and neck measurements must be right."[143]

Race thus marked vaudeville's status within the cultural hierarchy and its progress away from the past in several ways. Black performers in vaudeville largely remained examples of low culture. Although some thrived in vaudeville, few escaped the suggestion that they were beneath the Keith circuit. The racial masks of the minstrel show reminded viewers of a nasty, messy entertainment tradition as well as a fantasy picture of the South as a preindustrial utopia. Furthermore, the tension between Ned Wayburn's modern, orderly chorus girls and their moments of chaos in blackface, between the many "slim, sweet maid[s]" of contemporary vaudeville and the old-fashioned, fat coon shouters, shows that images of present and past femininity in vaudeville depended heavily on race (on images of the feminized black male and the mammy). Whereas working-class, masculine camaraderie, sexuality, and vigor were the primary symbols of vaudeville's past (a history that many administrators and fans longed for), white women's racial masquerades disclosed an alternative subtext of race and gender in vaudeville nostalgia. Gross white women, who combined elements of black masculinity and the mammy in their racial masquerades, seemed outdated in twentieth-century vaudeville compared to the chorus girls. Not only was the contrast between white women's racial masks and the chorus girls a juxtaposition of past and present, but also these different types of women addressed patriarchal authority in contrasting ways. Whereas the chorus girl of modern vaudeville was likely to be an anonymous body in a dance system arranged by male directors, other white women in vaudeville exploited racial hierarchies to take charge of pickaninny choruses or used well-worn racial caricatures to make themselves too ugly or wild for the traditional chorus line. Race shaped the images of vaudeville's progress and white women's power in vaudeville's patriarchy.

THE UPSIDE-DOWN LADY

RUTH BUDD'S CIRCUS ACROBATICS
IN VAUDEVILLE

When a reporter asked vaudeville acrobat Ruth Budd for her opinion of woman suffrage in 1916, Budd directed the reporter to touch her biceps: "Does this arm feel like a clinging vine?" The writer bashfully obliged, discovering that Budd's arms were as tough as "nails." The acrobat's muscular body, the reporter quickly learned, was a symbol of her feminist stance. "The Upside-Down Lady" supported woman suffrage (she was known as the "suffragist of the steel biceps"), and to prove that women were not the weaker sex, she bragged that she "could pick up any man of twice my own weight and set him out on the sidewalk."[1] Her athleticism and support for suffrage indicated that she was a New Woman, a modern woman who sought a broader public role, demanded greater political power, and experimented with romance and sex.[2] These new icons of female independence were highly visible in the commercial leisure empires of the turn of the century; bold female performers paraded across stage and screen, and eager female patrons filled these public spaces, perhaps petting with their boyfriends in the movie houses or flirting with strangers in the dance halls. Was the New Woman a sexy and assertive improvement over the frail feminine ideal of the nineteenth century? Or was she mannish and sexually deviant? As Ruth Budd's story shows, the images of refined and rough womanhood, of elite women versus low women, shaped the answers to these questions.

Ruth Budd and her brother Giles first performed in circuses and fairs in the early 1900s, and by the 1910s, the duo, known as the Aerial Budds, appeared regularly in vaudeville. In 1915 Giles dropped out of the act, and Ruth found greater success as a single act in vaudeville than the Aerial Budds had ever achieved, emerging as a "feature" act by 1919.[3] With her brother and in her solo act, Ruth Budd structured her performances around gender reversals. Her use of gender inversions onstage also shaped her image offstage, as her masculine reputation placed her in disreputable positions. Her association with two scandals demonstrates the specific elements of Budd's questionable reputation: as Darwa—the "female Darwin"—in the 1919 silent film *A Scream in the Night*, she appeared to be an animal, and after her well-publicized and controversial engagement to a female impersonator, Karyl Norman, in 1921, she was described as sexually deviant. In many ways, her gender inversion made her a low woman.

It is tempting to make a female acrobat a symbol of women's liberation. As female acrobats defy—momentarily—physical limitations by flying through the air, they seem to rise above social constraints. But the female fliers return to the ground; they are drawn back into the social structures that their soaring feats seem to resist. In her analysis of the promise and perils of the New Woman, Carroll Smith-Rosenberg describes Djuna Barnes's fictional acrobat—Frau Mann—in her 1936 novel *Nightwood* as a symbol of the possibility of flying free of all gender codes as well as the penalty imposed on women for soaring above these prescriptions. Frau Mann "violates all social categories and gender restraints," and her name suggests the label "Mannish Lesbian," the category used to marginalize many New Women.[4] Like the fictional Frau Mann, Ruth Budd was not an unequivocal symbol of either freedom or restraint. She took advantage of the increasing freedoms for women—in sports and sexual expression—but also faced the attacks on women and their public gains. Budd's story, furthermore, calls attention to the hierarchical distinctions among women in these debates about gender roles. A woman linked to the circus and with animals, Budd drew criticism because she was a low woman (a mannish woman, an immoral woman). She thus joins rude ethnic comediennes, like Kate Elinore, and the "dirty" women in blackface in revealing how female performers drew on and were caught in the disreputable traditions of vaudeville.

Many vaudeville acrobatic acts contained a "sexual enigma," a tradition extending back through the history of the circus. In the late nineteenth century, as theater historian Laurence Senelick explains, the acrobat Farini made up one of the boys in his troupe as a woman, billing him as "M'lle Lulu." He sang a song in his routine that included the line "Wait till I'm a man!" and was celebrated as an amazing female gymnast for seven years until a medical examination revealed the truth.[5] The following discussion of acrobatic acts in vaudeville uncovers in more detail the elements of androgyny and gender disguise so prominent in this type of performance. These routines were often the occasion for gender reversals in which women undertook "masculine" feats of muscle and men dressed in women's clothes. Feminine apparel and display were thus central to these acts for both men and women. Given this context, it is not surprising that Ruth Budd incorporated the reversal of gender roles in her act along with a manipulation of feminine sexual spectacle; both elements brought her fame as well as controversy.

There was a clear gender division of labor in acrobatic acts that some performers, including Budd, violated in order to make their acts novel. Women were supposed to remain largely dependent on the maneuvers of male acrobats, who were expected to be the muscular anchors of the stunts. Women usually posed while men held, twisted, and swung them.[6] The masculine role—including stationary poses—was to undergird these moments of feminine spectacle. Keith managers' reviews of acrobatic acts support this portrait of the gender division of labor, but they also reveal anxiety about the malleability of these conventions. Charles Lovenberg noted a striking difference between men's and women's levels of participation in Rudo and Bertman's acrobatic act:

"The man in this act does some very good contortion work and some novelties in the way of acrobatic dancing. . . . [T]he woman is excess baggage."[7] Of LePage and Florence's act on December 29, 1902, Lovenberg wrote: "Man in trick jumping, kicking and volting[;] woman is merely an assistant to hold the stuff."[8] Almost as often, however, Keith managers commented on the reversal of gender roles. The manager of Keith's theater in Boston, M. J. Keating, discussed the novelty of two acrobats, Tony Wilson and Mademoiselle Heloise: "Another great sight act, which scored a hit. The novelty of it is the woman doing the work usually performed by the male partner and doing it well."[9] And the performance of the Sandwinas, a male/female acrobatic team that toured on the Keith circuit in 1907–8, was "novel" because the woman undertook the male role: "Quite a novel equilibrist act on account of the size of the woman and her doing the understanding."[10] Although managers often praised the novelty of women performing men's roles, they did note instances in which such reversals were excessive. One Keith manager, for example, found the Patricks' gender reversals somewhat troubling: "A big strapping woman and an undersized man in an equilibrist exhibition. Woman does all the understanding. Man is rather awkward."[11]

Female acrobats who performed alone or with other women also used their mastery of "male" feats as a surprising element of their otherwise feminine performance and persona. Describing circus star Lillian Leitzel's trademark series of one-armed plange turns, historian Wilton Eckley wrote: "As her body rolled over and over, the effect was saved from monotony only because the crowd counted the turns. . . . And when she returned to the ring and curtsied as prettily as a fairy princess, the audience applauded because so little a girl had proved herself at once so dainty and so strong."[12] The combination of masculine action and daring with a feminine manner and appearance made women's acts more shocking to audiences, but the balance of masculine and feminine was sometimes difficult to maintain, as many female acrobats faced criticism because they appeared to be too masculine. Lovenberg remarked that trapeze artist Dainty Marie was not "as dainty as one expects from her billing," and Keith theater manager Carl Lothrop found that a female acrobat was too "coarse" in his review of Seymour and Hill: "A corking good acrobatic comedy act, although inclined to be a little rough in spots. The man is a great clown and a wonderful tumbler, while the woman is certainly a great female acrobat, but disposed to be a little coarse in her methods. In fact, she works almost like a man."[13] As this description shows, managers accepted the play with gender expectations in acrobatic acts only within certain limits; a woman's femininity, for example, should remain visible regardless of her accomplishment of masculine stunts. Despite a few disparaging comments, however, most managers' descriptions of gender inversion in vaudeville attest to administrators' approval of these acts. They wanted these acts to be unusual, exciting, and playful. But managers and publicists also helped support the traditional gender division of labor when they marked these acts as exceptions to the rule. Thus, by expressing standards indicating when acts went too far and by defining these acts as novel, administrators and advertisers made sure that these instances of gender inversion actually clarified the traditional gender hierarchy of the acts.[14]

Although on one level the field of acrobatics encouraged women to master male skills and roles, it also incorporated the sexual objectification of women. Sexual spectacle in general could hardly be termed novel, but acrobatic acts did offer unusual enhancement of the sexualized display of women's bodies. Acrobatic acts justified and broadened sexual display in several ways. Keith managers, at times reluctant to allow revealing costumes, could justify skimpy athletic attire as a necessity for this type of work.[15] In 1915 the manager of Boston's Keith theater commented that he hoped aerialists Fred and Lydia Weaver would be able to continue to feature revealing costumes and a disrobing scene: "The mayor has forbidden disrobing acts in Boston. We were obliged to put a sash on the lady, who works in full white fleshlings. Whether we can get away with the disrobing stunt remains to be seen."[16] Along with being an excuse for putting women in tights, bathing suits, and short skirts, acrobatic work promised new views of women's bodies. Performers on a trapeze and rings could soar over the audience, offering different angles of vision to the audience. Ruth Budd, for example, wrote that she "worked over the audience in Aberdeen and bumped the proscenium with my knee."[17] The trapeze could swing over the traditional limits of a theater audience's view of the stage, and the movements of acrobats often gave audiences unusual glimpses of women's bodies.

Although seemingly packed with masculine acts of strength and courage, these acrobatic routines were in fact showcases for femininity, with men and women both wearing flowing, frilly costumes for some portion of their acts. When one of the partners in the Alfaretta Sisters' act died, a male acrobat, Barbette, answered the remaining sister's call for a new partner: "She told me that women's clothes always make a wire act more impressive—the plunging and gyrating are more dramatic in a woman—and asked me if I'd mind dressing as a girl."[18] Lovenberg believed that the illusion that a woman was performing Barbette's feats was even more compelling than the surprise of Barbette's unveiling at the end of his act. On February 2, 1920, Lovenberg advised "Mr. Barbette" not to "remove your wig at the end of the performance, rather leaving the impression that it was a woman doing the act."[19] Describing Leach and Wallen, one Keith manager wrote: "Supposedly two women, but really man and woman. The woman holds one end of the wire in her teeth, while the man, dressed as [a] woman does stunts which are very good on the wire."[20] The impression of femininity thus seemed to embellish not only women's but also men's athleticism, adding fancy dresses and skirts to the visual array onstage and increasing the audience's amazement at the performers' physical feats. According to some scholars, male acrobats' scorn for and distrust of women may have motivated their female impersonation; male circus performers preferred to perform with other men, whose strength and skill they respected.[21]

Ruth Budd's act shows how an individual performer manipulated the central elements of spectacle, sports, and gender inversion to gain more success in vaudeville. Her juvenile acrobatic act with her brother, Giles, the Aerial Budds, worked circuses, fairs, and vaudeville in the 1910s. Their style of work differed from that of their competitors in several ways. This duo, first, was a novel act because of the performers' youth: one review in the *Toledo Blade* in 1909, for example, found that the "Aerial Budds, two exceedingly clever juvenile trapeze performers, gave a succession of thrills . . . that not only compares favorably with that of the best adult performers in the line but excels many of them."[22] In addition, the Budds, often billed as "America's Fastest Trapeze Artists," worked with lightning quickness, shunning the bows and pauses that punctuated other acrobatic acts.[23] After watching the Aerial Budds' January 14, 1909, performance in Crawfordsville, Indiana, a reviewer praised the "clever team of child artists, whose aerial feats are marvelous and their act is entirely lacking in the customary 'stalling' which attends most acts of this kind."[24]

Most important, Ruth and Giles Budd reversed gender roles. The act featured Ruth in the traditionally masculine position in an aerial act. Because Ruth was several years older and many pounds heavier than Giles, she undertook the tasks of carrying and manipulating her brother in the act. Giles, on the other hand, displayed his body more passively, frequently posing. Although Ruth's and Giles's ages made their positions in the act "natural," they nevertheless exploited the reversal of gender roles. A 1909 advertising pamphlet depicts them in costumes for a song-and-dance routine, and in one photo, Giles is dressed as a girl.[25] The extent to which Giles cross-dressed onstage is unclear. Ruth's letters suggest that the Budds rarely performed the nonacrobatic portion of their act at this stage of their career. On January 31, 1912, Ruth wrote that "we very seldom have to do [the singing]," suggesting that Giles's cross-dressing was a possibility but not a staple of their act.[26] Nevertheless, the appearance of transvestite Giles in a publicity montage corresponds with many reviewers' remarks about Ruth's controlling masculine role in the act and Giles's decorative position.

Publicity about the Aerial Budds often commented on Giles's vulnerability and Ruth's strength. One reviewer observed, "The little fellow is juggled about by the girl in a manner that makes the audience hold their breath, lest he should fall to his death."[27] Another critic noted with surprise Ruth's strenuous role in the act: "The young woman was never at rest during the continuance of the act and she had all the hard work, too, suspending the man from ropes attached to her neck or held by her hands, and allowing him to whirl or gyrate with abandon."[28]

Giles's series of accidents from 1912 to 1915 demonstrate that his vulnerability was more than inflated advertising rhetoric. Whereas Giles had four serious falls—the last of which broke his leg and forced

Ruth and Giles Budd, the Aerial Budds, circa 1910.
The Budds reversed gender roles in their acrobatic act, with Ruth,
approximately fifteen years old, holding and swinging her younger brother.
Courtesy of the Allen County–Fort Wayne Historical Society.

him out of the act—his sister suffered only a single injury during this period. On October 9, 1913, Ruth recounted her brother's recent fall: "Giles fell the first half of the week in Joliet. The first trick that I hold him in he missed my hand. He hurt his arm and head but is O.K. now."[29] Ruth's lone injury during the last three years of their double act, on the other hand, resulted not from falling off a trapeze or slipping out of her brother's hands but being struck by equipment onstage. "I had a very bad accident last week," explained Ruth in 1913; "a ring fell down and hit me on the forehead. . . . Our costumes were covered with blood and they had to scrub the stage that night. It fell in the middle of our act but I finished the act."[30]

Giles's 1915 injury precipitated many changes in the Budds' act. But even if Giles had not left the act, the Aerial Budds would have faced questions about how to make the transition from a juvenile to an adult act. At the time of her brother's final accident, Ruth was twenty years old, stretching the limits of a juvenile performer, and Giles's maturity meant a change in the weight distribution in the act. In 1915 Ruth explained that their different weights and his leg injury made the act increasingly difficult: "Giles can't work very well since his leg was broken and I have to help him so much and he is quite heavy. He weighs 120 and I only weigh 106."[31] Without the weight difference that encouraged their role reversal in their juvenile act, the Budds faced a transition in the novelty of their acrobatic routines.

Prior to Giles Budd's career-ending injuries, the Aerial Budds performed a circus-oriented act in vaudeville. Their success in crossing from the circus to vaudeville, however, was limited. When the Aerial Budds first played Keith's big-time in November 1914, they filled the second position—one of the least prestigious spots—on a ten-act bill. According to managers' philosophy for structuring vaudeville bills, the first act was the least important act. Managers on the Keith circuit regularly "buried" inexperienced acts in the first spot to avoid the danger of their being embarrassed by a more skilled act preceding them.[32] The second position was only slightly more prestigious. Ruth Budd described her opinion about the differences between the first and second positions in a 1914 letter: "We are on second here, some position. Anyhow it isn't opening."[33] The first and last positions were usually reserved for a certain type of act—a sight act or an act that could be appreciated despite the noise of arriving or departing customers. Performers disdained the final spot because in that position they risked being humiliated by departing patrons, particularly if the show ran over the scheduled closing time. Ruth Budd complained about being the closing act at the Palace Theatre in New York City: "I am getting along as good as possible closing the show at the Palace[.] [I]t is impossible to hold that audience as they start out on the third from the last act."[34] The Aerial Budds tried to extricate themselves from their low positions on vaudeville bills. In 1911, for example, Ruth Budd explained her reasons for canceling an upcoming appearance: "Next week they wanted us to open the show the first half [of the week] at the Clark but we would rather lay off as we go to the Casino the last half and are featured."[35] The Budds' weak position on vaudeville bills was only partly a reflection of managers' evaluation of their talent; it was also a result of the type and length of their act. The Budds were suitable for opening and closing positions because theirs was a brief sight act. Starring acts in big-time vaudeville almost always spent at least fifteen minutes onstage and often played for as long as thirty minutes.[36]

A sight act like the Budds' was firmly rooted in circus traditions, an association that marked the Budds as "low" in vaudeville. Their circus training made them a sight act that could be appreciated from afar. By the late nineteenth century, the circus had expanded to three rings. In this large space, performers relied on spectacle rather than speaking parts to reach their audiences. Clowns, for example, eliminated the banter and joking that had been popular in the early nineteenth century and relied primarily on physical stunts.[37] But the Budds had more to battle in their attempts to advance in vaudeville beyond the common fate of sight acts (being buried on the bill); they were also linked to animals, dirt, and rural America, all elements tied to the circus. Vaudevillians seemed to be well aware of the stigma of the rural circus. Managers derided the "rubes" and "yokels" who came to their theaters (these out-of-town visitors seemed to have no appreciation for high-class vaudeville), and vaudeville performers were often eager to demonstrate their superiority over animal acts.[38] Homer Lind, an opera singer, insulted the orchestra during his 1909 vaudeville act, snapping, "And you have not got any further than to be here playing for trained animals." The theater manager ordered Lind to omit this remark because he felt it was an "unnecessary knock to the orchestra."[39]

Two managers' comments about the Budds' appearances on the Keith circuit in 1914 suggest both the limits of the Budds' success in vaudeville and the possibilities for enhancing their crossover from the circus to vaudeville. Lovenberg compared the Budds favorably to the Flying Martins, noting that the Budds worked faster and even concluding that "they work a little too fast to get the best results."[40] Later that same season, the Budds appeared last on the program on January 11, 1915, at Keith's theater in Boston. Again, the manager compared the Budds to the Flying Martins, but in this case, he differentiated between the two aerial acts on the basis of gender: "A good fast act after the style of the Flying Martins, except that a rather attractive girl adds an element of novelty that the Martins have not."[41] Uninterrupted by songs and dances—the staples of other variety acts—the Budds' act was a brief, vigorous athletic display, a routine not likely to move up on the Keith circuit. But Ruth Budd, the "attractive girl," seemed to be the key to enhancing the act's success in vaudeville. She did in fact garner more success in vaudeville when she slowed down her acrobatic work and embellished the act with song-and-dance numbers that accentuated her as a feminine icon.

"I am breaking in a single," Ruth Budd reported on September 25, 1915. "There is so much to learn all new to me."[42] She diversified her skills, emphasizing new comic talk and songs as well as more dancing in her single act.[43] About a month later, Budd described the new song-and-dance routine and the less rigorous acrobatic work:

> I open in one[44] with a dance and have my velvet drop in one then on the side the curtain opens and there is a dressing table and chair where I sing or rather talk a song written about make up and myself then as I finish it mother dressed as a maid after changing my shoes just goes to drop my dress as the lights go out and when they go up the rings show and I run out in Leotards and do songs on the rings while I work (not fast like our old act) then the lights go out (leave me in spot light) again when I swing hanging by my

neck I drop from that run to the front and catch my rope that I go up on and do the webbing work very slow. I finish sliding down the rope head first real slow with the music.[45]

Her single act thus marked a transformation of her double act in several ways. By extending the song-and-dance segments and decreasing the pace of her acrobatic work, Budd was no longer a sight act and could thus expect to move out of weak positions on vaudeville bills. She also began to present herself in a more conventionally feminine way. Appearing at a dressing table and singing about makeup, she began her act as a pleasing young woman eager to show off her beauty. But this feminine display, similar to other women's acts in vaudeville, was only temporary in her act since Budd discarded her vanity and dainty persona when she launched into her aerial act. The organization of the material in her new act—the song-and-dance prelude to the acrobatics—intensified the previous gender novelty of the Aerial Budds. Whereas Ruth Budd had played the masculine role in contrast to her younger brother, she created the split between femininity and masculinity chronologically in her new solo act.

By camouflaging her acrobatics with a song-and-dance opening, Budd hoped to make the acrobatics more remarkable. Her new trademark song, "The Girl with the Smile," did not mention acrobatics at all:

[W]ith good luck, at last I struck,
    On a plan that ran like this.
Just a little vaudeville,
    And a little dance and song;
Just some little costumes,
    And an act that would not take long.[46]

In 1916 Budd protested her accidental billing as Queen of the Air, explaining that "[i]t spoils my opening. My opening song is 'The Girl with the Smile' and then if I am billed like a aerial artist they wonder why I am singing and dancing."[47] Two years later, she reiterated her strategy: "I want everybody to think my act is a song and dance act, when in reality it's a bit of surprise—because it's purely acrobatic and aerial."[48]

Publicity photograph of Ruth Budd in her white union suit, circa 1916.
Around this time, Budd began her solo act by adding new dances and songs,
such as "The Girl with the Smile."
Courtesy of the Allen County–Fort Wayne Historical Society.

Contrasting her song-and-dance opening with her acrobatic work, Budd increased the audience's awe at her athletic feats. A 1917 *Variety* review described the disjunction between Budd's femininity and her athleticism: "The house is surprised when they see the girl go from dresses to acrobatics and that surprise is intensified when noting what a finished gymnast Miss Budd is."[49] Central to the surprising second half of her act was Budd's sexual spectacle. To introduce the acrobatic portion of the act, she peeked out from behind the curtains, naked arms and shoulders exposed, and flirted with the audience: "Suddenly the curtain dropped whereat Miss Budd poked her head and bare arms through an opening to say: 'Soon you will see more of me.' Up went the drop curtain and Miss Budd was revealed in a closely fitted union suit of white."[50]

Budd's act thus captures the ways women's incursions into athletics and public amusements were tied to women's sexual spectacle. Women's athleticism was often transformed into sexual displays more pleasing and less threatening to male viewers. Journalists and spectators in the early twentieth century frequently focused more on women's clothing and appearance than on their skill.[51] The setting of popular entertainment also fostered the simultaneous increase in women's public activity and objectification. Although women were urged to become more daring and sexually expressive in turn-of-the-century amusement parks, for example, they were also made into "sights" themselves.[52] Certain rides at Coney Island enabled viewers to catch glimpses of parts of women's bodies that were usually hidden as female patrons' skirts flew up in the air when they whisked down a slide, and women also appeared as chorus girls on stages in amusement parks. Women were situated as both "sexual spectacle and sensory pleasure seekers."[53]

By introducing herself as a sexy, vain woman, Budd may have been trying to define herself as a "lady" athlete. The "lady" athlete and the "mannish" athlete were two characterizations of the sportswoman that emerged in the late nineteenth century through the 1920s. In the 1880s and 1890s, middle-class and elite white women like reformer Frances Willard who became involved in the bicycle craze were able to claim their femininity and refinement in contrast to rough, working-class women. Later, in the 1920s, glamorous stars in acceptably feminine sports such as tennis publicly espoused their sports' ability to enhance women's beauty and charm in contrast to the dangers of masculine sports and the image of the unkempt, "mannish" female athlete. Tennis champion Suzanne Lenglen epitomized a modern feminine ideal—active, sensual, trim, and uninhibited. She promoted this ideal not only by winning tennis matches but also by offering fashion tips and makeup advice.[54] By emphasizing her feminine appearance in the first part of her act, Budd may have been trying to appropriate the fresh sexuality of "lady" athletes such as Lenglen. Whatever her intentions, it is clear that her masculine identity, built on her gender inversion, overpowered the ladylike dimensions of her act. She remained primarily a "mannish" athlete associated with the taint of sexual immorality and circus animals.

Many observers felt that her disrobing and sexual innuendos did not match vaudeville's public notion of refinement. Her pert song and dance at the start of her act may have depicted a more conventional woman than the young female acrobat who twirled her brother in midair, but the new Ruth Budd also introduced elements of sexuality that remained somewhat controversial in relation to the Keith circuit's "Sunday school" image. For example, acrobats' disrobing scenes were often identified as salacious displays for male patrons. In 1903 the manager of Keith's theater in Philadelphia described the male response to an act similar to Ruth Budd's: Bella Veola "opens with a dainty French dance; does some dancing, then discards dress entirely and appears in black burlesque tights and does some contortion stunts, using a metal ring. Received a good hand from the men."[55] Emerie and Silvern's acrobatic routine also contained an innovative disrobing scene that the manager found to be provocative. The woman, Emerie, and her male assistant, Silvern, began their act in evening clothes, but after her partner pretended to drug her glass of wine onstage, she kicked off his hat and climbed up to her trapeze, where she began to strip down to tights. The Keith manager in Philadelphia concluded that "[t]his part of the act is a little tart, but, on the whole, inoffensive."[56] The Cleveland manager, however, found that the disrobing in this couple's routine went too far: "We were compelled to cut out the disrobing act of the lady member of the team."[57]

It is not surprising, then, to find that viewers focused on the sexual nature of Budd's disrobing. "We waited, we saw," wrote one critic. "It was worth the time. . . . Ruth is billed as the girl with the smile. I didn't notice the smile. Her ankles are lovely."[58] An audience member's letter to Budd on October 30, 1917, pointed to her lack of refinement because of her sexual suggestions and undressing onstage. Criticizing her trapeze work as second class and declaring, "Just listen, Ruth! You can't sing," this disgruntled patron was most upset by Budd's "immoral" attempts to arouse the audience. He referred specifically to the transition to her acrobatic uniform, beginning at the end of her "makeup" song when her maid starts to unzip her dress: "[T]hat make-up business spoilt our idea of your act and your character. What you chanted and what you did was silly enough, but the last part of the thing was disgusting (I am no wowser—but a soldier, an officer and a man). Of course the whole thing was specially devised for that smack of immorality. There was nothing wrong with your acrobatic dress," he concluded, "but *come on* like that. The dirty part is the disrobing" (emphasis in original).[59] The use of sexual spectacle was thus complicated for Budd. She could reveal a sexual knowingness in contrast to her previous juvenile identity and in keeping with the sexual assertiveness of the New Woman, but these additions left her open to charges of immorality. For Budd, feminine respectability was indeed tenuous.

As Ruth Budd earned success with her single act in vaudeville, she gained notoriety outside of vaudeville because of her appearance in a film about Charles Darwin's theory of evolution and her engagement to a female impersonator. These events articulate two interlocking strands of anxiety about shifting gender roles and the proper boundaries of sexuality in the early twentieth century: the consternation over "race suicide" and the rising attention to the parameters of sexual deviance. Darwin had been optimistic about natural selection in the 1870s, but by 1899, he pessimistically saw Americans as "beaten men from beaten races."[60] Such cynicism and xenophobia laid the foundation for the notion of race suicide. Theodore Roosevelt and others believed that women of the better classes were squandering their reproductive energies on careers and politics, whereas women of less civilized races produced more and more unfit children. The birth control movement, for example, drew on these theories as Margaret Sanger, the movement's leader, argued that birth control would bring "more children from the fit, less from the unfit."[61] This concept was so popular that comedians joked about it on the vaudeville stage. In fact, one theater manager ordered a performer to cut his "Roosevelt squib regarding race suicide."[62] Women who entered the traditionally male realms of sports, politics, and education increasingly faced the criticism that they were wasting their reproductive energies and injuring the "race." Ruth Budd's romance with Karyl Norman shows that charges of sexual deviancy—often intertwined with concerns about race suicide—were leveled at pioneering or unconventional women.

On March 14, 1919, Budd wrote from Miami: "You will be surprised when I tell you . . . I am down here working in a picture. . . . It is to be called the *Female of the Species* and I am Darwa."[63] Eventually retitled *A Scream in the Night*, the film examined women's place in Darwin's scheme: Was Darwa a mother fit to advance the race? A scientist, Professor Silvio, kidnaps a small girl, Darwa, and places her in the jungle near the Amazon River for eleven years in an attempt to prove Darwin's theory of evolution.[64] When Darwa returns to society, she soon becomes engaged to an aristocrat, but Professor Silvio disrupts the marriage plans by exposing Darwa as a "crossing of the species, not a true woman."[65] In Silvio's view, Darwa's successful assimilation into society is proof of Darwin's theory. But still unsatisfied, Silvio again abducts Darwa and imprisons her with an ape. Her intellect triumphs over the ape as she tricks the ape into shooting himself: after Darwa points a gun at her head and "pulls the trigger against the empty chamber," the ape imitates her, but this time the chamber is loaded.[66] Darwa resists the crossing of the species, or as one publicist wrote, she escapes "a thing worse than death."[67] A *Variety* review recognized that the film was confusing, pointing out that Darwa's survival in the woods and in high society offers no proof of evolutionary theory: "What [Silvio] seeks to prove by the experiment is hard to fathom."[68] The filmmakers seem to have sacrificed scientific consistency for "sensationalism."[69] Promoters of the film, however, tried to clarify the confusion about the film's message by emphasizing that the film refuted Darwin's theories. The advertisements they suggested for the film asserted that Darwa's intellectual superiority over the ape (her ability to think creatively as opposed to the ape's limited, imitative skills) disproved Darwin's connection between monkeys and humans. "He did not consider the fact that mankind's mentality is a God-given gift unto itself," stated one editorial that publicists recommended printing in newspapers to create interest in the film.[70]

Critics not only called attention to the confusions in the film but also claimed that it was somewhat trashy. Reviewer W. Stephen Bush explained that it did not "supply suitable entertainment for any classes."[71] In particular, images of the ferocious ape, Bush claimed, were frightening to women.[72] Adding to the film's questionable status, Bush reported, was the lack of women in the audience: "[T]he absence of women [was] particularly noticeable."[73]

Although some advertisements pointed out that Darwa distinguished herself from ape ancestry at the film's conclusion, other accounts of Ruth Budd and her vaudeville and circus associations clearly positioned her as a monkey. This acrobat continued to convey the darker side of athletic women and evolutionary scenarios: she was a monkey in the hierarchy of civilization. A newspaper headline proclaimed, "Movies Made Ruth Budd Real 'Monkey.'" In the article, Budd complained about the dangerous swinging acrobatics she performed and the real monkeys on the set, who threw coconuts at her.[74] Budd's particular Darwinian drama was corroborated by other vaudeville attractions. A monkey known as Lady Betty who was a headliner on the Keith circuit displayed her skills at shopping, dressing herself, and caring for children onstage. Advertising claimed that she was "not a monkey though born a monkey."[75] Furthermore, in an act called the Monkey Hippodrome, for example, monkeys played in an orchestra, juggled with their feet, performed feats of strength, and disrobed during their aerial act, according to a manager's review in 1913.[76]

The correlation between women and monkeys had been established earlier by Victorian scientists in their accounts of evolution. Although *A Scream in the Night*, released in 1919, should not be considered in a Victorian context, this film about evolution starring a woman swinging through trees in the jungle was a powerful reminder of this late-nineteenth-century framework. In the evolutionary scheme, women

Ruth Budd as Darwa, the female Darwin, from her feature film, A Scream in the Night *(1919). Budd complained about being treated like a monkey on the set. Courtesy of the Allen County–Fort Wayne Historical Society.*

often appeared as "arrested males," occupying a position beneath European men in the evolutionary hierarchy and seething with the race's base characteristics. Victorian scientists often saw women as children and savages; they pointed out that women, like children, were physically smaller and more delicate than men and argued that women's skulls, skeletons, and behaviors resembled "savages." Unlike men but like primates, they were apt to "resort to biting and scratching," according to one scientist.[77] The woman/monkey may have solidified the status of European men, many of whom were troubled by the implications of evolution. "Kinship with animals," explains historian Cynthia Russett, "raised disturbing reflections, not least the possibility that civilization was no more than a thin veneer over the savage self."[78] Women like Ruth Budd, then, symbolized an evolutionary stage that white men had already surpassed and provided evidence of "masculine excellence."[79]

Indeed, as these examples show, Budd was probably the wrong performer to disprove the human connection with a primate past. Her inversion of gender roles in the film and in vaudeville marked her, for example, as a less civilized creature. As Gail Bederman has demonstrated, the stages of evolution from "simple savagery" to "advanced and valuable civilization" were distinguished by the extent of their "sexual differentiation." Whereas "civilized" men and women embraced divergent spheres of activity and had different identities, gender differences were not as pronounced among "primitives." "Savage women," explains Bederman, "were aggressive, carried heavy burdens, and did all sorts of 'masculine' hard labor."[80]

This film's resemblance to the popular Tarzan narratives of the early twentieth century implies that Budd was less a female Darwin than a female Tarzan. *A Scream in the Night* was an adaptation of the well-known book *Tarzan of the Apes* by Edgar Rice Burroughs. *Tarzan of the Apes* was first published as a magazine serial in 1912 and then released as a book in 1914. The first of forty-five movie versions was produced in 1918, one year before Budd began working on *A Scream in the Night*. Orphaned by aristocratic parents in Africa, Tarzan is raised by an ape to become a great fighter in the jungle. He educates himself by reading books left behind by his parents and successfully uses his father's hunting knife in his battles with stronger, bigger apes. As a young adult, this human "king of the apes" falls in love with a white woman, Jane Porter, who is stranded in Africa after mutineers take over the ship on which she was a passenger. He follows Jane to America, where he realizes his noble heritage. Like Tarzan, Darwa grows up in the jungle, becomes quite proficient in the athletic skills of survival, and then embraces her position among socialites in America. Tarzan's primitive upbringing and elite family background combine to make him a particularly powerful symbol of the masculine ideal in the early twentieth century. He exemplified the notion that men could be revitalized by adopting some aspects of savagery. Tarzan's boyhood among the apes made him strong and aggressive because he escaped the feminizing influences of civilization that many observers believed sapped the virility of most men. Even though the film's conclusion tried to show that Darwa rose above her savage upbringing, for Darwa the jungle interlude was a liability, whereas for Tarzan it became a masculine badge of honor. Budd's association with Tarzan thus encouraged viewers to see her less as a virtuous woman than as a masculine woman.

Much of the portrait of Darwa casts a negative light on Budd's appropriation of masculine roles onstage and on the screen, but some positive discussions of Budd's athleticism show that the characterization of female athletes as masculine and savage did not stand alone. Darwinian concern about the fitness of the Anglo-Saxon race—the source of much criticism of women in sports and careers—was also the basis of the promotion of athletics for women and of Ruth Budd's film role in particular. The producers of *A Scream in the Night* tapped into the support for women's sports as a way to improve maternal health and thus stave off race suicide. For example, a pioneer in women's physical education, Dudley Sargent, argued that "good form in figure and good form in motion . . . tend to inspire admiration in the opposite sex and therefore play an important part in what is termed 'sexual selection.'"[81] Ruth Budd had contributed to the nation's well-being by appearing in an earlier film, *Building Up the Health of a Nation* (circa 1916), in which she and Giles performed their acrobatic routine.[82] Furthermore, advertisements for *A Scream in the Night* bragged that the star was a "perfect specimen of womanhood" and emphasized that acrobatics had helped Budd overcome ailments. In particular, publicity compared Budd favorably to vaudeville swimmer and diver Annette Kellerman, another woman who had benefited from the healing powers of sports.[83] Athletic regimes allegedly cured childhood illnesses of Budd and Kellerman, remaking them into perfect specimens of womanhood. Kellerman reportedly began to swim because of her weak legs, and Budd's father put her "through a course of calisthenics, later setting up rings and horizontal bars" to build up her slight physique.[84] "I started acrobatic work when a very small child," explained Budd in 1919, "by the doctor's orders."[85] The phrase "specimens of womanhood" signals that these women were hailed by scientists—and presumably fit for motherhood. The athletic woman—perhaps the intimidating acrobat who could lift men twice her size—could be softened through discussions of her maternal service to the race. Women's expanding roles in education, sports, and various professions may have inspired fears of race suicide, but the sporting woman's maternal "fitness" was a soothing concept.

Sexually attractive and assertive, Ruth Budd exemplified the end of weak femininity. Such a daring performer represented the strong woman that female reformers and physical education professionals had hailed as a model of emancipated womanhood since the late nineteenth century. The producers of *A Scream in the Night* recommended publicizing Budd's claim that "women are not the weaker sex." "In this picture . . . Miss Budd accomplishes feats requiring strength and agility that appear to be beyond a girl so winsomely feminine," asserted one article. "Certainly no member of her sex and few of the opposite sex can swing through 40 or 50 feet of space."[86]

Despite some positive interpretations of and justifications for Budd's gender inversion, her masculinity brought her sexuality into question. The film had raised questions about Budd's fitness as a mother and doubts about women's roles outside of motherhood, and her affair with a female impersonator suggested that women who crossed into "male" social realms were sexually abnormal. In one case, Budd was a primate; in the other case, she was a "pervert." But in both scenarios, Budd seemed to reject maternity and thus threaten the gender order and the health of civilization.

During a tour of Australia in the summer of 1917, Budd met George

Peduzzi, a female impersonator billed as the Creole Fashion Plate. Three years later, Budd again crossed paths with Peduzzi, who by this time had changed his stage name to Karyl Norman. They announced their engagement in August 1921, set a wedding date for the following June, and often performed together on the same vaudeville bill, with Norman joining Budd from his seat in the auditorium or appearing as a separate act on the bill. When Norman and Budd called off their marriage a month before the wedding, they ignited curiosity about the nature of their relationship and the cause of the breakup. The affair stirred up gossip about Budd; for example, one acquaintance wrote to Budd that someone "had said a number of catty things against you" after she and Norman split up.[87] Their performances together, the accompanying reviews, and discourse about their upcoming marriage and hostile breakup fused these two figures in the public spotlight.

The engagement of an "unnatural" woman and an "unnatural" man pointed not to a heterosexual union but to gay and lesbian subcultures of the early twentieth century. Definitions of sexual perversion in the early twentieth century depended most on the reversal of gender roles. Historian George Chauncey has shown that early-twentieth-century definitions of abnormal sexual identity were tied to the inversion of gender status rather than to a binary of homosexuality and heterosexuality based on the choice of sexual partner. Normal men, for example, were contrasted with "fairies," who were identified not by their sexual activity with other men but by their womanliness. Chauncey explains further that "an inversion of any one aspect of one's prescribed gender persona was presumed to be symptomatic of a much more comprehensive inversion, which inevitably would manifest itself in abnormal sexual object-choice as well."[88] Sexologists, in addition, linked women's "unnatural" sexuality to their masculine traits as well as their feminist political aims. They often interpreted women's cross-dressing and athletics as signs of "sexual inversion" and described lesbians as being masculine in appearance and personality.[89] In the hands of sexologists, the label of sexual inversion became a tool for challenging and discrediting the New Woman, including women's romantic friendships and feminist goals. To counter women's expanding roles, some sexologists tied their definitions of unnatural, inverted sexuality to their eugenicist

*George Peduzzi (known as Karyl Norman or the Creole Fashion Plate).
Peduzzi met Ruth Budd during their tours of Australia in 1917. He probably
sent her this picture when they were traveling in different parts of the United
States and England in 1918–21. They announced their engagement in 1921 and
broke up in 1922. Courtesy of the Allen County–Fort Wayne Historical Society.*

beliefs. Havelock Ellis, for example, claimed that professional and political women were selfish because they neglected their primary roles as childbearers and childrearers.[90]

Published accounts of this failed romance hinted at the abnormality of Budd and Norman's inversion of gender roles and hence their "perverted" sexuality. One author explained the reversals of Budd and Norman in terms of eagles and doves: "Eagles and doves have tried to mate before without success. But always the eagle was a man . . . and the dove was a maid—some gentle, cooing creature who wanted nothing save a cozy love nest."[91] The author tied Budd's gender inversion to the physical inversions in her acrobatic act: "Ruth Budd takes that breath-catching swoop at full speed, darting head first down the thread-like cable."[92] Karl K. Kitchen, in addition, explained: "[I]f the Creole Fashion Plate was known to possess certain feminine characteristics, his prospective bride was equally noted for certain masculine traits. For while Karyl Norman affected feminine furbelows on the stage, Miss Budd appeared in the most mannish 'tailor-mades' in private life."[93] The suggestion of Budd's offstage transvestism and her well-known athleticism clearly point to the category of the sexual invert, a label that many late-nineteenth-century sexologists attached to women who attempted to pass as men.

Budd alleged that the affair was actually a publicity stunt, claiming, "I'm glad I found out in time." This phrase was ambiguous since it referred on one level to Norman's desire to keep "himself in the eyes of the public," as Budd put it, but it also hinted at a secret sexual life, a link with a gay male subculture that Norman referred to in other ways.[94] An outraged and apparently heartbroken Budd sued Norman for "breach of promise" and reportedly won $8,000.[95] Norman countered with the alternative explanation that there was "[t]oo much mother-in-law," complaining that Budd had "insisted on having her mother travel along with them on the honeymoon and afterward when they were on the road."[96] His reason for the failed engagement would have been familiar to fans of vaudeville comedy; he relied on vaudeville's popular "mother-in-law" jokes.[97] Indeed, both performers' mothers worked closely with their children, helping with their acts and managing their professional engagements. Kitchen noted that "when the two performers found themselves together their mothers were not far distant."[98] The discussion of their mothers actually called more attention to Norman's effeminacy. His attachment to his mother marked him as weak and feminine, whereas Budd, as an unmarried woman, would have seemed more "naturally" in need of a chaperone.

Descriptions of the breakup also undermined the New Woman. Attacking Budd's career, Norman allegedly had tried to transform her into an ideal wife. She claimed that Norman had demanded that she give up her overprotective mother, leave the stage, and travel with him as his dresser: "Well, I even went so far as to agree to that," confessed Budd; "to give up everything . . . and just travel about helping him dress himself."[99] Some observers speculated, however, that she was not qualified to be Norman's dresser. The *Baltimore American* reported that Norman "questioned whether she would be altogether successful in dressing him."[100] Budd did not appear to be sufficiently feminine, caring, or subservient.

Like other female impersonators, Norman was linked in a variety of ways to a gay male subculture. Female impersonator Julian Eltinge reportedly was popular with gay men, although he publicly distanced himself from disreputable female impersonators who were more openly associated with gay men.[101] Eltinge proclaimed his virility in the press, circulating publicity photos that showed him in athletic garb and boxing gloves jabbing at another man. Such attempts to assert his "true" manhood contrast with Bert Savoy, a female impersonator who regularly used feminine pronouns to identify himself and included slang from the gay subculture in his routine. One line from his act, "dishing the dirt," was identified as "fag parlance" in a theatrical publication.[102] Vaudeville historian Anthony Slide notes that Norman was jokingly called the "Queer Old Fashion Plate."[103] Norman, in addition, became a performer at the Pansy Club, which opened in 1930 and offered entertainment resembling "drag balls," occasions that featured the effeminate homosexual or the "fairy" on display in glamorous women's clothing.[104] This club and Norman's career exemplify what Chauncey has called the "pansy craze," the period from 1920 to 1933 in which gay men were increasingly visible in New York City's central entertainment district—Times Square.[105] A few comments from Keith managers reveal that they discouraged the appearances of "pansies" on their stages. In 1910 Ned Hastings, the manager of Keith's Hippodrome in Cleveland, criticized the Clipper Quartette for their effeminate act: "Most of the time is taken up by a Dutchman chasing a 'sissy' about the stage. They were laughed at and applauded, but the act would have a more intelligent appeal if . . . much of their brand of comedy [was] eliminated."[106]

Although a lesbian subculture was less established than a gay male subculture, lesbians were increasingly visible in the 1920s as sexual experimentation, particularly bisexuality but also lesbianism, was in vogue. Several male impersonators who worked in variety and vaudeville in the late nineteenth century had long-term romantic relationships with women, but their private lives were not well known to the theatergoing public.[107] By the 1920s, however, performers' offstage romances were more visible. The lesbian onstage was one attraction of Harlem to those seeking adventure in the 1920s. Male impersonator Gladys Bentley, for example, wore men's clothes onstage and on the street and was married (dressed in a tuxedo) to a woman in a civil ceremony in New Jersey. The broader cultural support for revolt also helped lesbians establish a community in Greenwich Village in the 1920s. But as Lillian Faderman has shown, bisexuality was more accepted than lesbianism; radical men in the Greenwich Village milieu often pressured women to give up relationships with other women. Despite the support for sexual revolt in the 1920s, the lesbian was a "pariah." In particular, the lesbian became an obstacle to the post–World War I standard of companionate marriage, a union that was supposed to feature cooperation, friendship, and sexual satisfaction for husband and wife.[108] In this period, then, it was quite easy to explain the failure of Budd and Norman's romance by intimating that Budd was a mannish lesbian and Norman was a "sissy."

Circus monkeys, Tarzan, Darwa, and Karyl Norman—all were links in a chain of deviance and disrepute for Ruth Budd. Her career certainly shows women's freedoms in vaudeville to perform in "men's" roles and to use a more sexually aggressive persona; Budd was also lauded as an emblem of the end of Victorian constraints on women. But the controversies surrounding her also indicate the price women like Budd paid for their gains. In many ways, Budd symbolized the dark side of the new

Ruth Budd's Circus Acrobatics

freedoms for women; her resemblance to a monkey and the suggestion of her perverted sexuality pointed to the dangers of women outside of and unfit for maternity and marriage. Her gender inversion onstage proved to be a powerful and enduring foundation for doubts about her morality and normality.

ARTISTS AND ARTISANS,
RATS AND LAMBS

♦ —— ♦

THE WHITE RATS, 1900–1920

In 1900 eight men established a fraternal order of vaudeville performers, the White Rats of America, taking the name from an English association of music hall players, the Water Rats, to encourage the American Rats to emulate the "brotherly love" of the Rats across the Atlantic.[1] The White Rats led two major strikes—one in 1901 and the other in 1916–17—to protest a variety of managerial practices, including pay cuts and the cancellation of acts without warning or pay. In these strikes, the White Rats faced a formidable opponent, the Vaudeville Managers' Protective Association (VMPA), a coalition of major vaudeville administrators that had been established under B. F. Keith's authority in 1900. Although they won some concessions from the managers in 1901, such as the end of commissions, the White Rats' power and popularity declined after this skirmish, and the managers soon reinstated the policies that the Rats had fought to eliminate. The White

Rats rebounded in 1910: they launched a new membership drive, merged with the more militant International Actors' Union to become the White Rats Actors' Union of America, and affiliated with the American Federation of Labor (AFL).[2] In the next few years, the growing union gained some ground with managers by staging walkouts in a few Chicago theaters (when managers canceled acts at the last minute) and threatening to launch a widespread strike.[3] During the strike of 1916–17, however, the White Rats Actors' Union made no headway with the managers. After this defeat, its numbers fell dramatically and its treasury was depleted, but the Rats tried once more to topple the vaudeville hierarchy by arguing before the Federal Trade Commission (FTC) that the Keith organization, then led by Edward Albee, held an unlawful monopoly in vaudeville. When the FTC sided with Albee and his associates, the White Rats' crusade was over. They had failed to stop Keith and Albee's consolidation of vaudeville and to derail their tale of vaudeville's feminization for the public good.

The White Rats' sense of themselves as men was central to the establishment of this organization as well as their battles with the Keith hierarchy. They drew primarily on the nineteenth-century ideal of the artisan (skillful, independent, and manly) but also incorporated the more modern notion of masculinity based on physical power. In these ways, the White Rats were part of the broad and diverse trend to remake manhood around the turn of the century. Fraternalism, which reached its peak in the late nineteenth century, tried to prop up a type of manhood (the artisan) and male sociability that was fading in wider society.[4] In the face of big business and mechanization, the skilled worker was losing footing, and at the same time, reformers, particularly women, were attacking male activities such as drinking. Middle-class men, responding to the perceived overcivilization and feminization of American society, sought a robust, even aggressive masculinity (often exemplified by strong bodies of "primitive" men) to replace the Victorian model of manhood, which emphasized character and self-control. The burgeoning industries of sports and leisure encouraged male patrons to express this vigorous masculinity and promoted the heroic symbols of this new masculinity, such as prizefighter Jim Jeffries, who won his first heavyweight championship in 1899.[5]

The White Rats' articulation of manhood often relied on inversions of cultural hierarchy. The low culture of vaudeville, according to the Rats, was a source of pride, not shame, since this physically strenuous field molded men who were superior to players from high-culture venues: they were more robust, independent, and even artistic. In contrast to Keith's claim that his aesthetically elevated vaudeville catered to women, the White Rats argued that they were the truly chivalrous ones, protecting women and vaudeville's art from Keith's ever-increasing greed. The White Rats, therefore, attacked Keith's feminization on several levels: they tried to unmask it as a hypocritical publicity ploy and attempted to show that manhood continued to thrive in an industry increasingly associated with women.

Gender and cultural hierarchy were also key elements of the White Rats' paradoxical ideology of equality and exclusion. Leaders of the White Rats proudly announced that the word "rats" was "star" spelled backward, claiming that members of the group were "all equal, and the humblest member may look for the same protection as the highest salaried star."[6] But although they promoted equality among their members and criticized managers' power over performers, the Rats also erected their own hierarchical divisions. The White Rats' AFL charter gave them the power to represent performers from all branches of entertainment, including the legitimate stage, but most members identified themselves primarily as vaudevillians. Many legitimate performers resisted the Rats' association with low culture and labor, and the White Rats often cast dramatic actors as effeminate and thus undesirable. Furthermore, the Rats carefully distanced themselves from women (who they believed could sap their manhood) and from African Americans (whose manhood was considered suspect). Like other labor unions with roots in fraternal societies, the Rats continued to have secret initiation rites for men only, and they reluctantly allowed women to become members of a subordinate auxiliary in 1910. The Rats, furthermore, excluded black performers for many years, although there is some evidence that they set up a "colored branch" that offered secondary membership to black performers. The distinction of "White" Rats, then, may well have been a declaration of the group's discriminatory racial policies. Such exclusions and subordinations enhanced their own manhood by emphasizing what they were not and allowed the Rats to construct equality among substantially similar members.

The White Rats resembled other fraternal orders in their exaltation of the ideal artisan—a skilled craftsman who was economically independent, in control of his work processes and his product, and faithful to his fellow craftsmen. In an account of their fraternal organization published in 1900, the leaders emphasized that the White Rats social order was "composed of vaudeville players who combine such excellence in their art as public entertainers, with such stable heart qualities as men, and such high standing as good fellows."[7] The Rats would pursue "all measures as shall . . . make us financially independent, free, and estimably respected in the eyes of our professional brothers."[8] The artisan's pride in his craft was inextricably tied to "masculine honor" and "male solidarity."[9] The White Rats pointed to the centrality of the performer as the creator, director, and set designer as proof that vaudevillians were manly and independent, particularly in contrast to performers from the dramatic stage. Unlike legitimate performers, who relied on dramatic scripts and the guidance of directors, vaudeville performers were often the sole creators of the acts. As vaudeville actor James Fitzpatrick argued: "The vaudeville manager . . . invests in nothing but the four walls of the theatre. . . . People do not go to vaudeville theatres to see the stage set or hear the orchestra play or admire the manager."[10]

Although vaudevillians defined themselves as more independent than dramatic actors, the basis of the establishment of the White Rats was the infringement on that independence and control. When the Rats emphasized that the vaudeville actor "should own and control [the theater] because he creates it and keeps it going," they actually acknowledged the erosion of their manly independence.[11] Like other workers in the early twentieth century, vaudeville performers protested the loss of their autonomy and the growing power of a cadre of administrators in a rapidly consolidating industry. "For more and more wage earners," concludes historian David Brody, "the power over their working lives receded far off into distant central offices and into the hands of men probably unknown to them even by name."[12] White Rats organizers, for example, charged that the increasing centralization of vaudeville through the United Booking Office (UBO) led to several injustices: unfair contracts (including managers' ability to cancel acts at will), the prohibitions against playing theaters outside of the UBO, and the high commissions performers paid to agents through the UBO (often 10 percent of a performer's salary). Managers made increasing demands about the content of a performer's act and then enforced their censorship by prohibiting offending acts from playing in UBO theaters—quite a serious penalty. Ruth Budd, for example, explained that her performing schedule suffered after she played in Shubert's theaters, houses outside of the UBO: "Doing three shows a day and split weeks has kept me so busy. . . . [W]e have one more week and then they are over. . . . I did play for Shubert so must take my punishments."[13] *The Player*, the weekly magazine of the White Rats, complained of the new practice of making performers punch a time clock to keep them in the theater for the entire length of a bill.[14] Fighting against these encroachments on their freedom, the White Rats elevated the model of the artisan to "assert or reclaim" economic independence.[15]

The artisanal ideal was also the basis of the White Rats' claim that they were artists as well as laborers. The link between art and labor had not been immediately apparent to the Rats and remained a sticking point when the Rats tried to recruit dramatic actors to their cause. Prior to their affiliation with the AFL in 1910, the White Rats had "taken a decided stand against becoming part of any organized labor organization, under the claim that its members do not come under that heading."[16] But after 1910, the White Rats attempted to unite the terms "art" and "labor." Max Corrigan, active in the labor movement for performers, explained: "There is the skilled mechanic, who goes to work in the shop and turns out a wonderful piece of machinery; he is an artist in his line of work, yet we must not forget that we are laboring people, and toil and labor to earn our living. But until recently the artist could not see why he should be classed as a laborer, and for that reason the artists of this city were compelled to work under such low degraded conditions that existed here."[17] J. Aldrich Libbey, an actor and singer, agreed with Corrigan. "'Art' and 'labor,' two words so much misunderstood," stated Libbey in 1911, "so different and yet so similar."[18] Writing in support of the White Rats, he tried to show that "art" and "labor" both meant "work," claiming that art was the result of labor—not the divine gift of genius—and that "proficiently executed" labor was art. According to the leaders of the Rats, talented performers worked hard, and these laboring performers—whether or not they were from the opera or the legitimate stage—earned the title of artist when they gained popular support from the crowd or "made good." The notion of "making good," popular with many rank-and-file vaudevillians, thus suggests a democratization of art: in this case, only a popular audience could bestow the title of artist on a performer.

The White Rats were not alone in celebrating art in labor. As Eileen Boris describes in *Art and Labor*, John Ruskin and William Morris promoted arts and crafts in nineteenth-century England as a way to reunite art and labor, and supporters of Ruskin and Morris extended and adapted their ideals in the United States around the turn of the century. Their followers protested the degradation of labor through industrialization and the cheapening of art in commercial society. As Julia De Wolfe Addison, an embroiderer from Boston, explained, "Labour should not go forth blindly without art, and art should not proceed simply for the attainment of beauty without utility,—in other words, there should be an alliance between labour and art."[19] The arts and crafts movement celebrated the individual craftsman who could shape his products according to his own vision and personality; the ideal craftsman was "free, creative and manly."[20] The proponents of arts and crafts believed that work in a factory subdued the worker's spirit and autonomy and that manufactured products were not as pleasing as products made by a craftsman. To resurrect the autonomous craftsman, the arts and crafts guilds in England advocated a fundamental transformation of the economic system and work processes through socialism. In contrast, the arts and crafts associations in the United States, which reached their peak in the first few years of the twentieth century, did not retain this link with socialism.[21] They turned more toward refining consumers' tastes than toward challenging the structure of industry and did not forge significant links with wage laborers. Since it focused more on the objects than on the workers, the arts and crafts movement in the United States was more successful in uplifting crafts to the status of art than in reconnecting art and labor.[22] The melding of labor and art also proved to be somewhat difficult and controversial for the White Rats, primarily because legitimate performers often rejected the idea that artists were also laborers.

Performers from the legitimate stage were slow to join the union, often advocating separate organizations for dramatic actors and vaude-villians.[23] The White Rats speculated that the scarcity of members from the legitimate stage could be a result of the White Rats' lackluster efforts at publicizing the cause among dramatic performers or a result of their failure to emphasize the ways the organization could ameliorate the complaints of dramatic actors. But most often, the White Rats charged that legitimate performers did not want to join because they felt superior to the low, laboring Rats.[24] According to one account, "Actors on the legitimate stage are disposed to regard the vaudeville performers with a certain condescension as their professional inferiors."[25] One woman in the ladies' auxiliary of the White Rats observed that legitimate players did not ally with the Rats because they did not fully identify with vaudeville. "[W]hy throw the bluff and tell us you don't intend to stay in vaudeville, etc., when in your own heart you know it's the only way you have of making a living at the present time, and perhaps for the next year or two to come. . . . [W]e all have but one aim in life, and that's to make good."[26] In this light, the argument that the White Rats were artists was partly a defense against the distinctions emphasized by legitimate performers, particularly their efforts to assert their own nascent artistic status in contrast to the cheap entertainment of vaudeville.

A large part of the legitimate performers' reticence stemmed from the Rats' merger with the AFL. One 1900 article captured the primary argument against the Rats' alliance of art and labor, stating that the "actor who calls his business a trade makes a trade of it. . . . [He is] artistically club-footed."[27] Organizations of dramatic actors did not affiliate with the AFL until long after the White Rats first joined the cause of organized labor partly because they believed that union activism detracted from their claims of artistic standing. The history of the Actors' Society of America (ASA) illustrates some of the controversy over art and respectability for dramatic actors. Established in the winter of 1893–94 to mold a professional image for actors and improve their working conditions, for example, by securing cleaner dressing rooms, the ASA emphasized that it was not a trade union but a professional organization. In 1897, however, the governing board raised the divisive question of whether or not to affiliate with the AFL. Some actors argued that unionization was the only way to counter the organization of the managers in the Theatrical Syndicate; others held that unionization threatened the individualism and artistry of actors. The issue split the ASA. The members opposed to union affiliation left the organization, and the remaining members voted to join the National Association of Theatrical Stage Employees (part of the AFL).[28] This affiliation, however, was never completed. In addition, Actors' Equity, an organization of actors established in 1913 to secure a fair standard contract from theatrical managers, disagreed with the White Rats' linkage of art and labor. In 1915, when the White Rats asked for the support of Actors' Equity and suggested that the two organizations merge, Equity refused.[29] After debating the compatibility of art and labor for many years, Actors' Equity finally voted to join the AFL in 1919—only after the White Rats Actors' Union had relinquished its charter.[30]

The sentiment that artists were not laborers, shared by many legitimate performers during the first two decades of the twentieth century, enjoyed widespread support during this period. According to Raymond Williams, the definition of "art" changed with the acceleration of industrial capitalism: "The word *Art*, which had commonly meant 'skill,' became specialized during the course of the eighteenth century, first to 'painting' and then to imaginative arts generally. *Artist*, similarly, from the general sense of a skilled person . . . had become specialized in the same direction, and had distinguished itself from *artisan*" (emphasis in original).[31] By the turn of the century, "art"—which was lofty and spiritual—was defined as the antithesis of "labor"—which was low and dirty.

This gap between art and labor, high and low culture, undoubtedly kept many legitimate performers away from the White Rats. But the union leaders did not give up entirely on trying to recruit their Shakespearean siblings. In fact, White Rats' publicity attempted to shame legitimate performers into joining by attacking their manhood. Lamenting that dramatic actors continued to tolerate poor working conditions, one observer saw the manly White Rats as the answer: "[L]et them join an order where the men have good RED blood in their veins, and then they can conquer all unjust conditions."[32] Libbey similarly noted that those at the bottom of the cultural hierarchy often displayed exemplary manhood: "Some have been more blessed by the 'Creator' with certain gifts or talents, than others. . . . They are fortunate, but in their good fortune they should never forget that we are all of one family in the broad sense of Humanity, and that 'brotherhood of man' should prevail in the hearts of all, with the exceptions of a few, who are naturally snobbish, and who affect a certain supercilious superiority over those who in reality are vastly their superiors in manhood and moral stamina."[33] Furthermore, in 1911 *The Player* published the potent suggestion that actors who did not join the Rats resembled needy and subjugated African Americans:

[A]n ought is an ought
an a figer is a figer;
all fo de white man,
an none fo the nigger.

That little rhyme sounds cute, doesn't it? But if you stood in the "Nigger's" shoes it wouldn't sound so cute![34]

Such claims cast the hesitant actor from the dramatic stage as cowardly and dependent in contrast to the manly Rats.

Although part of the White Rats' campaign, therefore, was a defense of vaudeville against its lingering reputation as dirty and wild in relation to the arts, the Rats often took a contrasting approach: they embraced vaudeville's association with low culture—its vulgarity, crude humor, and physical aggression—as proof of vaudeville's manliness, particularly in contrast to performers from the legitimate stage. Acknowledging that the average man in vaudeville had a reputation as a "rough, uncouth, crude bit of eccentric manhood," the White Rats, on several occasions, turned toughness into virtue.[35] When performers mastered the vaudeville aesthetic—"Wow! Siss! Boom! Zing!"—they developed the traits of the modern masculine ideal, namely, physical power and even aggression, and once performers had proven their mettle in vaudeville, they could conquer the fields of high culture as well.[36] According to the White Rats, vaudeville was a proving ground for masculinity and artistic talent. As one White Rat explained proudly, "It is not soft for anybody in vaudeville."[37]

Although Keith's vaudeville indeed preserved some elements of male sociability and continued to encourage male-dominated styles of performance (such as slapstick), some White Rats found that their masculinity could best be established by proving their triumphs in an industry with less polish and comforts than the Keith circuit: vaudeville's close relative—variety. Frank Conroy, a veteran vaudevillian and enthusiastic Rat, wrote about how he had survived many tough years touring in the male-dominated and unashamedly lowbrow industry of variety. The dressing rooms in the variety theaters were "cold, dismal and a great deal out of order in every respect," and the audiences "were men, strictly stag, who attended the performance nearly every night, not to see the show, but just to have a few drinks and see how loud they could talk while we were trying to make a 'hit.'" Despite the inconvenience and discomfort, Conroy and his partner actually relished the "rough and ready life." By succeeding in variety, Conroy became a better performer, invigorated by the atmosphere and strengthened by the rude, demanding crowds. Conroy looked back on variety as the industry that made him a manly performer (implying that feminized vaudeville was somewhat weak by comparison) but still asserted the superiority of vaudevillians, as men and artists, over legitimate performers.[38] After enduring the rigors of vaudeville (and perhaps variety) and learning how to grab the audience with a rough-and-tumble style, the average White Rat was prepared to battle the managers, ineffectual men who had grown fat on the performers' honorable labor. A 1917 cartoon, for example, showed one White Rat as a tall, muscular boxer jabbing at a slouching manager with a double chin and a potbelly.[39]

Considering that the honorable White Rat often avoided association with legitimate performers and African Americans (groups that did not display exemplary manhood, according to the Rats), it is not surprising that the White Rats excluded white women for many years. Although the White Rats had announced in 1901 that they would admit female members as "ratlambs," this policy was short-lived, and the Rats returned to an all-white-male admission policy and allowed white women to become part of an auxiliary beginning in 1910.[40] "Ten years ago I

The White Rats, 1900–1920

marched around with them and took the oath that made me one of you," explained actress and former "ratlamb" Mattie Keene in 1910; "[t]hen you bad boys sorta dropped us out."[41] The odd word "ratlamb" suggests some of the reasons that the men of the White Rats rejected women as full members: docile lambs hardly blended well with feisty Rats.

Many vaudevillian women were restless and dissatisfied with the White Rats' male-only policy, however. *The Player* announced in April 1910: "Usually anything feminine detests a rat, but of late some Rats . . . are very popular with the ladies and some of them wish that they were Rats."[42] The observation that many female performers, despite the feminine fear of rodents, wanted to be part of the White Rats appears to have been true. Beginning in April 1910, women wrote frequently in *The Player* advocating the inclusion of women in the White Rats. These female performers followed the precedent of other women who had demanded inclusion in fraternal orders in the late nineteenth century. When women pressed for access to all-male groups (such as the Freemasons), leaders of the orders found a way to placate them while preserving the status of the orders: they created women's auxiliaries. The Order of the Eastern Star, the women's auxiliary to the Masons, was open to the wives, mothers, sisters, and daughters of Master Masons (the highest-ranking members), and several of the offices of the auxiliary were reserved for Masons. The auxiliaries were thus clearly subordinate to the fraternal orders, and the guidelines for membership reinforced women's primary family identification, even as the auxiliaries granted women an active role, including public speaking, in the associations.[43] This tradition of the formation of women's auxiliaries to fraternal orders is important for understanding women's relationship to the White Rats because although the group was a labor union when it established its women's auxiliary, it retained many qualities of a fraternal order. But as we will see, the women's auxiliary of the White Rats, although still secondary in some ways to the men's organization, gave women greater autonomy than the earlier women's auxiliaries had offered.

In September 1910 the White Rats responded to women's demands by forming the Associated Actresses of America (AAA), which, according to Harry Mountford, the executive secretary of the White Rats, gave women the same rights and privileges that male White Rats enjoyed, including legal advice, emergency railroad fares, and death benefits.[44] In contrast to earlier auxiliaries to fraternal orders, membership in the AAA was not based on a familial relationship with a Rat; the AAA was open to any "fit and proper" white actress who had been employed in the "dramatic, vaudeville, circus or entertainment profession for at least twelve months."[45] Although the White Rats extended many of the benefits of the organization to women, the leaders enhanced the virility of the White Rats and the vestiges of secret brotherhood by maintaining all-male rituals and spaces. For example, women were regularly barred from sections of the White Rats' club in New York City. Franklyn Gale, a female correspondent for *The Player*, was able to see these rooms only with a male escort, a member of the board of directors of the White Rats. She went to the rooms "where mere woman is not allowed even to peep through the slot. . . . I followed my guide just as brazen as you please, and, would you believe it, as soon as those dreadful male men saw a female they became quiet as mice."[46]

Barring women from the initiation rites seems to have been more important than securing space for men only. Mountford, for example, explained that AAA members "will be White Rats in all but initiation and sex."[47] Although the exact nature of the White Rats' initiation ceremonies remains unclear, they seem to have been based on a version of Masonic rites.[48] Masonic initiation ceremonies were elaborate pageants, involving role playing, costumes, and lighting, in which new members embarked on a symbolic journey to learn about the order and to prove that they were worthy of inclusion. Initiates were blindfolded to create confusion and were given some type of uniform to strip away their previous identity. They then had to survive a test of harassment and intimidation in the ritual to secure membership. Along with proving their bravery and endurance, the initiates also learned about the symbols of the order—tools associated with the traditional mason's manual labor—and about the importance of a member's "duty to his brethren."[49] Such initiation rites reinforced the exclusionary policies of fraternal orders, namely, the barring of African Americans and white women, intensifying the masculine, collective identity of the order.[50] As historian Mark Carnes explains, the ceremonies of most fraternal orders gave the "un-

The White Rats, 1900–1920

ALL WOMEN ARE NOT AFRAID OF RATS, TAKE THE A.A.A.'s FOR INSTANCE.

*Cartoon supporting the Associated Actresses of America (AAA), the ladies'
auxiliary to the White Rats. From* The Player, *May 12, 1911, 22C.*

masculine" initiate his manhood, bringing him into a "new family of ap-
proving brethren and patriarchs" and often separating him from maternal influence.[51]

White Rats leaders and supporters used references to feminine vulnerability and virtue as a basis for organizing female performers into

The White Rats, 1900–1920

the women's auxiliary, as an inspiration for male action, and as a critique of employers' unjust power over workers. The White Rats' promotional literature was filled with tales of women in sexual danger. One woman charged that a manager attempted to seduce her, further complaining that "unprotected women cannot go to an office to seek employment to earn her daily bread without being insulted and assaulted."[52] Advocates of a women's auxiliary to the White Rats used such descriptions of women in sexual danger to argue that women needed to be included in the White Rats so that men would be better able to defend them. Gale explained in *The Player* that "[e]veryday the White Rats are showing the real manhood that is in them by the protection they try to give their sisters in the profession."[53] Mountford similarly hailed the chivalrous duty of the Rats toward the AAA: "The very sex of the women in this business, which should appeal to all decent minded and honest men, and give them added claim to fair treatment and chivalrous behavior, makes them in the majority of cases more open to insult and abuse, moral and physical."[54] These comments reveal that the portrayal of female victims was a tactic for bringing women into the White Rats (if only in a secondary position) as well as a means of drawing men closer together in their defiance of managerial power.[55]

The discussion of the vulnerability of women in vaudeville often focused on the status of the woman performing a solo act. As actress Marion Blake wrote to Gale, "Many women need protection in this business more than a man, especially women doing a single act."[56] In August 1910 Gale argued that the woman who performed alone in vaudeville was more vulnerable than female performers in other theatrical venues: "In dramatic, opera, burlesque, all other branches, they form companies, rehearse and in most cases are all well acquainted before starting out and on the road they cling together either on a whole or in a clique but the single woman in vaudeville is alone, except for the few moments she is doing her act in the theater."[57] Several other female performers wrote to *The Player* emphasizing the dangers faced by the "single woman." Collis LePage, for example, explained: "[I]t is some comfort to know that one 'single act' woman found the White Rats ever ready to protect us."[58] The single woman in vaudeville joined other women who left their families to live and work alone in growing cities around the turn of the century.[59] The "women adrift" (as reformers called them) were controversial figures, labeled naive and vulnerable by nineteenth-century reformers but increasingly identified as dangerous and opportunistic as well. Not surprisingly, some accounts of stranded actresses used the language of the reformers; as one White Rat explained, when women's acts were canceled in cities far from their homes, they were "turned adrift to get back as they can."[60]

This concern about the isolation of the female performer in vaudeville, particularly the solo performer, was tied to the vaudeville performer's usual detachment from directors and ensembles of performers. The centrality of the performer to the routine and the sense that the performer could and should control all facets of the production had helped bolster male workers' sense of manhood, but for women ("women adrift"), these elements of independence took a sinister turn. Far from enhancing their womanhood, the vaudeville performer's autonomy (crucial to the vaudeville aesthetic) threatened female players, often bringing their reputations into question. Vaudevillian men embraced the ideal of the "solo" performer with pride; vaudevillian women tried to rise above it.

Union activists used the accounts of endangered women, such as solo female players, to illustrate the unjust power of managers and agents over the workers. "I went up to his office and he at once put his arms around me and tried to kiss me," wrote one actress. "It is high time something should be done to put such agents in Chicago out of business who make their living off us artists. Were it not for the artists' ability the agents could not exist."[61] When the White Rats walked out of Oklahoma City theaters in 1916 to protest the abrupt and arbitrary cancellation of acts, they used the female performer forced into prostitution or liaisons with managers or agents as the symbol of the degradation of employment in vaudeville. In his criticism of contracts, Mountford described how managers canceled acts with little notice to performers, "throwing them out on the pavement, the men to get back to where they came from, as best they could, AND THE WOMEN—GOD KNOWS WHAT BECAME OF SOME OF THEM." He urged the White Rats to consider the fate of women "stranded in a far off town, perhaps to earn their living on the streets."[62]

The White Rats, 1900–1920

Cartoon depicting one of the main reasons for joining the AAA—the vulnerability of the female performer on the road. From The Player, *May 19, 1911, 22.*

By drawing attention to the exploitation of female performers, the leaders of the White Rats also tried to undermine Keith's claim of providing morally uplifting entertainment for women. Although Keith announced that he catered to and pampered women in his theaters, his circuit was, according to the White Rats, a dangerous place for female players. When the White Rats extended the strike from Oklahoma City to Boston in 1917, the union denounced Keith's forces for mistreating the women on the picket line in front of Boston's Olympia Theatre: "[T]o drive the AAA pickets off, thugs bombarded them from the roofs of the theatres with chunks of ice. This is another example of the noble regard managers have for the women of the profession."[63]

In these ways, the White Rats drew on a traditional strategy of labor activism in which the "corruption of women and the need to protect them were important symbols in the critique of industrial relations."[64] In a variety of confrontations between unions and employers, for example, the portrayal of innocent women victimized by evil employers was a prominent means of encouraging male participation in labor activism and attacking the employers' immoral exploitation of workers. The Leo Frank case provides one example. After Mary Phagan, a young employee at a pencil factory, was murdered (and reportedly sexually abused) in 1913, Frank, a Jewish supervisor at the plant, was arrested. Although a black janitor with a criminal record was also a suspect, Frank was convicted of the crime and later lynched in 1915. Anti-Semitism played a role in Frank's fate because he was cast as one of the "shylocks of high finance"—a symbol of the excess and cruelty of capitalism's elites.[65] Phagan became, for many observers, an apparent "victim of capitalism." The *Journal of Labor*, a prolabor publication in Georgia, wrote that Phagan was similar to "the girl who has her life sapped away slowly by occupational disease or is maimed or killed by machinery at her work."[66]

Although often intended to help women, the calls to protect vulnerable female performers presented a limited view of women and their work on the vaudeville stage. Female players were depicted primarily as victims, not resourceful workers or strong leaders. Similar to other discussions of women's work during this period, the White Rats' campaign focused on the ways work in vaudeville threatened women's morals and on women's inability to defend themselves in the labor market as vigorously as men. In the late nineteenth century, social reformers began to support legislation that set limits on the type of employment women could pursue as well as the number of hours they could work. Some states, for example, barred women from night work; others did not allow women to sell alcohol or become messengers. The supporters of such laws believed that female wage earners needed special protection because of their roles in childbearing and childrearing; women should not be exhausted by long hours or endangered by hazardous conditions. Other rationales focused on the ways particular types of jobs, such as those that involved serving liquor, could corrupt a woman's morals. Protectionism was a paradoxical framework for addressing the needs of working women.[67] On the one hand, protective legislation was aimed at ameliorating harmful working conditions. On the other hand, this approach reinforced the assumption of women's weakness. The vaudevillian women found themselves in a similar ideological bind: tales of their exploitation identified the hardships and dangers of women's vaudeville tours, but female performers appeared to be somewhat timid in these accounts.

Nevertheless, the notion of the female performer as the defenseless prey of aggressive men and greedy capitalists did not stand alone. White Rats' leaders and new AAA members, in fact, found themselves in the awkward position of advocating the protection of virtuous female performers while also acknowledging (and, in some cases, refuting) the widespread criticism of actresses as morally corrupt and sexually adventurous women. In a 1917 letter, James Fitzpatrick, then president of the White Rats Actors' Union, captured this dilemma well: "I do not say that all the women of the business are angels. The percentage of good and bad is the same as in any other walk of life. What I do say is this: That, as long as there is a drop of blood in my body, and a bit of strength in the White Rats Actors' Union, every atom of both will be directed to seeing that women, who are good, and trying to remain decent, shall not be annoyed, threatened, tricked or blackmailed into yielding their decency before they can secure work."[68] Just as Fitzpatrick noted the existence of decent and indecent women in the profession, other pleas to protect women included the image of the flirtatious female performer. *The Player* reported that when two chorus girls agreed to take a car ride with some wealthy young men, the men propositioned the women, then pushed them out of the car after they resisted. The author of this report to *The Player* concluded that "the whole matter is simply the result of chorus girls accepting introductions from strangers."[69] Questioning the judgment of the seemingly bold performers, this tale diverges in many ways from the accounts of agents and managers taking advantage of innocent women in the theater.

Thus, in contrast to middle-class women, who attained leadership roles in a variety of civic reform organizations based on their assumed moral superiority, working-class women, lacking the impeccable reputation of their elite sisters, had to establish and defend their upstanding moral character as they moved into public campaigns, such as union drives.[70] Along with being working women and thus somewhat suspect morally, actresses were also identified as being on the forefront of sexual changes in the early twentieth century. By the late nineteenth century, the notion of white women as passionless was eroding, and accounts of naive women being coerced into "white slavery" were matched by stories of women pursuing romance, experimenting sexually, and enjoying the heterosocial environment of burgeoning commercial leisure. It was not altogether clear, then, whether female performers were sexual victims or vamps.[71]

AAA members were aware that female performers seemed to be sirens at the forefront of loosening sexual mores, not naive victims of predatory managers. During the AAA membership drive in 1910, *The Player* published several articles that defended actresses' reputations. Mrs. Everett E. Knotts, an actress who had heard a preacher criticize women in the theatrical world, asked: "Why should a minister of God quote one example of immorality in our profession and hold it up to the ridicule and denunciation of the whole? Why not on the other hand take some one of the ministers who have 'fallen' and hold that up as an example of what the church produces?"[72] Gale answered similar charges by asserting that a woman in a theatrical company is safer than a "girl who is closeted all day with one man in an office."[73] Managers also defended actresses' reputations, challenging the White Rats' portrayal of vaudeville administrators as lecherous men. They charged that Mountford betrayed women in vaudeville by classifying them as "easy prey for managers."[74] According to the employers, this was an unnecessary tarnish on actresses' reputations, not an indictment of managers' power over performers.

Although the primary justification for the AAA was the claim that women needed protection from managers and agents, other reasons for supporting the AAA also emerged. Members of the AAA, for example, at times expanded the critique of male power over female performers to include not only circuit administrators but also male players and patrons as threats to women. Several articles in support of the AAA criticized aspects of the male culture in and around the theater. One account complained about men who loitered outside of shops and theaters and ogled women: "I think ladies passing and going in and out of stores on the block would gladly dispense with some of the gentlemen barring the doors and in some cases expectorating over the place."[75] One woman reported her discomfort with men smoking in theaters, and another asked that men who approached women at hotels be "muzzled."[76] The members of the AAA thus broadened the paternalism of the White Rats by arguing that many widely accepted behaviors should be stopped and that many men, not just managers and agents, needed to be restrained. Also in contrast to the argument that women should join the AAA to receive the protection of the White Rats, some of the AAA's publicity noted that the auxiliary would fight for greater equality among actors and actresses. One article in *The Player* revealed, for example, an actress's anger that men obtained superior theatrical roles. Irma La Pierre protested that "men are usurping all the salaries. . . . [N]ine out of ten of the plays now being produced on Broadway employ male actors to a far greater extent than they do women."[77]

The portraits of weak women that dominated the White Rats' membership drives and strikes did not mesh with female vaudevillians' activism and leadership during the union's confrontations with managers. In the Oklahoma City strike of 1916–17, the White Rats attempted to close nonunion theaters by picketing, pressuring performers and customers to boycott theaters, and operating a theater with union performers. Wearing white satin sashes, the picketers tried to keep performers and patrons out of nonunion theaters. Newspaper reports indicated that women were "particularly active" on the picket lines.[78] The *Daily Oklahoman*, for example, described the arrest of union picketers, including a woman who walked down the middle of the sidewalk and "blocked traffic."[79] Striking performer Hazel Hall threw an onion onstage from her seat in the gallery as part of the White Rats' effort to stop a show put on by strikebreakers at the Fulton Theatre in Brooklyn in the spring of 1917.[80] In fact, the male leaders of the White Rats used women's prominence in the strikes to shame men into action. On August 18, 1916, Mountford announced that women seemed to be eclipsing men on the front lines of the White Rats' battles with managers: "It seems as if the women are to be the leaders in the fight for justice for the actor. . . . Are men going to let the women get all the glory and honor of freeing the actor?"[81]

Women's participation in the White Rats' strike of 1916–17 occurred at the peak of women's labor activism in the 1910s. During this decade, women's membership in trade unions increased fivefold.[82] Although

most female unionists were members of male-led unions, female garment workers and telephone operators created national unions in which
women held prominent leadership positions, and the female garment
workers and telephone operators were often more militant than the
men in their organizations.[83] In the 1909 "Uprising of 20,000," the
young immigrant women in the International Ladies' Garment Workers' Union walked out on their jobs, and women in the Telephone Operators' Union struck in New England in 1913 and 1919. The telephone
operators marched in parades, launched twenty-four pickets, and, in one
case, encircled a hotel filled with strikebreakers, holding hands and
blocking the front doors of the hotel. In 1919 these striking women
won several concessions from their employers, including a pay raise and
the right to bargain collectively.[84]

Cora Youngblood Corson, identified as a district manager for the
White Rats during the Oklahoma City strike, was the most prominent,
outspoken female labor activist for the vaudevillians' cause. Even before
the Oklahoma City strike, Corson, a Native American, was making
news with her attacks on the managers. When her act was canceled at a
Rochester theater, she sued the manager (her court case was postponed
indefinitely).[85] In 1913 she referred to Pat Casey, the representative of
the VMPA, as "Czar Patrick Casey" and "Patrick Casey (THE GREAT)."[86]
Described as the "heroine of Oklahoma City," Corson was featured on
the cover of *The Player* in 1917. In that year, she was arrested for her allegedly disruptive behavior while walking the picket line in Chicago
after the Oklahoma City strike had spread to other midwestern and
eastern cities. At her trial in April 1917, the judge dismissed the case
against Corson and several other women after police testified that the
picket line had, in fact, been "quiet and orderly." When the judge released them, he asked them if they wanted to speak. They declined, only
shaking their heads. The judge then commented sarcastically on the apparent timidity of the female activists: "This is the first time in my experience that a woman didn't want the last word. I am more than surprised to meet such a modest lot of young women from reading the
accounts of your lawless acts in the daily press."[87]

Hardly conforming to the appearance and behavior of a refined
woman, Corson actually had many traits of the ideal White Rat: she

was manly, and she was not ashamed of her talents in "low" culture or her rough physical labor. For example, her specialty was playing the tuba, a skill not usually associated with female performers. Publicity about Corson focused on the gender novelty of her musical talents, particularly her physical strength. One reporter asked, "Why shouldn't the 'champion lungs of the world' be owned by a woman who devoted most of her spare time to coaxing haunting melodies out of huge, kinky and rotund brass instruments?" This author continued to describe her as a rough performer: "She is decidedly athletic, tall and handsome. She can ride a bucking bronco until the girth about the equator of the cayuse breaks from its plunges. Her lung development has been declared by men versed in anatomical mysteries to be a wonder of the medical world."[88] This portrait of Corson as an anatomical freak and her association with a Wild West show indicated her distance from East Coast, urban sophistication and respectable femininity. These characteristics also reinforced her identification as a Native American since women who were not white were usually excluded from refined acts in vaudeville and were often considered manly onstage and offstage. Her status as a freak corresponded not only to her standing as a low performer but also to her lack of femininity.[89]

Along with the physical exertion of playing the tuba, Corson's allegiance to striking stagehands in Oklahoma City reinforced her association with manual labor. Some performers, critical of the White Rats' decision to walk out of Oklahoma City theaters in support of striking stagehands, attacked Corson in particular. After performing in Oklahoma City during the strike, performer Al Harvey wrote an angry letter to *Variety* on August 11, 1916. He explained that he had learned about the strike from a stagehand and had decided not to grant the stagehand's plea to stay out of the theater. "I didn't see where I was to take orders from a stage hand," snapped Harvey.[90] He saved most of his criticism, however, for Corson: "Afterward we found out Miss Cora Youngblood Corson, who lives in Oklahoma City or neighborhood, and who had nothing to lose, thought she'd call a strike because a couple of stagehands wanted $3 a week more, and I should pull out and lose a few hundred."[91] According to Harvey, Corson lacked credibility in large part because she resembled a laborer, not an artist.

The White Rats, 1900–1920

The White Rats' final strike, the protest that began in Oklahoma City in 1916, was a disaster for the vaudevillians' union. A New York State court issued an injunction against the striking Rats, and the VMPA promoted a company union, the National Vaudeville Association (NVA), and maintained a blacklist. Performers who were not members of the NVA and who participated in White Rats' protests were barred from playing theaters booked through the UBO.[92] In the winter of 1916, for example, the managers announced that they would "not recognize the White Rats, nor [would] they book White Rats," promising to permanently blacklist any striking actor.[93] Largely because of this threat, the White Rats could no longer keep performers out of nonunion theaters, and theater business returned to normal, despite union pickets. A 1916 article in *Variety* concluded that "[t]he people have money, want entertainment and are willing to pay for it. Therefore most of the houses are filled to capacity at night, while the majority also enjoy liberal afternoon patronage."[94] VMPA representative Pat Casey explained that the managers "had plenty of extra acts right in town to go into the theatres. . . . In fact, in most of the theatres we had a double show, and had one set in the audience while the other was on stage."[95] On April 12, 1917, the White Rats announced the suspension of the strike. The vaudeville managers had won.

Whereas the wild women of low culture such as Corson emerged at the forefront of the disastrous Oklahoma City strike, another type of woman appeared as the White Rats' enemy in the union's final stand, the FTC's investigation into the White Rats' claim that Keith's empire was an unlawful monopoly. The 1919–20 FTC hearing, which lasted approximately four months, involved the testimony of many performers, including White Rats, as well as managers and leaders on the Keith circuit. In particular, actresses from the legitimate stage and musical comedy were important witnesses on behalf of the managers for several reasons: their mobility through many entertainment industries, including vaudeville, suggested that Keith's offices did not monopolize the employment options of players in vaudeville; they denounced the White Rats' linkage of art and labor; and they symbolized, according to managers, the kind of artistry that would be lost if the White Rats gained a union shop in vaudeville.

The White Rats, 1900–1920

The attorneys for the FTC charged that Keith's organization suppressed competition between theaters and held absolute control over performers' career paths. They claimed that theaters in opposition to Keith's circuit collapsed because they could not book enough quality performers and that performers, under the threat of Keith's blacklist, had only one viable employment option: play for Keith's UBO. In contrast to this portrait of a theatrical labor market under Keith's authority, managers' attorneys drew attention to performers who had diverse careers, playing for Keith then starring in musical comedies and dramas on the legitimate stage. Managers' attorneys called Elizabeth Murray, Emma Carus, and Valerie Bergere, all of whom had successful careers in musical comedy, and George McFarlane, a singer who also frequently played in musical comedy, among others. The lawyers established that each of these witnesses had great success in moving among the legitimate stage, musical comedy, and vaudeville. "There was part of that time that you were in something other than vaudeville?," asked one lawyer early in his examination of Bergere. She replied that she had performed in "stock companies and a season with Mr. [David] Belasco in 'Madame Butterfly.' "[96] Murray, a singer specializing in dialect songs, provided similar evidence of the fluidity of the labor market for performers. An attorney for the vaudeville managers asked Murray, "When I ask you if you have any trouble getting from vaudeville to musical comedy, what I want to ask about particularly is this, whether there is anything peculiar about the work in musical comedy or in vaudeville that renders it difficult for an artist, if she has ability, to frame up an act so that, if she cannot get work in vaudeville, she can go into musical comedy?"[97] She answered, "[I]f you have the material, I think you are in demand in [either] one."[98] As we have seen, the ability of performers from other industries to move into vaudeville was a barrier to building a strong union since many performers who were crucial to the vaudeville labor market did not identify themselves as vaudevillians. In the FTC hearing, this mobility was again an obstacle for the White Rats because the vaudeville managers pointed to performers' movement through the theatrical hierarchy and made a definitive vaudeville labor market disappear.

Keith's officers also argued that it was the White Rats, with their push for a closed shop, who attempted to restrain competition. The managers' attorneys elicited a great deal of anxiety about who and what types of performers would be shut out of a closed shop of "vaudevillians," suggesting that highbrow performers, particularly women, would no longer be able to appear in vaudeville. Frederick Schanberger, the manager of the Maryland Theater in Baltimore, testified that a closed shop "would shut off the supply of new material, the material so necessary to keep up this high standard that we have established now in high class vaudeville. . . . [I]n a few years why we would be driven back to the show now presented by the cheap vaudeville theatre."[99] Casey was even more specific in his denunciation of the closed shop: "The new act would not get a chance, or a woman like [Sarah] Bernhardt or Adelaine [sic] Genée. . . . [I]t would be impossible for them to secure work unless they joined a labor union, as it would be absolutely up to the executives and heads of that labor union as to whether or not they would admit them to membership."[100] The idea of stars like Bernhardt and Genée in a labor union with women like Corson obviously seemed ridiculous to Casey.

This reference to Bernhardt and Genée suggests that the disembodied female star—rising above commerce, low culture, and physical work—was one symbol of the vaudeville managers' claims of cultural uplift. Such stars provided an important contrast to the manly White Rat who acknowledged (and even celebrated) his physical labor. Far from the White Rats' portrait of degraded working women or endangered women's bodies, the vaudeville managers' depiction of the female performer was as an artist removed from labor, a personality removed from the body. When she testified at the FTC hearing, actress Nan Halperin concluded that "I am an individual artist. I have not a voice, nor a wonderful pair of dancing feet, but I am what they call an artist. God has given me a talent to entertain people through a personality and individuality."[101] Bergere explained her opposition to the closed shop in similar terms, largely denying the physical labor of vaudeville and emphasizing her unique personality: "As far as I see I would think [a closed shop] was sort of [a] restriction because I am not an artisan. I depend on an individuality, on a personality, on work. I did not know I would have to carry a card to sell my brains or my personality."[102]

The White Rats, 1900–1920

Such characterizations of artists supported managers' contention that they had uplifted vaudeville to serve the public. In their brief, attorneys introduced the heads of the Keith circuit, A. Paul Keith and E. F. Albee, by emphasizing their efforts to improve vaudeville: "That Mr. Keith in his lifetime and his father before him, with the aid and cooperation of Mr. Albee, strove to elevate the vaudeville profession and business by conducting their own business in a high plane of business and moral legitimacy and respectability is also beyond question."[103] Some performers embellished this favorable portrait, explaining that the UBO made it easier for them to book routes since they no longer had to contact individual theaters and made it possible for them to construct longer routes through the circuits of theaters. Testifying before the FTC, Carus stated that when she first performed in vaudeville in 1899 "there were not many circuits. I had to write to the various managers. . . . And I booked a week here and a week there as best I could."[104] As vaudeville became more popular, theater managers invested more money in their facilities and in performers' salaries.[105] For example, Samuel K. Hodgdon, an administrator at the UBO who was a former theater manager for Keith, testified that the offices of the UBO were exemplary because they had a ladies' waiting room for female artists that had a maid.

The familiar rhetoric of artistic progress and feminization offered important support for Keith's claim that the expansion of his business was lawful because it did not harm the public. The respondents in the FTC hearing (the executives of Keith's organizations) held that the case should be dismissed because it was not in the public interest, based on the clause in section 5 of the 1914 Federal Trade Commission Act that held that the FTC could only intervene in practices that harmed the public generally, such as price hikes and false advertising. In particular, the vaudeville managers' attorneys referred to the holding in the federal appeals court decision *Federal Trade Commission v. Gratz* (1919) that "the unfair methods . . . must be at least such as are unfair to the public generally."[106] The notion of trusts that worked for the public good had rescued many corporations in the past. Indeed, the managers probably hoped to tap into legal support for "reasonable" trusts since the Supreme Court had ruled in 1911 that only "unreasonable" combinations were unlawful.[107] In this light, the Keith circuit's proclamations about cultural ascendance and hospitality for women were not simply strategies for expanding the vaudeville audience; they were also planks in Keith's defense against the White Rats' and the FTC's attempt at trust-busting.

On March 26, 1920, the FTC dismissed the complaint against Keith and the VMPA with little comment. Albee released one letter from the Department of Justice explaining that theatrical enterprises did not fall under the category of interstate commerce and that Keith's enterprises therefore were not in violation of congressional laws prohibiting the restraint of such commerce.[108] This conclusion was probably based on the argument (made strongly by the managers' attorneys) that performers' labor should not be considered commerce, based on section 6 of the Clayton Anti-Trust Act (1914), which states that "[t]he labor of a human being is not a commodity or article of commerce."[109] Attorneys for the managers relied on this provision, designed to exempt labor unions from the antitrust statutes, as well as their claim that individual theaters and the UBO conducted only local and intrastate business.[110] Other accounts of the hearing suggest that the managers were successful in turning the accusation of restraining trade back on the White Rats and their demand for a closed shop. Several articles cast the White Rats as the instigators of hostilities between performers and managers, thus supporting the view that managers' tactics, including their blacklist, which they described as an innocent list of "unreliable" performers, were simply defensive. A newspaper article in April 1920 reported that "the controversy had its origin in differences between an actors' organization . . . and the vaudeville managers. The White Rats demanded that no persons be engaged as actors except members of their organization."[111] The vaudeville managers exalted the decision, declaring that the FTC "left vaudeville wide open to rule, regulate and run itself without government interference."[112]

When the FTC ruled in favor of the managers, the White Rats' hopes for a revival were crushed. Already suffering from the loss of the Oklahoma City strike, the Rats sold their clubhouse in 1919 to Albee, who allowed the NVA to use it, and they relinquished their AFL charter. By 1923, *Equity* concluded that the White Rats were "almost defunct."[113]

The White Rats, 1900–1920

Although they were bitter rivals, Keith's organization and the White Rats shared more of an agenda than they perhaps realized. Both attempted an alliance of high and low culture—Keith by putting acrobats and Shakespearean actors on the same vaudeville bill and the White Rats by bringing artisans and artists into the same union. The apparent permeability of the lines dividing high and low culture harmed the Rats in two ways: Keith's managers pointed to the fluidity of the vaudeville labor market to refute the Rats' claim that they had a monopoly on vaudeville, and antipathy between high and low performers and ongoing disagreements about the identity of artists as laborers made it difficult for the Rats to recruit legitimate performers. Both sides also used women as symbols in their attempts to infuse their campaigns with moral and manly rectitude. For the White Rats, the virtuous female performer victimized by managers' sexual advances was the symbol of exploitative vaudeville labor, whereas for the managers, the portrait of the artist as a lady exemplified Keith's public triumph. The opposing groups—both led and dominated by men—granted women little authority or voice in their campaigns, although the moralism that was so important to their drives was often expressed through feminine icons or justified by men's duty to protect women. However, a few women, such as Cora Youngblood Corson, proved that flesh-and-blood women could not be wholly represented or contained by the dichotomous symbols of feminine virtue and depravity, art and cheap labor, that pervaded the conflicts between the Rats and managers.

CONCLUSION

During the 1919–20 Federal Trade Commission (FTC) hearing investigating whether Keith's organization was a monopoly, Frank Fogarty, a character actor and a leader of the White Rats, remembered that he had once revered the Keith circuit: "I recall some years ago looking to Keith's as a golden temple and I hoped one day to be able to play at Keith's." But with the White Rats' losing campaigns behind him, he no longer looked to Keith's with such awe. He lamented that "[n]owadays you can work in a butcher store and snap your fingers and do a dance and you can be working at Keith's tomorrow."[1] Fogarty's description of a crumbling Keith dynasty probably did not seem accurate to most observers in 1919. In fact, when the Keith circuit emerged unscathed from the FTC hearing, the vaudeville industry looked unstoppable. It still seemed to be a "golden temple." The leaders of the Keith circuit bragged about their benevolent public service, they demolished the White Rats, and their company union (the National Vaudeville Association) was flourishing. Without fear of union opposition, administrators like E. F. Albee implemented many policies that had previously been opposed by the White Rats, such as requiring players to perform a staggering five shows per day.[2] And the circuit continued to expand. In 1920 Albee spent $1 million to build and decorate the new B. F. Keith Theatre in Syracuse.[3] He also opened a new theater in Toledo in 1923 and later acquired six more theaters in Canada.[4] But vaudeville's future was not as bright as it probably seemed to administrators at Keith's offices around 1920.

Several years after the FTC hearing, the vaudeville empire began to show signs of weakness. In 1922 a manager on the Keith circuit hinted at a drop in business when he asked one performer to "eliminate any references to the number of people in the audience, such as the expression, 'We could use them.'"[5] Following a few reports of declining ticket sales (mainly outside of New York City) and lackluster shows in 1922 and 1923, vaudeville's troubles multiplied rapidly around 1926.[6] Around this time, many vaudeville theaters announced that they would begin to give motion pictures top billing ahead of the live acts on their programs, and by 1926, only fifteen big-time theaters offered straight vaudeville in the United States.[7] Perhaps most humiliating to vaudeville's live performers was the 1926 announcement that managers in the Keith chain would stop using drum crashes and spotlights during vaudeville acts to avoid disturbing customers who wanted to sleep through these acts and wake up only for the movies.[8]

The Palace Theatre in New York City, once the most prestigious vaudeville house in the country, was declining fast in the late 1920s. In 1926 Albee, then in control of the Palace, reportedly cut employees' salaries and fired other workers in an effort to make the theater competitive with the posh new movie houses that had moved into the neighborhood. The Capitol Theatre had opened in 1919, and the Paramount, owned by Adolph Zukor, opened in 1926.[9] After 1926, the Palace no longer had problems with the ticket scalpers who had previously capitalized on patrons' willingness to pay high prices for the popular shows, and in 1928 *Variety* reported that there was "a line in front of the Palace's Monday matinee—on its way to the Roxy [movie theater]."[10] In the 1930s the Palace began to experiment with various combinations of vaudeville acts and films, briefly playing only films (a double feature and previews of coming attractions), returning to a combination of vaudeville acts and motion pictures in 1935, and then ending with a film-only policy. In his recollections of vaudeville, Joe Laurie Jr. remarked that the Palace's transformation from being the pinnacle of "top-notch two-a-day" to being a "pic house" was "like a fine Shakespearean actor who just mumbles his lines, and like a dancer who couldn't find the rosin box."[11]

As these examples indicate, vaudeville was losing ground to the motion picture industry. By the 1920s, vaudevillians found that their power and popularity in relation to the films on the bills were declining. Vaudevillians were more likely to provide the accompaniment for the main attraction—motion pictures—than to be the main attraction themselves. Furthermore, vaudeville's dramatic decline after 1926 corresponds roughly to the introduction of sound to motion pictures. The first sound picture, *The Jazz Singer* (which opened in 1927), was a box office hit, and, with a series of successful sound movies, the motion picture industry thrived until the Depression. In 1928 Joseph P. Kennedy, head of the political dynasty, bought a large share of stock in the Keith-Orpheum circuit, hoping to use the chain of theaters as outlets for the films he booked through the Film Booking Office (FBO), which he administered in cooperation with the Radio Corporation of America (RCA). Two years later, Kennedy merged Keith-Orpheum interests with RCA and the FBO, forming Radio-Keith-Orpheum (RKO). The Keith-Orpheum circuit provided the theaters for the films that were made and distributed by RCA and the FBO. The Keith vaudeville circuit had worked to standardize live acts and subsume local groups into a national audience, but vaudeville did not have the technology necessary to fully develop a mass-production enterprise. The substitution of the mass media commodity of film for live performers, however, fit well into the Keith circuit's bureaucratic organization and national network.[12] As Robert Snyder concludes, "A major force in the American media had risen out of the ashes of vaudeville."[13]

Vaudeville was also facing greater competition from full-length revues, such as the *Ziegfeld Follies*. Whereas vaudeville bills often included spectacular revues as a single act on a bill, full-length revues increased in popularity after 1915, employing vaudevillians and stealing many of vaudeville's middle-class customers along the way. Between 1907 and 1931, for example, there were twenty-one editions of the *Follies*. Such productions, actually reviewed as vaudeville shows through the early twentieth century, used thin narratives (like a trip through New York City) to give players the opportunity to do comic bits or song-and-dance routines. Borrowing the chain of intense performances from the structure of a vaudeville bill, the producers of revues added lavish scenery to give their shows an air of "sophistication."[14]

Just as the revue borrowed vaudeville performers and expanded on spectacles that had been popular acts on vaudeville bills, the motion picture industry also incorporated elements of the vaudeville aesthetic. Film historian Henry Jenkins has shown that Hollywood began to recruit vaudevillians, many of whom had already moved from vaudeville to starring roles in revues. When performers such as Bert Wheeler, Robert Woolsey, and Winnie Lightner, who had all spent time in vaudeville, took leading roles in comedies of the 1920s and early 1930s, they brought some of vaudeville with them. Their films, along with many others of the period, relied on "self-conscious showmanship" and emphasized "emotional immediacy over narrative coherence."[15] Some of the vigor, nonsense, and rebelliousness of vaudeville lived on in these Hollywood films. Motion pictures, therefore, drew on the traditional acts of vaudeville and, with the aid of technology, perfected vaudeville's early efforts at mass marketing commercial leisure.

Most of the women featured in this study outlived vaudeville; they experimented with other entertainment media and then retired. Only Kate Elinore was still performing in vaudeville at the end of her life. Kate Elinore married Sam Williams, an amateur songwriter and schoolteacher, in 1906, and three years later, the Elinore Sisters broke up. They teamed up with new partners, and Kate, working with her husband, earned far more success than May, who had several different partners and sunk into small-time vaudeville. Kate Elinore later played the role of Lizette in the musical comedy *Naughty Marietta* in 1910–11. Reviews for the show fittingly noted: "Vaudeville invades comic opera."[16] She continued to play in vaudeville in between her roles in musical comedy, sometimes replacing male performers. While working with her husband at the Orpheum Theatre in Los Angeles, Kate Elinore became ill and, on the train ride back to the East Coast, was hospitalized in In-dianapolis and died after abdominal surgery on December 31, 1924.[17]

Julia Arthur did not play in vaudeville again after her 1923 tour as Hamlet, but vaudeville lurked in the background of her subsequent en-gagements. When she returned to legitimate drama as Joan of Arc in George Bernard Shaw's *Saint Joan* in 1924, some critics praised her for lifting the audience above vaudeville: "Certainly there has been nothing like it since the Public's taste became depraved to the level of the movies and cheap vaudeville."[18] In subsequent years, she turned down several movie roles, explaining that although she believed a "spirit of uplift" had swept through the industry, she still thought the parts offered her "had all the characteristics of a fifth rate vaudeville act."[19] Her vaude-ville appearances were only a small part of her career, but vaudeville re-mained an evocative reference point throughout her professional life. Following *Saint Joan*, she retired permanently and died in 1950.

Like the other women considered here, May Irwin moved beyond vaudeville in her career, alternating between vaudeville and musical comedy through the mid-1920s. Her last Broadway appearances were in *On the Hiring Line* (1919–20) and *The 49ers* (1922). In one of her final appearances, for the Palace's "Old Timers' Week" in 1925, she shared the bill with Cissie Loftus, Marie Cahill, and Marie Dressler, among others. This "Old Timers' Week" and several other similar bills in 1925 were quite successful, although the Palace by this time was losing ground to the competing movie houses. Despite her extensive stage ca-reer, Irwin is perhaps best remembered for her role in an early Edison film, *The Kiss*, which was originally a scene from her stage hit, *The Widow Jones* (1895).[20] Irwin not only tried to preserve vaudeville as a plucky old-timer but also helped inaugurate vaudeville's competitor—motion pictures. The second achievement proved to be her legacy. Irwin spent most of her retirement on her farm in upstate New York with her husband and manager, Kurt Eisfeldt, and died in 1938.[21]

Ruth Budd's fame in vaudeville faded by the late 1920s. In 1927 she married Ray Hanna, a stagehand and electrician in Fort Wayne, Indi-ana, who had corresponded with her for sixteen years. After her mar-riage, she continued to perform, but her star on the Keith circuit had fallen. Considering the gender novelty of her routine and the gossip surrounding her affair with Karyl Norman, perhaps it is fitting that she was replaced on the Keith circuit in 1927 by a transvestite male acrobat, Barbette. A review of Barbette's appearance at the Palace late in his career jokingly commented that the theater management had forgotten to obtain the "endorsements of Ruth Budd and Karyl Norman" for Barbette's act.[22] Budd's scandal thus lingered on after she had embarked on her married life in the Midwest. Budd often wrote to her husband that she regretted being on the road: "I count the days away and even the day seems long I count the hours until it is over."[23] She appeared in circuses and vaudeville in her later career but apparently was embarrassed about performing in circuses because this aspect of her career was often omitted from accounts of her life. She preferred to tell people she had retired after her marriage in 1927. After she injured her wrists in a fall at a Los Angeles theater in 1929, she sued the theater and used the settlement to finance her retirement, although she did return to the stage (mainly in Fort Wayne) several times in the 1930s. Along with performing intermittently, she ran a small grocery store with her husband and her parents. She died on December 11, 1968.

Vaudeville passed away along with these women. Although some elements of vaudeville crept into modern culture (as some of these performers brought their vaudeville experience to new media), the massive vaudeville circuits, the opulent theaters, and the exciting vaudeville bills receded into the shadows of a new mass culture in which entertainment was increasingly generated or mediated by technology. Vaudeville had helped to create a world that made it obsolete. But vaudeville did not go quietly. In fact, the passing of vaudeville was the topic of a wide-ranging discussion in which many observers blamed vaudeville's decline on the industry's femininity. It is clear that questions of gender and cultural hierarchy were central not only to vaudeville's growth (as this book has already shown) but also to interpretations of vaudeville's death. A 1925 editorial attributed vaudeville's troubles to its earlier efforts to acquire class with "bunk draperies and bunk settings" instead of obtaining fresh material and recruiting new performers. The author described the result in highly gendered terms: "Instead of vaudeville and variety, it was vanity."[24] Another article pointed to the "timidity" of agents, who were not taking enough initiative in recruiting new vaudeville talent, as well as the frailty of the producers of "girl acts." These producers, according to this article, "prefer to wait until the situation insures them a guarantee of a profit before they invest in scenery, royalties and production expenses."[25] This critic tied vaudeville's problems to these men's feminine weaknesses as well as the extravagant, flashy elements of the girl acts. Similarly, many critics argued that vaudeville's original appeal (the vigorous and implicitly male performer) had been replaced by fake, flat, and overwhelmingly feminine trifles. The ladies of vaudeville had toppled from high to low culture.

The attack on the femininity of the decrepit vaudeville industry was part of a broad critique of mass culture as feminine. This hostility toward mass culture drew on long-standing traditions in American culture. The ideal republican citizen, as envisioned by such early thinkers as Thomas Jefferson, was independent, truthful, and productive. The citizen should reject the temptations (and assumed trickery) of the marketplace because these pleasures could sap a citizen's strength and therefore undermine the Republic.[26] The tension between masculinity and femininity, authenticity and artifice, shaped the critique of mass culture around the turn of the century as well. American modern writers launched "an explosive protest against maternal suffocation and infantilization," in which some intellectuals, like T. S. Eliot, decried mass culture as passification and celebrated a virile and cynical art.[27] Constance Rourke, furthermore, criticized the "false feminine" in American culture, attacking the sentimental (and popular) female authors of the nineteenth century in particular.[28] An antifeminine backlash also occurred in American theater around the turn of the century. The female theater patrons who had previously been linked to cultural ascendance (to moral rectitude and polite manners) were in the early twentieth century lambasted for eroding high culture because of their childlike tastes and lack of education.[29] Walter Prichard Eaton described the "bad influence of American women on the drama" in 1910, and Ludwig Lewisohn identified the "American girl" as the cause of the lack of "virility" in the legitimate theater.[30]

Although many American modernists held themselves at a distance from mass culture, others embraced mass culture as a vibrant wellspring of American creativity, particularly as a source of racially mixed, indigenous American art, and many drew on mass culture forms as they developed their careers in literature and the arts. According to Ann Douglas, popularity in and of itself was not the source of most American modernists' disgust; rather, these cultural rebels abhorred hypocrisy, denial, and repression—whether in high or in low culture—and linked these traits with the nineteenth-century tradition of feminine uplift.[31] To get rid of these cultural impediments, they attacked the symbol of the matriarch. Some modern American artists embraced vaudeville's ragtime, hard-edged comedy, and sexy slang as antidotes to sappy, maternal Victorian culture, but this raw vaudeville was also entangled in a cloak of matriarchal ascendance and feminine finery. Vaudeville, then, was both friend and foe to modern American writers and artists of the 1920s.

Ultimately, the uneasiness about mass culture and an antagonism toward feminization (sometimes powerfully intertwined) contributed to a reinterpretation of gender and cultural hierarchy in vaudeville's history—to a regendering of vaudeville's value. Although many people depicted the Keith-Albee vaudeville empire as a mass culture machine catering to women, they also hailed early vaudeville as undiluted, masculine art. From the vantage point of the late 1920s, some observers argued that vaudeville had not evolved from a raunchy, low male culture to a respectable feminine culture, as Keith would have proudly said; rather, they argued, vaudeville had decayed from a robust, authentic masculine aesthetic to a low culture of feminine sentimentality and artifice.

The White Rats were important early critics of vaudeville as feminized mass culture. During the 1919–20 FTC hearing, several years before vaudeville's actual collapse, the Rats predicted vaudeville's demise and presented an enduring hypothesis for that failure. They blamed the decay of vaudeville primarily on circuit administrators' unfettered drive for profits but also pointed to the ways these unscrupulous managers used particular female performers—sexually corrupt amateurs—to bolster profits. They argued that the eye-catching and famously disreputable female star degraded vaudeville, supplanting the comedian's razor-sharp wit and finely honed dance steps. In these ways, the White Rats linked women in vaudeville to what they saw as vaudeville's debased status as mass culture.

Conclusion

In the FTC hearing, several White Rats criticized the administrators of the Keith circuit for placing commercial concerns over aesthetic value and for introducing machinelike standards in the expansion of vaudeville. Some leading Rats argued that managers' demand for three shows a day reduced players to cogs in a mass culture machine, destroying the art and exuberance of vaudeville: "I believe [three shows a day] means killing the actor's talent and art, if he has any. . . . [H]e becomes an automaton, is careless in his work."[32] This language resembles earlier White Rats' complaints about contemporary vaudeville as opposed to variety. Frank Conroy argued that whereas the variety performer had to learn many skills and not only perform his or her own act but also join a larger cast in variety's afterpiece, the vaudeville performer focused only on his or her routine—"the same old act day in and day out, week in and week out." Probably using jokes from a mass-produced joke book, the new vaudevillian relied on imitation and standardization, according to Conroy. Not surprisingly, Conroy identified the audience for such watered-down entertainment as feminine. He described "[t]he nice, pleasant lady audience laughing at [the new vaudevillians'] clean jokes" and explained that "the newcomer of today does not have to be versatile; all he has to do is learn a song, learn a few dancing steps, and *borrow* several jokes with another newcomer" (emphasis in original).[33]

Just as the audience for this enervated vaudeville was female, the unskilled, fraudulent vaudeville star—the epitome of the decline of vaudeville—was often a woman. The White Rats faulted modern vaudeville for employing immoral stars (criminals and suspected criminals) who were valuable in vaudeville not because of their skills but because of their names, particularly the sexual scandals associated with their names. They exemplified the ascendance of glittering surface appeal in vaudeville rather than the rigorous skill of veteran vaudevillians, developed over years of "making good." "I . . . still claim . . . that no man should be permitted to appear in the variety business . . . who is a notorious criminal or the principal figure in a notorious scandal," James Fitzpatrick argued, pointing first to a female performer. "I knew that, first, at Hammerstein's, a woman named Diss de Bar had played, who was a notorious international crook, a woman who had been exposed in

London for some unspeakable dealing with children, and a woman who had an international reputation as a swindler, a confidence woman and crook; and yet she appeared at Hammerstein's as the headline attraction of the bill. . . . I think the presence of a man like Jack Johnson was an unspeakable insult to every decent man and woman in the profession."[34] Jack Johnson, a black boxer who had won the heavyweight championship in 1909, created controversy during his 1910 vaudeville tour because of his well-publicized involvement with white prostitutes and his marriage to a white woman.[35] Johnson and de Bar were fitting symbols of the corruption of vaudeville for several reasons. Black performers and white women had long been "other" to the White Rats' artisanal identity, and these stars also symbolized the open selling of sexual scandal, a core of vaudeville's mass production of stardom, which many White Rats deplored.

Surpassing Johnson and de Bar, however, Evelyn Nesbit was the premier symbol of illegitimate stardom, according to Fitzpatrick, who repeatedly pointed to her as a sign of vaudeville's deterioration. "I think Evelyn Nesbit was booked on the Keith Circuit, and she had no business in the theatre," Fitzpatrick said. "I played the bill with her many times, and she never was an applause hit."[36] While working as a chorus girl in the early 1900s, Nesbit had an affair with prominent architect Stanford White, but soon after the tryst, she married Harry K. Thaw, a Philadelphia millionaire. Obsessed with his wife's previous affair, Thaw shot White in June 1906 and was tried for murder but declared insane. The crime and the trial were widely publicized, creating new opportunities for Evelyn Nesbit Thaw's theatrical career. After turning down several lucrative vaudeville contracts, she finally accepted vaudeville agents' offers of engagements in Great Britain and the United States in 1913. Nesbit received some valuable free publicity when Thaw escaped from a mental institution during her tour, making headlines across the nation. In her trademark dance, Nesbit held onto her partner's neck and swung around with a "transparent yellow dress" billowing around her. By 1914, Harry Thaw's mother began to finance a coalition of reformers who objected to Nesbit's "immoral" dancing.[37] Publicity for Nesbit's appearance at Keith's theater in Providence claimed that she was booked "absolutely on her own . . . merit" and that she had not taken advantage of her role in the "most sensational criminal case in the annals of the American courts."[38] By denying that her association with the murder trial was a reason for her appearance, Keith publicists still called attention to the fact that the scandal was part of her notoriety.

The White Rats' hostility to scandalous female stars builds on earlier trends in this group's history. Although Keith had long celebrated the female socialite as the target of vaudeville's uplift and offered the amateur lady artist a chance on the stage in part to elevate vaudeville, the White Rats, as early as 1910, told the story of the debutante who usurped the veteran vaudevillian. A 1910 cartoon showed a well-dressed woman (identified as the "debutante") at an agent's office. With a joke book under her arm, she tells the agent that she has "never appeared in public." The agent does not seem to mind; he looks at her lustfully, gives her a route, and promises that "the jumps [between towns] are all small." In contrast, the other frame of the cartoon shows a veteran male vaudevillian, with twenty years' experience, pleading unsuccessfully with an agent. "We're looking for big names and new faces," the agent explains. The problem with the debutante in vaudeville was twofold: she exemplified stardom—based on name recognition, social status, or perhaps scandal—and because of her inexperience, she was easy prey for agents and managers (she did not realize, for example, that the guarantee of an easy route was often a lie).[39] The White Rats' criticism of the debutante was part of their broader campaign against the exploitation of performers in vaudeville. They protested the increased pace of work and their declining independence in the expanding bureaucracy of vaudeville. Although they often seemed disgusted with the feminine influence in vaudeville and the allegedly inauthentic female stars, the leaders of the White Rats placed the primary responsibility for vaudeville's slide on the men in charge of the industry. They saw Keith, Albee, and their corps of managers and agents—not women—as the true engineers of feminization in vaudeville.

The concern about the fate of the individual (such as the talented male performer) in a vast bureaucracy that manufactured culture was not limited to vaudeville. Similar debate, also infused with gender, surrounded the Book-of-the-Month Club, a central industry in the newly identified "middlebrow" culture of the 1920s. In the eyes of many crit-

Cartoon showing the debutante's rise in vaudeville at the expense of the veteran male vaudevillian. From The Player, *March 25, 1910, 18.*

ics, the Book-of-the-Month Club was dangerous because it standardized and corrupted culture by forcing all members to read the same books, selected by "literary experts" and distributed through the hierarchy of the club. Although almost half of the Book-of-the-Month Club subscribers were men, criticism of the club usually referred to a female consumer who was easily duped by this commercial enterprise. One critic decried the book club as feminization when he protested, "No literary wet nurses for me!"[40] "However much they were welcomed by middle-class consumers," explains Janice Radway, "the book clubs were greeted by their critics as a profound threat to independent American writers and readers, individuals gendered always as male and represented as endangered by the interminable flow of materials issuing from the new cultural agencies."[41]

This gendered critique of mass culture peaked during the 1920s but continued to a lesser extent through the twentieth century. Some music critics, for example, saw the popularity of girl groups in the late 1950s and the rising influence of teenage girls as rock 'n' roll fans as the cause of rock music's decline—its "emasculation." A magazine article in Brit-

Conclusion

ain pleaded with girls to stop buying records. "Borrow records from your boyfriend instead," the article advised.[42] Several histories of vaudeville from the 1940s carried on these gendered metaphors, explaining the decay of this entertainment industry as the result of its excessive femininity. In his 1940 account of vaudeville, Douglas Gilbert placed most of the blame for vaudeville's lapse on chorus girls and evening gowns:

> The backbone of vaudeville was low comedy. When dialect, eccentric, and nut comedians in exaggerated costumes and facial make-ups predominated, the dumb acts and sensational presentations gave balance to the bill. When dinner coats, white tie and tails, and evening gowns replaced the baggy pants, slapshoes, and fright wigs; when faces were made beautiful instead of grotesque . . . when manufactured acts, consisting of a number of girls who changed costumes frequently, ousted the really nimble and effective old-time dance acts; when fashion-plate comics entertained between numbers instead of a roaring slapstick turn — vaudeville was devitalized. Cycloramas, drapery and gorgeous drops added to the glamour, but not to the comedy.[43]

Reminiscent of mass culture critics of the 1920s, Gilbert links "manufactured" culture to women, hinting at the machinelike precision of the chorus girl acts. These masses of women in vaudeville, he says, overwhelmed the traditional vaudevillian. Women also symbolized the shallow appeal of mass-produced vaudeville. From this perspective, Keith's achievement of his primary goals (appealing to white women and reaching a mass audience) was his downfall.

The transformations of the Keith circuit identified by Gilbert are accurate: Keith managers catered to women by including fancy interior designs in their theaters; grotesque ethnic comedy, such as that of Kate Elinore, declined in favor of more restrained humor onstage (although this rough style was never wholly eliminated); and producers like Ned Wayburn increasingly took the headliner position on vaudeville bills with elaborate girl acts. But it is difficult to determine the extent to which these transformations actually contributed to vaudeville's demise. After all, musical comedies and revues, which emphasized all of these elements, thrived, whereas vaudeville declined. Perhaps, as other historians have suggested, vaudeville was not quite feminine or showy enough. One historian, for example, concluded in 1946 that the lone vaudevillian was defeated by the hordes of women in musical revues: "The funniest of funny men cannot hold his own against eighty or a hundred 'lovelies,' descending a golden staircase in an Earl Carroll or Florenz Ziegfeld review."[44] Vaudeville historian Shirley Staples wonders: "Why go to vaudeville for spectacle when you could see bigger and better for a bit higher price in musical comedy and review?"[45] Other theories about the decline of vaudeville pointed to trends other than feminization. Some argued that vaudeville had become too coarse and crude; others noted that action had supplanted the ingenious, often subtle comic talk of early vaudeville. Comedian and dancer Pat Rooney II (son of veteran vaudevillian Pat Rooney Sr.) stated in 1929 that "color and action have taken the place of whimsical talent on stage."[46]

The criticism of the bloated debutantes and illicit female stars of vaudeville rose above other theories in large part because it fit a modernist ideal, a longing for a raw, masculine art. The image of a lone male vaudeville comedian on a bare stage, hustling the audience with his charismatic personality and quick feet, fulfilled this ideal. Such a tribute to vaudeville is not unwarranted. Vaudeville, as this study has shown, encouraged a masculine resistance to the official program of feminization and cultural uplift. Managers could not (or did not want to) suppress the gallery's jeering of lady artists, they allowed Kate Elinore and Mike Haggerty to ridicule "civilizing women," and they lifted Ruth Budd's boyish, often primitive athleticism to the headliner position in vaudeville. In these ways, vaudeville had cultivated the seeds of the attack against it in the 1920s.

The exaltation of the feminine to uplift a culture industry and the denigration of mass culture as feminine deserve careful examination because these opposing trends are powerful reminders of the centrality of gender to social changes around the turn of the century as well as the reactions to these trends. But they do not capture women's status in entertainment industries, their motivations as consumers, or their varied embodiments of gender onstage. As this study has shown, the investigation of women as performers, patrons, and workers in vaudeville uncovers a complex social and cultural history beneath the sometimes simplistic gender imagery in the publicity and criticism surrounding this industry. Furthermore, this study demonstrates that it is worth analyzing the persistent use of the feminine to uplift or insult mass culture industries to uncover the alternative tales of gender that are lurking beneath the official stories of progress and decline. In vaudeville, as we have seen, labor leaders, performers, and customers often rejected the administrators' plans for feminization and offered alternative impressions of women's significance in the industry.

The split image crafted by vaudeville's modernist critics and mourners (the portrait of early vaudeville as authentic and masculine versus the image of late vaudeville as feminine glitter) is a tidy image of vaudeville's history that supports a widespread devaluation of the feminine in American culture. But this portrait is just as misleading as Keith's celebration of his circuit's feminine progress was decades earlier: vaudeville was richer and more complicated than either of these gendered dichotomies and chronologies allows. It had always been an odd mixture of Shakespeare and slapstick, refined and rough women, artists and artisans. The rank ladies and ladies of rank did not always share center stage, but the shifting balance between them was an enduring preoccupation of publicists, managers, and labor leaders. Although the women onstage and in the audience did not control the bureaucracy of vaudeville, they emerged as key symbols in the industry's power struggles, the stories of vaudeville's elevation and decline, and the interpretations of vaudeville's legacy—the new mass culture.

NOTES

◆ ——————————————————— ◆

Abbreviations

The following abbreviations are used throughout the notes.

BRTC Billy Rose Theatre Collection, New York Public Library for the Performing Arts, New York, New York

DBS Daniel Blum Scrapbooks, Wisconsin State Historical Society, Madison, Wisconsin

ESVAP Elinore Sisters' Vaudeville Act Papers, Department of Rare Books and Special Collections, University of Rochester Library, Rochester, New York

FTC v. VMPA *Federal Trade Commission v. Vaudeville Managers' Protective Association et al.,* Docket 128, Record Group 122, National Records Center, Suitland, Maryland

HC Harris Collection, Special Collections, John Hay Library, Brown University, Providence, Rhode Island

HRHRC Harry Ransom Humanities Research Center, University of Texas, Austin, Texas

HTC Harvard Theatre Collection, Houghton Library, Harvard University, Cambridge, Massachusetts

JAC Julia Arthur Collection, Harvard Theatre Collection, Houghton Library, Harvard University, Cambridge, Massachusetts

KAC Keith/Albee Collection, Special Collections Department, University of Iowa Library, Iowa City, Iowa

LC Library of Congress, Washington, D.C.

RBC Ruth Budd Collection, Allen County–Fort Wayne Historical Society, Fort Wayne, Indiana

RLC Robinson Locke Collection, New York Public Library for the Performing Arts, New York, New York

Chapter One

1. The description of this entertainment is based on the theater manager's account in Report Book 10, 28, KAC.

2. *New York Dramatic Mirror*, October 23, 1909, quoted in Slide, *Selected Vaudeville Criticism*, 91.

3. "Keith Bill Headed by Yvette Guilbert," *Philadelphia Inquirer*, November 16, 1909, 6. Epes Sargent (Chicot) described her "personal charm" in *Variety*, April 28, 1906, quoted in Slide, *Selected Vaudeville Criticism*, 90.

4. Report Book 10, 28, KAC.

5. Guilbert was not simply a cardboard caricature of feminine snobbery. During her first vaudeville tour, she agreed to incorporate several "coon songs" (syncopated songs with African American characters usually sung in African American dialect) after her agent convinced her that the usual fare would not draw a broad enough crowd. Critics noted that as she progressed in vaudeville she abandoned some of her typical restraint; one reviewer was pleased to see that by 1906 Guilbert was no longer standing motionless onstage while she sang. See Gilbert, *American Vaudeville*, 142.

6. Report Book 10, 28, KAC.

7. *New York Dramatic Mirror*, October 23, 1909, quoted in Slide, *Selected Vaudeville Criticism*, 91.

8. "Yvette Guilbert Raps American Audiences," *New York Times*, October 17, 1909, 13. For information on Guilbert's appearances in Britain, see Geraldine Harris, "Yvette Guilbert."

9. Report Book 2, 231, KAC.

10. "Mrs. Fiske's Anger Aroused," *The Player*, November 25, 1910, 37; "The Matinee Girl," *New York Dramatic Mirror*, June 11, 1904, 2. Furthermore, the police reportedly became involved in maintaining cultural order when they forbade blackface, acrobatic, and animal acts to appear at the Actors Fund Benefit, a charity production that included many vaudeville as well as dramatic performers. See "Big Actors' Fund Benefit Given by White Rats," *The Player*, May 6, 1910, 17.

11. Frank Fogarty testimony, box 71, 1134–35, *FTC v. VMPA*.

12. DiMaggio, "Cultural Entrepreneurship in Nineteenth Century Boston, Part II," 308–13. See also DiMaggio, "Cultural Entrepreneurship in Nineteenth Century Boston: The Creation of an Organizational Base for High Culture in America"; Bright and Bakewell, *Looking High and Low*; and Lamont and Fournier, *Cultivating Differences*.

13. Levine, *Highbrow/Lowbrow*, 101.

14. Neil Harris, "Four Stages of Cultural Growth," 22. See also Levine, *Highbrow/Lowbrow*.

15. Butsch, "Bowery B'hoys and Matinee Ladies," 376.

16. Ann Douglas, *Feminization of American Culture*; Cott, *Bonds of Womanhood*; Ryan, *Cradle of the Middle Class*.

17. Butsch, "Bowery B'hoys and Matinee Ladies." See also Claudia Johnson, "That Guilty Third Tier," and Tracy C. Davis, *Actresses as Working Women*. Hansen notes that, by the end of the nineteenth century, middle-class leisure was usually family centered (catering to women and men), whereas popular entertainment (saloons and burlesque, for example) was still male dominated, a threat to women's reputations (*Babel and Babylon*, 115).

18. Butsch, "Bowery B'hoys and Matinee Ladies," 387.

19. McLean, "Genesis of Vaudeville," 86.

20. Levine, *Highbrow/Lowbrow*, 197; Kasson, *Rudeness and Civility*, 250. Kasson also acknowledges some debate over refinement in American vaudeville, pointing to the activity of the "guerilla fighters of male working-class culture" (ibid.).

21. Oberdeck, "Contested Cultures of American Refinement," 42. See also Oberdeck, "Religion, Culture, and the Politics of Class." The manager of Keith's theater in Providence noted a class difference between the patrons who came to see Ethel Barrymore one week and those who came to see the Edison talking pictures the next, but he admitted that "as they both pay the same price, I presume it is all right" (Report Book 14, 246, KAC).

22. Oberdeck, "Contested Cultures of American Refinement," 53.

23. Rubin, *Showstoppers*, 14–18. William Taylor has described the aggregate amusements around the turn of the century as the "commercial culture of pastiche." Such offerings, he argues, were a profitable combination of "plasticity and suggestiveness," open to varied interpretations and broad markets (*In Pursuit of Gotham*, 74, 90). See also Snyder, *Voice of the City*, 3–12.

24. Ibid., 16. See also Toll, *On with the Show*, 86.

25. Mahar, "Ethiopian Skits and Sketches," 269. See also Toll, *Blacking Up*.

26. Toll, *Blacking Up*, chap. 3.

27. Snyder, *Voice of the City*, 9.

28. Ibid., 10.

29. Nasaw, *Going Out*, 14.

30. Ibid., 18. Dennett notes that "typical late nineteenth century middle-of-the-road dime museums [catered] to a working-class and lower-middle-class clientele" (*Weird and Wonderful*, 56).

31. Nasaw, *Going Out*, 18. See also Dennett, *Weird and Wonderful*, 61.

32. Harlow, *Old Bowery Days*, quoted in Dennett, *Weird and Wonderful*, 61.

33. Nasaw has identified the late nineteenth century as the beginning of an "era of public amusements," including the dramatic rise of world fairs, amusement parks, baseball parks, vaudeville, and motion picture houses (*Going Out*, 1). And Ohmann has described the rise of mass culture in relation to magazine publishing and marketing around the turn of the century in *Selling Culture*.

34. Butsch, "Introduction: Leisure and Hegemony," 14–15.

35. Snyder, *Voice of the City*, xv.

36. Gorn, "Sports through the Nineteenth Century," 1639.

37. Leach, *Land of Desire*, 23.

38. Ibid., 25.

39. Nasaw, *Going Out*, 27. Sometimes, however, vaudeville theater managers noted that popular baseball games hurt vaudeville's business. On the opening day of the baseball season in Cleveland, Keith's manager there wrote, "The sun shone, and the theatre starved to death. At one time I thought of asking our audience if he would go out and have a cigar, but as he seemed about to laugh at something, I resisted the temptation" (Report Book 5, 4, KAC).

40. Describing the innovations planned by the "great department store proprietors," a reporter for the *New York Dramatic Mirror* revealed that "[o]ne of the novelties . . . is a vaudeville theatre within the walls of the new building" ("What Next?," *New York Dramatic Mirror*, August 15, 1896, 12).

41. Fox, "Discipline of Amusement," 86; Levine, *Highbrow/Lowbrow*, 197; Kasson, *Rudeness and Civility*.

42. Peiss, *Cheap Amusements*, 65; Uricchio and Pearson, *Reframing Culture*; Frith, "The Good, the Bad, and the Indifferent."

43. Cohen, *Making a New Deal*, chap. 3. See also Peiss, *Cheap Amusements*, chap. 3.

44. For the debate over the feminization of culture in the nineteenth century, see Ann Douglas, *Feminization of American Culture*; Tompkins, *Sensational Designs*; and Merish, "'Hand of Refined Taste.'"

45. Modleski, "Femininity as Mas(s)querade," 34. See also Huyssen, "Mass Culture as Woman"; Petro, "Mass Culture and the Feminine"; Radway, "On the Gender of the Middlebrow Consumer"; and Joyrich, "Critical and Textual Hypermasculinity."

46. Modleski, "Femininity as Mas(s)querade," 34.

47. Hansen, *Babel and Babylon*, 120.

48. Peiss, "Commercial Leisure and the 'Woman Question,'" 106.

49. For a discussion of Victorian passionlessness, see Cott, "Passionlessness."

50. Peiss, *Cheap Amusements*, 6–7. See also Enstad, "Dressed for Adventure"; Rabinovitz, *For the Love of Pleasure*; Todd, *"New Woman" Revised*; Rupp, "Feminism and the Sexual Revolution"; and McGovern, "The American Woman's Pre–World War I Freedom."

51. Hansen, *Babel and Babylon*; Rabinovitz, *For the Love of Pleasure*.

52. Eva Tanguay was known as a "cyclonic" comedienne. See, for example, the cover of *Keith's Theatre*, April 19, 1909, clipping, Clipping Book (February 20, 1909–November 15, 1909), 37, KAC.

53. Smith-Rosenberg, "Puberty to Menopause," 27.

54. Ibid., 24. See also Douglas Wood, "'Fashionable Diseases,'" and Rosen, *Lost Sisterhood*, chap. 1.

55. Natalie Zemon Davis, "Women on Top."

56. See Russo, "Female Grotesques," and Rowe, *Unruly Woman*.

57. The influx of women into the male realms of theater and politics and women's attacks on such male preserves as the saloon were not uniformly appreciated or accepted. Middle-class men became increasingly concerned with strengthening and defending masculinity in a variety of ways, partly because they felt besieged by female reformers. Men joined exclusively male groups such as the Freemasons and the Boy Scouts and supported male activities like the Young Men's Christian Association's programs for teaching boxing to men and boys. Men countered what they saw as "excessive femininity" in other venues as well. Many observers, for example, were critical of the predominance of female students and teachers in public high schools, reasoning that education was losing its vitality and that boys were becoming "effeminate." Educators in Los Angeles established several programs to combat the perceived effects of feminization, including plans to recruit male teachers and draw truant boys back into the school system. See Bederman, *Manliness and Civilization*, 16–17; Kimmel, "Men's Response to Feminism," "Consuming Manhood," and *Manhood in America*; and Brown, "Fear of Feminization."

58. "The Colonial," *Variety*, January 21, 1911, 14.

59. As Glenn has shown in "'Give an Imitation of Me,'" Tanguay was one of many comediennes who imitated others and who was often imitated herself on the vaude-

ville stage. One vaudeville manager offered this revealing description of Tanguay's enigmatic popularity in 1907: "Homely and no voice, but that Vaudeville something that makes her worth every dollar" (Report Book 6, 7, KAC). Tanguay also held a grudge against legitimate performer Ethel Barrymore because Barrymore had received a larger salary during her tour of the Keith circuit. In December 1914 Tanguay set out to prove that she was worth more money by attracting more fans to the Palace Theatre than Barrymore had, and she reportedly succeeded. See Robert Grau, "Grau's Gripping Grist," *Billboard*, January 16, 1915, 5.

60. Slide, "E. F. Albee," 5.

61. "The Growth of Vaudeville in the United States," *Providence Tribune*, November 30, 1913, clipping, Clipping Book (December 29, 1912–December 8, 1913), KAC. Albee eventually became the general manager of the United Booking Office and of B. F. Keith's New York Theatres Company.

62. Slide, "E. F. Albee," 5–6.

63. "The Growth of Vaudeville in the United States," *Providence Tribune*, November 30, 1913, clipping, Clipping Book (December 29, 1912–December 8, 1913), KAC.

64. McLean, "Genesis of Vaudeville," 90.

65. Allen, "B. F. Keith and the Origins of American Vaudeville," 110–11. In this combination, Keith followed the lead of Moses Kimball, who in the 1840s established the Boston Museum and Gallery of Fine Arts, which had museum exhibits downstairs and a theater upstairs.

66. Snyder, *Voice of the City*, chap. 2.

67. Allen demonstrates that Keith's experiences with variety in dime museums in Boston differed from the development of vaudeville in New York City. Whereas variety was considered "immoral" in New York City, it was considered a respectable alternative to dramatic arts in Boston. Keith's problems with variety in dime museums had more to do with the working-class identity of dime museums than with a disreputable image of variety acts. As Allen concludes, "[T]he function and meaning of variety acts differs as we move from one institutional context (the concert saloons) to another (the dime museum). Keith's problem was not removing the taint of immorality from variety, but removing a working-class stigma from the dime museum" ("B. F. Keith and the Origins of American Vaudeville," 114).

68. Bernheim, "The Facts of Vaudeville," *Equity* 8 (September 1923): 34. The Keith contract for the spring of 1923 listed thirty-two theaters on the circuit. See Ruth Budd contract, March 3, 1923, box 2, vol. 11, RBC.

69. Ruth Budd contract, March 23, 1923, box 2, vol. 11, RBC. See also McLean, *American Vaudeville as Ritual*, 45.

70. Bernheim, "The Facts of Vaudeville," *Equity* 8 (September 1923): 32.

71. Report Book 7, 172, KAC.

72. Report Book 6, 103, KAC. Performers evidently realized that if they upset a manager at one theater, their future with the entire Keith organization was in jeopardy. When one performer known as Vinton refused to appear in Philadelphia's Keith theater in 1914, the manager there reportedly "asked him how about his future time and he said he did not care to play for the United Booking Office any way, that he was through" (Report Book 16, 89, KAC). Another report in 1909 revealed the cooperation among managers: "Billy Van at rehearsal this morning, didn't like his place

on the bill, preferring to resign, which I permitted him to do. He refused to go on in that place, violating his contract and those who want to lose him can now do so" (Report Book 9, 27, KAC).

73. Snyder, *Voice of the City*, 95.

74. Prill, "Small Time King," quoted in Snyder, "Big Time, Small Time," 128.

75. Snyder, *Voice of the City*, 95–96.

76. Marston and Feller, *F. F. Proctor*, "Keith on Top," *Variety*, May 19, 1906, 2.

77. "Vaudeville War on Now," *New York Times*, February 17, 1907, 9.

78. "Keith and Beck in Vaudeville Combine," *New York Times*, July 17, 1910, 9.

79. *Equity*, furthermore, reported the financial linkages between the two circuits, with Keith holding 51 percent of stock in New York City's Palace Theatre, originally built by Beck, and Orpheum owning 49 percent (Bernheim, "The Facts of Vaudeville," *Equity* 8 [September 1923]: 36–37).

80. Ibid., 32.

81. "Vaudeville Managers Unite," *New York Times*, March 2, 1911, 7. The original directors of the VMPA were B. F. Keith, Martin Beck, Morris Meyerfeld Jr., Harry Davis, Sylvester Poli, F. F. Proctor, E. F. Albee, Percy Williams, and Michael Shea. In July 1911, Proctor won a suit to dissolve his partnership with Keith. Proctor received control of the 125th Street Theatre, the Fifty-Eighth Street Theatre, and the Twenty-Third Street Theatre in New York City, whereas Keith got the Union Square Theatre and the Jersey City theaters.

82. Report Book 1, 5, KAC.

83. Report Book 9, 169, KAC. Charles Lovenberg wrote that Benjamin Chapin's sketch, *At the White House*, "made a hit at 5th Avenue. Thank heaven the Providence audiences have a little more grey matter" (Report Book 10, 59, KAC). See also Report Book 16, 147, KAC.

84. Singer explains that many elements of East Coast vaudeville were exported to the West Coast (including standard bills and identical performers), but he adds that managers on the West Coast had more opportunity to try innovations outside of the corporate controls of the East Coast ("Vaudeville in Los Angeles").

Chapter Two

1. Quoted in McLean, "Genesis of Vaudeville," 93–94.

2. This account has been reprinted in various forms in Levine, *Highbrow/Lowbrow*, 196; Allen, *Horrible Prettiness*, 184; McLean, *American Vaudeville as Ritual*, 207; and Snyder, *Voice of the City*, 31. Kasson notes similar instances in *Rudeness and Civility*, 250–51.

3. The manager of Keith's theater in Philadelphia also listed other elements, in addition to "ladies and nuts," that he ordered Fitzgibbon to cut from his routine: "'What the h——,' the word 'cock roach' . . . speaking to the persons entering and leaving the theater" (Report Book 21, 239, KAC).

4. For an excellent discussion of vaudeville's struggles over refinement in the "social milieu of urban rivalry," see Oberdeck, "Contested Cultures of American Refinement," 42.

5. One article in Keith's publicity newsletter in Providence explained that "[w]e

aim to have our prices at all times within the reach of everyone's pocketbook" ("The Girl behind the Pen," *Keith News*, October 25, 1909, 3, clipping, Clipping Book [February 2, 1909–November 15, 1909], 232, KAC).

6. Cohen, *Making a New Deal*, chap. 3; Carbine, "'Finest outside the Loop'"; Levine, "Folklore of Industrial Society"; Waller, *Main Street Amusements*, chap. 7.

7. William Taylor has reached similar conclusions about other settings of controversial intermixture around the turn of the century. The Metropolitan Life Insurance building in New York City, for example, housed a variety of male and female workers in its new offices but segregated employees by "function and gender" (*In Pursuit of Gotham*, 72).

8. *Variety*, 1908, quoted in Nasaw, *Going Out*, 168.

9. Clipping, Clipping Book (October 25, 1914–August 9, 1915), vwyz, KAC. The *Attleboro Sun* also advertised a 10 cent admission price for Keith's bargain matinee in September 1918 (clipping, Clipping Book [April 1, 1918–December 14, 1918], 185, KAC). A survey of New York City's recreation also found that three Keith theaters had 10 cent gallery prices in 1911 (Michael Davis, *Exploitation of Pleasure*, 25). In 1911 one Keith manager reflected on the competition from 5 cent movie houses: "Five cent picture shows both sides of Euclid Ave. were advertising pictures as coming direct from the American Press Association. This took the edge off any advertising we could do on a 50 cents basis for a feature" (Report Book 12, 163, KAC).

10. "The Girl behind the Pen," *Keith News*, September 18, 1911, 3, clipping, Clipping Book (March 17, 1911–January 28, 1912), 142, KAC.

11. "The Girl behind the Pen," *Keith News*, October 25, 1909, 3, clipping, Clipping Book (February 2, 1909–November 15, 1909), 232, KAC.

12. Blumin, *Emergence of the Middle Class*, 270–75, 283.

13. Nasaw, *Going Out*, 5. For a comparison of the wages and status of saleswomen and other types of workers, see Benson, *Counter Cultures*, 177–209. Benson explains that most department store women earned more than women in manufacturing, although there were some exceptions in industries with union wages for women (needle trades and tobacco, for example). Benson also shows that women in department stores usually worked less hours than women in manufacturing (often eight hours or less), as stores ended evening shopping hours around this time.

14. More, *Wage-earners' Budgets*, 142–43, 168–69; Chapin, *Standard of Living*, 211; Peiss, *Cheap Amusements*, 53.

15. Nasaw, *Going Out*, 163.

16. Keith's top price of $1.00 in Boston in 1909–10 contrasted the Park Theatre's maximum from 1896 to 1910 of $1.50 and was dwarfed by the Hollis Street Theatre's price for a box seat—$2.40. All price comparisons are based on the figures listed in *Julius Cahn's Official Theatrical Guide* (1896, 1900–1901, 1902–3, 1905–6, 1906–7, 1907–8, 1908–9, 1909–10); *The Cahn-Leighton Official Theatrical Guide* (1912–13, 1913–14); and *The Julius Cahn–Gus Hill Theatrical Guide and Moving Picture Directory* (1921).

17. The Colonial, Hollis Street, Park, and Tremont theaters in Boston had top prices that were between $1.25 and $2.15 higher than their gallery prices. Keith's New Theatre in Boston, on the other hand, had only a 50 cent gap between its top orchestra price and the rate for gallery seats until 1909. In Boston, Keith's theaters

maintained a four-tiered price scale, whereas legitimate theaters advertised approx-imately five different price levels. In New York City, three of Keith's theaters main-tained three-tiered price scales between 1908 and 1911 (three seasons). Syndicate theaters in New York City, on the other hand, maintained an average of four to five gradations between 1896 and 1910.

18. *B. F. Keith's New Theatre*, brochure, B. F. Keith Clipping File, BRTC.

19. Ibid.

20. Archie Bell, *A Little Journey to the B. F. Keith Palace, Cleveland* (1913?), 7, HTC. After a detailed description of the colors and shading in Josef Israels's *Shoal Fisher*, Bell instructed spectators to "pause again to realize what you are seeing. An Israels in an American vaudeville theatre!"

21. He comments further that Jacobus Simon Hendrik Kever's paintings were housed in art galleries in Holland and graced the walls of Keith's theaters. See ibid.

22. "The Girl behind the Pen," *Keith News*, February 24, 1908, 3, clipping, Clip-ping Book (November 6, 1907–April 29, 1908), KAC.

23. "The Girl behind the Pen," *Keith News*, November 23, 1908, 3, clipping, Clip-ping Book (February 25, 1908–February 19, 1909), KAC.

24. "The Girl behind the Pen," *Keith News*, April 6, 1908, 3, clipping, Clipping Book (November 6, 1907–April 29, 1908), KAC.

25. Irving, *Letters of Jonathan Oldstyle, Gent*, quoted in Kasson, *Rudeness and Civil-ity*, 219.

26. Poggi, *Theater in America*, 41.

27. Levine, *Highbrow/Lowbrow*, 206–7.

28. Ibid., 207.

29. "The Girl behind the Pen," *Keith News*, January 31, 1910, 3, clipping, Clipping Book (November 16, 1909–May 27, 1910), 88, KAC.

30. "The Girl behind the Pen," *Keith News*, April 6, 1908, 3, clipping, Clipping Book (November 6, 1907–April 29, 1908), KAC. In the October 25, 1909, *Keith News*, "The Girl behind the Pen" presented the story of two women discussing their the-atrical preferences. Whereas the older woman preferred Keith's, her younger com-panion complained that she could not afford Keith's. When the Keith patron argued that Keith's offered a much higher quality of entertainment for only 5 cents more than competitors, her friend responded: "Yes but for fifteen cents you have to go up in the gallery at Keith's." The older woman then offered the familiar defense of the Keith gallery: "Have you ever been up in that gallery? Loads of people better dressed and with more money than you and I have go up there every week. If you go up there once, you'll never go anywhere else. It's just as good a show up there as the people who sit downstairs get" ("The Girl behind the Pen," *Keith News*, October 25, 1909, 3, clipping, Clipping Book [February 2, 1909–November 15, 1909], 232, KAC).

31. "Women's Influence in the Theatre," ca. 1916, clipping, Clipping Book (May 15, 1916–January 20, 1917), 98, KAC.

32. Report Book 8, 245, KAC.

33. Blair, *Torchbearers*, 27.

34. "The Model Playhouse of the Country" (1894), brochure, Clipping File, "Boston Theatres," HTC. See also Butsch, "Bowery B'hoys and Matinee Ladies."

35. "Special Reception for Ladies and Children," April 15, 1911, clipping, Clipping

Book (March 17, 1911–January 28, 1912), 15, KAC; "Girl Usher Reaches Providence and Tells How She Likes Her Work," *Providence Journal,* October 16, 1910, clipping, Clipping Book (May 28, 1910–March 17, 1911), 115, KAC.

36. Archie Bell, *A Little Journey to the B. F. Keith Palace, Cleveland* (1913?), 37–38, HTC. For excellent discussions of the historical processes of demasculinization, domestication, and feminization in American theater, see Butsch, "Bowery B'hoys and Matinee Ladies," and Peiss, "Commercial Leisure and the 'Woman Question.'"

37. "The Girl behind the Pen," *Keith News,* October 17, 1910, 2, clipping, Clipping Book (May 28, 1910–March 17, 1911), KAC.

38. "The Girl behind the Pen," *Keith News,* September 18, 1911, 3, clipping, Clipping Book (March 17, 1911–January 28, 1912), 142, KAC.

39. Kasson explains that Keith's was known as the "Sunday School Circuit" (*Rudeness and Civility,* 249–50).

40. Renton, *Vaudeville Theatre,* 121.

41. Ibid.

42. A survey of fourteen Keith managers' obituaries in *Variety* reveals that the most common career path for these administrators was a move from employment with newspapers to jobs at Keith theaters. Five of the fourteen managers came to Keith's after working as reporters: Ned Hastings (Cleveland), John J. Hastings (Philadelphia), John C. Peebles (Union Hill, N.J.), Edward P. Lyons (Philadelphia), and Robert G. Larsen (Boston). Journalists and theater managers shared the status of new professionals at the turn of the century. Wiebe notes that journalists sought to professionalize their status in the late nineteenth century by emphasizing, among other issues, the goal of scientific inquiry. Journalists and theater managers attempted to establish their prestige and employed "scientific" methods to regulate their respective businesses (*Search for Order,* 120). For discussions of reception studies, see de Cordeva, "Ethnography and Exhibition"; Sholle, "Reading the Audience"; Lenz, "'Ethnographies'"; and Radway, "Reception Studies."

43. Report Book 2, 105, KAC.

44. Report Book (1902–3), 122, KAC. Another manager wrote of Press Eldridge: "Personally I think him coarse and suggestive and occasionally have complaints about him, but he goes by with the large majority" (ibid., 272).

45. In several instances, managers noted that patrons had spoken directly to them about the quality of the shows. F. J. O'Connor wrote that "[a]cts like Kennedy and James and Van Lear and Duke would be better left out of our bills. They are simply fierce. People telephoning from our booths were actually saying up to the time . . . Van Lear and Duke went on, 'it was one of the worst shows they had seen in this house,' and I must agree with them" (Report Book 3, 182, KAC).

46. Renton, *Vaudeville Theatre,* 15.

47. Lane describes a Pennsylvania law, passed in 1887, making it a criminal offense for restaurants, hotels, and other places with public accommodations to discriminate (*Roots of Violence,* 17).

48. Spear, *Black Chicago,* 42.

49. *Broad Ax,* May 28, 1910, quoted in Spear, *Black Chicago,* 42.

50. Report Book 16, 169, KAC.

51. Report Book (1902–3), 335, KAC. Carbine in "'Finest outside the Loop'" notes

that African American patrons successfully sued Chicago movie theaters for equal access to seats in 1910. Despite these suits, discriminatory practices continued, according to Carbine.

52. "Colonial Theater Refuses Colored Gentlemen—Fined," *Chicago Defender*, June 11, 1910, 1.

53. "Wallace Paldrow," *Chicago Defender*, May 20, 1911, 1.

54. "Courts," *Crisis* 9 (September 1912): 221. Renton, in addition, noted that some black customers had refused to sit in a "second balcony" for blacks only. "It is well to remember," Renton counseled, "that in some cities the better class of negroes have declined to patronize a 'second balcony' reserved for them exclusively" (*Vaudeville Theatre*, 15).

55. *Two Knights of Vaudeville* (Ebony Films, 1916), Motion Picture, Broadcasting, and Recorded Sound Division, LC.

56. Nasaw writes that "'[d]ecency' remained the essential element in determining who would and would not be permitted within the public amusement sites, but decency in the abstract was too evanescent a notion. To sustain its integrity and utility, it had to be concretized through reference to an immutably 'indecent' other. This was the role assigned to African Americans" (*Going Out*, 47).

57. Report Book 3, 173, KAC. In 1904 the aging actress Annie Irish appealed "to the better class" in New York City with a "quiet [sketch] containing but a few laughs" (Report Book 2, 141, KAC).

58. Report Book 3, 127, KAC. See also ibid., 119.

59. Snyder, *Voice of the City*, xiii.

60. Report Book 14, xiv, KAC. The review of Daniels and Conrad, furthermore, states: "High class instrumental musical act. . . . Most of their numbers are classical but they use some popular airs" (Report Book 18, 136, KAC).

61. Report Book 21, 144, KAC.

62. Report Book 7, 241, KAC. Laurie credits Caron and Herbert with originating the dive into the backdrop gag. When the backdrop came down, the audience would see "stage hands playing cards, a gal fixing her stocking, etc, all supposed to be a surprise to them" (*Vaudeville*, 29). Gilmore and Leonard's Irish cross-fire act was a "good gallery act," according to one Keith manager. "A bit coarse for our orchestra patrons," he continued; "the orchestra and box patrons will never be able to 'see' acts of this style" (Report Book 2, 107, KAC).

63. Jenkins, *What Made Pistachio Nuts?*, 34.

64. Ibid., 35.

65. Report Book 4, 237, KAC. See also Report Book 5, 151, KAC.

66. Report Book 5, 64, KAC. Barnes also remarked on the cuts he made in their act: "The cuts which had to be made on Coakley and McBride were particularly flagrant and offensive. By referring to cuts in Boston and New York, we find that they cut out several things, but their substitutions were even more vulgar and worse than the matter formerly eliminated. One or two things were not even fit to print" (Report Book 5, 54, KAC).

67. Report Book 20, 4, KAC.

68. Report Book 7, 241, KAC.

69. Report Book 5, 159, KAC. See also Report Book 12, 190; Report Book 13, 96;

and Report Book 6, 73, KAC. One manager found that Harry Breen "succeeded in getting a lot of laughs. He, however, depends partially upon a song to the audience, which is in cases embarrassing, for his fun. He was instructed to stop referring to people in the boxes, who took exception to this method of securing mirth at Monday's matinee" (Report Book 13, 235, KAC).

70. Report Book 17, 117, KAC. The manager of the Grand Opera House in Pittsburgh found a performer's position in the gallery "coarse, noisy and distracting. . . . [T]he ballyhoo business in the audience, especially the comedy of Bosco in the balcony, could be eliminated in houses where the clientele is refined" (Report Book 15, 171, KAC).

71. Report Book 12, 155, KAC.

72. Report Book 4, 189, KAC. Describing Ben Reinhold's "distinct fall-down" on November 4, 1907, Keith's Philadelphia manager explained that the "gallery started to guy him" (Report Book 7, 68, KAC).

73. Report Book 4, 238, KAC. See also Report Book 5, 121, 241, KAC.

74. Report Book 8, 30, KAC.

75. Report Book 12, 113, KAC. At the Columbus theater, Howard and Howard "were a riot all the way through and to them must be given the distinction of being the first act that has ever played this house which went so big that they stopped the show. They took any number of bows at the finish and the audience would not let them go and simply would not permit the introduction of 'At the Waldorf' to be heard" (Report Book 10, 162, KAC). See also Report Book 3, 112, KAC.

76. Report Book 4, 38, KAC.

77. Report Book 5, 39, KAC.

78. Report Book 8, 161, KAC. Describing *The Fall of Port Arthur*, manager H. T. Jordan noted that patrons expressed their delight with the act during the show but criticized it on their way out of the theater. The playlet "is very rough from start to finish. . . . [W]hile the people laugh while it is on, it did not make a favorable impression as I know from the comments made by people going out. It is not an act of the calibre our audiences are accustomed to" (Report Book 3, 230, KAC).

79. Caffin, *Vaudeville*. For fascinating background on Caffin, see Glenn, "'Give an Imitation of Me.'"

80. Caffin, *Vaudeville*, 18–19.

81. Report Book 18, 63, KAC. Five months later, this manager reiterated the gulf between art and his vaudeville patrons in his evaluation of Henrietta de Seris and Company, another group offering "art reproductions": "For beauty approaching gorgeousness as to scenic investiture and all that makes for true artistry the act is the most stupendous and brilliant affair ever offered in local showdom. But their reception was not quite so enthusiastic as I had hoped for. There was some applause of course, but nothing equal to what the act deserves. . . . [M]ost of our patrons know little or nothing of art, ancient, medieval or modern and they refuse to learn" (ibid., 133).

82. Report Book 20, 143, KAC.

83. Report Book 11, 196, KAC.

84. Report Book 18, 99, KAC. See also Report Book (1902–3), 18, 192, KAC. Robert Larsen replaced theater manager Carl Lothrop in Boston in 1909.

85. Report Book 2, 220, KAC. In Boston in 1903, Charlie Case's reception was weakened by the presence of Dr. Carl Louis Perin on the same bill. According to the Boston manager, Case "did not finish at all strong. This may be caused by the fact that Perin drew a class who are not regular vaudeville patrons and did not understand him" (Report Book 1, 63, KAC). Three years later, one manager estimated that Auguste van Biene "will bring a good deal of money to the house, and not only that, but many of them are not our regular patrons" (Report Book 4, 188, KAC).

86. Report Book 5, 147, KAC.

87. Ibid., 198. Langtry's imprint on the vaudeville audience may have intensified when Arnold Daly followed her on November 12, 1906. Predicting that Daly would "certainly draw box business," one Keith manager argued that Daly was "especially valuable in following Langtry by bringing back many new patrons whom Langtry brought to the house for the first time" (ibid., 162). See also Report Book 15, 235, KAC.

88. Report Book 20, 143, KAC; Report Book 3, 127, KAC. The wealthier patrons are defined as "better" in Report Book 2, 141, KAC.

89. Report Book 22, 169, KAC. The manager of the Columbus theater felt intimidated by a grand opera production: "[M]usic so far above the usual thing in vaudeville that I fear to comment on it without the aid of a musical dictionary. I was afraid that it might be over their heads but it seems not judging from the reception accorded it" (Report Book 8, 225, KAC). See also Report Book 15, 84, KAC.

90. Report Book 9, 232, KAC.

91. Report Book 15, v, KAC. Other acts with themes or characters from Dickens apparently were not as successful with the various groups in the audience. Describing Bransby Williams's presentation of Dickens characters, one manager wrote: "I think that he will draw business with the orchestra crowd. Act a little over the heads of the gallery but wins big with the better class of patrons" (Report Book 7, 48, KAC).

92. Report Book 7, 243, KAC.

93. Report Book 11, 232, KAC.

94. Report Book 10, 104, KAC.

95. Report Book 3, 178, KAC.

96. Report Book 4, 228, KAC.

97. Report Book 9, 232, KAC.

98. Report Book 4, 28, KAC.

99. Report Book (1902–3), 298, KAC. Another manager remarked that the comedy team of Mullen and Coogan "has nothing to offer but very aged jokes. . . . Their best joke 'how does a goat smell?' we cut, while 'what grows larger the more you take from it?' answer 'a hole' still remains. The offering will go well with a burlesque show but not where women and children attend frequently as they do in this theatre" (Report Book 14, 89, KAC).

100. Report Book 1, 146, KAC.

101. Report Book 6, 244, KAC. See also Report Book 10, 210, KAC.

102. Report Book 2, 68, KAC.

103. Report Book 4, 236, KAC.

104. Report Book 16, 24, KAC.

105. Report Book 20, 158, KAC. See also Report Book 14, 156, and Report Book 15, 246, KAC.

106. "The Girl behind the Pen," *Keith News*, October 15, 1906, 3, clipping, Clipping Book (January 7, 1906–November 25, 1906), 205, KAC. The author continued, "It is really worth the price of admission to watch them and it seems to me that we grown ups, who are constantly suppressing outward signs of enjoyment and emotion, might learn from them how to best enjoy ourselves."

107. "Majestic Chicago," *Variety*, ca. 1919, clipping, Envelope 2073, RLC. For more information on Shaw's career, see Kibler, "Nothing Succeeds Like Excess."

108. "Lillian Shaw Stars at Keith's," *Philadelphia Telegraph*, March 11, 1913, and "Alhambra Drawing Crowds," *New York Telegraph*, December 28, 1911, clippings, Envelope 2073, RLC.

109. "Lillian Shaw, Character Singer," n.d., clipping, Envelope 2073, RLC.

110. Report Book 6, 26, KAC.

111. Report Book 13, 102, KAC.

112. Ibid., 176.

113. Ibid., 156. Another act, *Court by Girls*, featured gender role reversals: "The women act as judge, jury and lawyer with one man as defendant to a suit for damages and the other as court officer. The man is sued for breaking the heart of a young woman. He is convicted by the jury, but the judge sets him free to marry herself" (Report Book 14, 45, KAC).

114. Report Book 9, 226, KAC.

115. Report Book 7, 232, KAC. Lovenberg also commented on Sandwina's particular appeal to men: "She is really a marvel, the ease with which she balances a man who weighs at least 160 lbs is most remarkable. She is a magnificent specimen of womanhood and will no doubt attract men in large numbers" (ibid., 142). W. W. Prosser, manager of Keith's theater in Columbus, also remarked that Miss Stuart, performing with her partner White, "is a little too 'fly.' I noticed that the ladies in the house sort of rebelled at a walk she executes also at the way she handles her skirts" (Report Book 6, 134, KAC).

116. Report Book 4, 59, KAC.

117. Juggler Paul Spandoni was featured on the cover of *Keith News* on December 12, 1904, displaying the muscles in his shoulders and back; his body, more than his juggling skills, seems to have been the main feature of his act (clipping, Clipping Book [August 13, 1904–February 14, 1905], KAC).

118. Report Book 9, 240, KAC.

119. Hansen, *Babel and Babylon*, 1–2. See also Musser, *Emergence of Cinema*.

120. Report Book (1902–3), 255, KAC. Snyder also notes Sandow's popularity among women (*Voice of the City*, 33).

121. Report Book 1, 48, KAC.

122. Hansen, "Pleasure, Ambivalence, Identification." See also Studlar, *This Mad Masquerade*. Studlar makes a similar argument about John Barrymore.

123. Report Book 9, 82, KAC.

124. *Rubes in the Theater* (Edison, 1901), Motion Picture, Broadcasting, and Recorded Sound Division, LC. Although the theater in this film is not specifically identified as a vaudeville theater, the portrait of different social strata and genders in the theater matches the composition of vaudeville audiences.

Chapter Three

1. Distler, "Exit the Racial Comics," 248.

2. Ibid.

3. Gilbert, *American Vaudeville*, 291.

4. Report Book 8, 124, and Report Book (1902–3), 297, KAC. See also ibid., 252.

5. Dormon, "American Popular Culture," 191. Dormon also suggests that ethnic stereotypes onstage reached different segments of the audience on different levels, particularly assimilated immigrants versus new immigrants. See also Dormon, "Ethnic Caricatures of the Mind."

6. See, for example, Snyder, *Voice of the City*, 113–20.

7. For more on how ethnic characterizations onstage addressed gentility in vaudeville, see Oberdeck, "Contested Cultures of American Refinement."

8. See Diner, *Erin's Daughters*.

9. See Walsh, "Lace Curtain Literature"; Fanning, "Short Sad Career of Mr. Dooley"; and William H. A. Williams, "Green Again."

10. Coquelin, "Have Women a Sense of Humor?," 67.

11. Burdette, "Have Women a Sense of Humor?," 598. In addition, Maurice defined women's humor as "wholesome" ("Feminine Humorists," 39).

12. Report Book (1902–3), 192, KAC. On December 2, 1921, one Keith manager noted the failure of a male/female comedy team (Maud Muller and Ed Stanley) that reversed gender roles: "Comedy woman with man foil which did not score at all" (Report Book 23, 7, KAC).

13. Robert Speare, "Plenty Doing at the Alhambra," *New Jersey Telegraph*, May 28, 1908, clipping, vol. 444, 65, RLC. Sochen has mistakenly argued that female performers did not engage in rough, physical comedy in vaudeville: "Women could be in the chorus line, or the featured singer, or finally as the romantic interest in the show, but as the comic attraction, assuredly no" ("Slapsticks, Screwballs, and Bawds," 143). Sochen not only ignores comedians like Kate Elinore but also overlooks nuances in the relationship between gender and comedy at the turn of the century.

14. Report Book (1902–3), 324, KAC.

15. The *New York Dramatic Mirror*, for example, described another female comedian, Evie Stetson, as "one of the funniest women on the stage. . . . [She] imitated wild Irish women, any sort of wild woman" ("The Matinee Girl," *New York Dramatic Mirror*, February 20, 1904, 2).

16. "The Elinore Sisters," December 20, 1906, clipping, vol. 444, 61, RLC.

17. "Kate Elinore without a Sister at the American," *New York Star*, September 11, 1909, clipping, vol. 444, 67, RLC.

18. Caffin, *Vaudeville*, 211. Describing her appearance in *The Adventures of Bridget McGuire*, one reviewer stated, "No woman ever made such a persistent attempt to look ugly" (*New Orleans Item*, n.d., clipping, box 3, vol. 3, 10, ESVAP).

19. Clipping, n.d., box 3, vol. 3, 9, ESVAP.

20. "American Music Hall," *Boston Herald*, November 30, 1909, clipping, vol. 444, 68, RLC.

21. Distler, "Rise and Fall of the Racial Comics," 52. Discussing a female performer's impersonation of an Irish maid, Charles Lovenberg, manager of Keith's the-

ater in Providence, commented that the "woman is decidedly coarse" (Report Book 1, 52, KAC).

22. *The Finish of Bridget McKeen* (Edison, 1901), Motion Picture, Broadcasting, and Recorded Sound Division, LC. Another film with a similar plot was titled *How Bridget Made the Fire.*

23. Obituary, *New York Times*, June 12, 1934, quoted in Distler, "Rise and Fall of the Racial Comics," 120.

24. Natalie Zemon Davis, "Women on Top," 125.

25. Ibid., 126.

26. Jenkins, *What Made Pistachio Nuts?*, 221–22. Jenkins uses the term "anarchistic" rather than "anarchic" to convey "a sense of the process in the texts, a movement from order to disorder," and to foreground "the active and central role of the clowns as bringers of anarchy" (ibid., 22–23).

27. Ibid., 232.

28. Elias and Dunning, *Quest for Excitement*, quoted in ibid., 217.

29. Ibid., 225.

30. George M. Cohan, *Dangerous Mrs. Delaney* (1898), box 1, folder 11, ESVAP. Page numbers for citations to this handwritten script are given in the text. Two vaudeville sketches from the Elinore Sisters' career are held at the Manuscript Division of the LC: *The Actress and the Maid* (written in 1907; performed in 1908) and *The Irregular Army* (1910). Three sketches are held at the Department of Rare Books and Special Collections at the University of Rochester Library: *The Irish 400* (1897), *Dangerous Mrs. Delaney* (written in 1898 and 1902), and *The Adventures of Bridget McGuire* (performed in 1902).

31. Maurice E. McLaughlin, *The Irish 400* (1897), box 1, folder 11, ESVAP. There are two handwritten versions of this sketch (probably transcribed by May Elinore). The quotations in this chapter come from the version with the additional subtitle, "Original Sketch for Elinore Sisters." This version does not have numbered pages but is more complete than the other text.

32. Paderewski had many successful tours of U.S. concert halls around the turn of the century. See Ann Douglas, *Terrible Honesty*, 365–66.

33. Eugene Ellsworth, *The Adventures of Bridget McGuire*, box 1, folder 10, 101, 111, ESVAP. Page numbers for further citations to this handwritten script are given in the text.

34. According to one Keith manager, Van Leer and Duke offered a similar sketch in which the woman impersonates "an Irish servant girl disguised as the mistress of the house" (Report Book 1, 65, KAC).

35. In *The Actress and the Maid* (1907) by Kate and May Elinore, actress Geraldine de Bluff tries to establish her superiority over her Irish maid, Nanette O'Hara. As the actress and the maid are preparing for a vaudeville appearance, de Bluff emphasizes her artistic superiority and her aversion to vaudeville. The maid, on the other hand, calls de Bluff's bluff, telling the audience that she will be the "big lemon" (Drama Deposits, reel 230, #9819, 4, Manuscript Division, LC).

36. Rowe, *Unruly Woman*; Russo, *Female Grotesque*. Rowe, for example, acknowledges that women's unruly spectacles may be read within a misogynist framework and concludes that "the unruly woman can be seen as prototype of woman as sub-

ject—transgressive above all when she lays claim to her own desire" (*Unruly Woman*, 31).

37. Jenkins, for example, celebrates Winnie Lightner's shattering of feminine codes through her awkward performance as Princess Mauna Kane in the film *Side Show*. He describes Lightner's exaggerated attempts to grasp male attention and her failure to uphold feminine beauty—she sings in a raspy voice and behaves aggressively, refuting the "demure" feminine ideal. Although she clearly uses grotesque imagery and behavior to undermine traditional feminine sexual spectacle, her rebellious performance draws some of its power from the "low" woman she impersonates—an "exotic, primitive" from Hawaii. Thus, Lightner's disguise permitted the critique of the social hierarchy of gender by reproducing ethnic hierarchies, particularly the notion that the low woman is overly sexual, loud, and unmannered (*What Made Pistachio Nuts?*, 265).

38. Allen, *Horrible Prettiness*, 32–33. Susan Davis, in *Parades and Power*, shows that native-born, working-class white men participated in often-violent street celebrations in Philadelphia at Christmas in the 1840s. They expressed their class antagonism and rebellion, however, through their disguises as blacks and German immigrants. These protesters—for the most part the laboring poor—took control of streets and taverns to express class hostility, but they also demonstrated racism and nativism as they attacked blacks and immigrants.

39. "Fifteen Lively Acts at Pastor's," *New York Telegraph*, January 31, 1907, quoted in Staples, *Male-Female Comedy Teams*, 84.

40. Maschio, "Ethnic Humor and the Demise of the Russell Brothers." In addition, George Monroe, a monologist, impersonated an "Irish Biddy" in his 1905 vaudeville act.

41. "This Comedienne Is Really Comic," *Newark Evening News*, n.d., clipping, box 3, vol. 3, 2, ESVAP.

42. Clipping, n.d., box 3, vol. 3, 9, ESVAP.

43. Ullman, *Sex Seen*, chap. 2. See also Slide, *Vaudevillians*, 52.

44. "The Theater: Breezy Kate Elinore; She Discusses Her Unique Rigs; Wagers Made as to Whether She Is Man or Woman," n.d., clipping, box 3, vol. 3, 4, ESVAP.

45. *New Orleans Item*, n.d., clipping, box 3, vol. 3, 10, ESVAP.

46. "Kate Elinore Dies in Indianapolis," *Morning Telegraph*, January 1, 1925. Elinore also stepped into a male comedian's role in *Dick Whittington* in 1910.

47. Maschio, "Prescription for Femininity."

48. Ibid., 45.

49. Clipping, April 11, 1913, vol. 431, 78, RLC, quoted in Ullman, "'Twentieth Century Way,'" 581. The interpretation of female impersonations has been complex. Ullman, for example, concludes that although female impersonators seemed to shore up male power, they also signaled gender confusion (as there was increasing concern about verifying Eltinge's masculinity by investigating his private behavior) and provoked anxiety about homosexual desire ("If Eltinge could be an object of heterosexual male fantasy, was he really a man?") (ibid., 583).

50. Senelick, "Boys and Girls Together."

51. Indeed, it is important to examine the ways Kate Elinore's alleged gender masquerade influenced her ethnic disguises because the figure of the transvestite often

followed and shaped the nature of other challenges to social categories such as ethnicity. Garber argues that "the possibility of crossing racial boundaries stirs fears of crossing boundaries of gender and vice versa" (*Vested Interests*, 274).

52. M. S. Robinson and H. S. Gibson, *The Mill Owner's Daughter—or—She Said She Wouldn't But She Did!* (1902), Drama Deposits, reel 52, #2454, Manuscript Division, LC.

53. Staples, *Male-Female Comedy Teams*, 84–85.

54. Ibid., 87.

55. Will Cressy, *Mag Haggerty's Reception* (1905), 16, BRTC. *Mag Haggerty's Father's Daughter* and *Mag Haggerty, M.D.* are also included in this collection. Page numbers for further citations to the Cressy plays are given in the text.

56. Maurice E. McLaughlin, *The Irish 400* (1897), box 1, folder 11, ESVAP.

57. Mike is again triumphant when he objects to Mag's instructions for refined dancing, substituting his own style of dancing. He responds to his daughter's charge that he can't dance by demonstrating a series of his "specialties" (18).

58. In addition, by 1900 Irish Americans (those born in Ireland and their offspring) had reached "relative occupational parity with native white America" (Doyle, *Irish Americans*, quoted in Miller, *Emigrants and Exiles*, 495).

59. Meagher, "Introduction," 2.

60. Diner, *Erin's Daughters*, 9. See also Meagher, "Sweet Good Mothers."

61. Miller, *Emigrants and Exiles*, 494.

62. Diner, *Erin's Daughters*, 94.

63. Meagher, "Sweet Good Mothers," 334; Diner, *Erin's Daughters*, chap. 4.

64. Diner, *Erin's Daughters*, 51–52; William H. A. Williams, "Green Again," 19.

65. Fanning, "Short Sad Career of Mr. Dooley," 175. Diner points out that Dunne portrays Irish American women as the primary status seekers. Diner, in particular, cites one of Dunne's Christmas scenes in which an Irish man begrudgingly thanks his wife for his Christmas gift: "How thought-ful iv ye Mary Ann, to give me th' essays of Emerson. I wuz sayin' on'y la' week to a friend iv mind in th' pork pit that iv all th' fellows that iver hurled the pen, Emerson f'r me money" (quoted in *Erin's Daughters*, 140). Diner also adds that Catholic clergy stressed that Irish women uplifted their families despite irresponsible, volatile men.

66. Edward Harrigan and David Braham, "I'll Wear the Trousers, Oh" (New York: Pond, 1890), quoted in William H. A. Williams, "Green Again," 8.

67. Diner, *Erin's Daughters*, 140. Miller echoes Diner on this point in *Emigrants and Exiles*, 494.

68. Meagher, "Sweet Good Mothers," 335.

69. Report Book 18, 126, KAC.

70. Report Book 2, 107, KAC. The career of the Chadwicks provides another example. This team, including the eccentric dancer Ida Chadwick, had a successful career in Keith's vaudeville despite managers' protests against their low comedy. Evaluating their performance on April 8, 1907, Lovenberg admitted that some audiences enjoyed their comedy but that he found it too rambunctious: "In any house, where the roughest kind of slapstick stuff is appreciated and where an artistic side is not considered very much, they would make a hit. . . . To say that it was boisterous would be putting it mildly. It is so coarse that it borders very strongly on vulgarity" (Re-

port Book 6, 83, KAC). Despite Lovenberg's negative review, the Chadwicks' career was by no means over. When the Chadwicks brought their act to Lovenberg's Providence theater in 1914, Lovenberg again criticized their style, although he acknowledged their success: "The roughest kind of a rough, slapstick act, absolutely devoid of merit. I will admit that the holiday audience with the yokels of Fall River, Attleboro and the other Massachusetts towns adjacent to Boston laugh at it somewhat, but I'm sure they are going to die when the regular crowd looks at them, especially as most of their laughs were got on vulgarity which was promptly cut out" (Report Book 16, 144, KAC).

71. Report Book 7, 207, KAC.

72. See Peiss, "Commercial Leisure and the 'Woman Question.'" As Peiss explains, leisure entrepreneurs approached the "'woman question' as bricoleurs, combining cultural elements to satisfy women's notions of respectability while still catering to the male audience" (ibid., 111). Although I agree with Peiss's point that commercial leisure addressed gender in multiple, contradictory ways, it is not clear whether vaudeville entrepreneurs responded to or constructed women's notions of respectability. Managers on the Keith circuit noted many instances in which female patrons disrupted managers' belief in female refinement.

Chapter Four

1. Jule Delmar (B. F. Keith Vaudeville Exchange) to Julia Arthur, February 3, 1923, Julia Arthur Scrapbook (January 1923–May 1924), JAC.

2. Woods, "Two-a-Day Redemptions," 14.

3. Report Book 18, 226, KAC. Lovenberg added: "Without any particular drawing feature, the first three weeks of our season we opened to big Monday business in warmer weather. On Monday of this week our business dropped a hundred dollars on the day." The following week, Lovenberg reiterated his assertion that "'broken down stars'" tended to keep people out of the theater (ibid., 235). The Boston manager wrote of Violet Black: "Miss Black announces herself as lately with Frohman, Daly and others. How lately and for how long is a question in my mind" (Report Book 5, 211, KAC).

4. One critic described Virginia Harned's turn to vaudeville: "Speaking of lovely actresses not as young as they used to be there's Virginia Harned. . . . [H]aving failed at the season's start with a long play, she writes a short one herself and goes into vaudeville" ("Virginia Harned Plays on Her Age," *Chicago Tribune*, September 20, 1908, clipping, vol. 262, 37, RLC).

5. Woods, "Sarah Bernhardt and the Refining of American Vaudeville," 23. See also Woods, "Two-a-Day Redemptions," "Ethel Barrymore and the Wages of Vaudeville," and "'Golden Calf.'"

6. Report Book 14, 115, KAC. In addition, Samuel K. Hodgdon wrote on September 12, 1904: "The offering is quiet, containing but a few laughs, although novel and dainty, it being rather deep for the Monday crowd and appeals to the better class" (Report Book 2, 114, KAC).

7. Report Book 2, 161, KAC. See also ibid., 134.

8. Jenkins, *What Made Pistachio Nuts?*, 84.

9. Ibid., chap. 3.

10. Ibid., 82–85.

11. Report Book 11, 238, KAC.

12. Ibid., 196.

13. Report Book 12, 113, KAC. Charles Barnes, manager of Keith's theater in Philadelphia, praised James T. Power's act as an exception to the usual fare offered by legitimate performers: "These legitimate stars fall down so often when they come on the Vaudeville-stage that it is quite a relief to have anyone come on the bill who really lives up to his big reputation" (Report Book 5, 16, KAC).

14. Report Book 2, 89, KAC.

15. Report Book 3, 129, 121, KAC.

16. Ibid., 115.

17. Woods, "Ethel Barrymore and the Wages of Vaudeville," 83.

18. Report Book 8, 198, KAC. The manager of the Grand Opera House in Pittsburgh agreed with his Boston colleague, calling Harned an "extremely disagreeable, incompetent actress whose name is not worth anywhere near the salary she gets" (ibid., 237).

19. "Julia Arthur, Stage Traveler Delux," *Los Angeles Morning Tribune*, July 26, 1917, clipping, Scrap Album (clippings and playbills from *Liberty Aflame*, *Out There*, *The Woman the Germans Shot*, *The Common Cause*, *Victory Loan*, and *Salvation Army Testimonial*), JAC; *Spokane Review*, February 27, 1910, clipping, vol. 98, 58, RLC.

20. "When Mrs. Pat Rehearses," *Chicago Tribune*, March 23, 1910, clipping, vol. 98, 66, RLC.

21. "The Theatres," *Providence News*, September 28, 1904, clipping, Clipping Book (August 13, 1904–February 14, 1905), 63, KAC.

22. Ibid.

23. Ashton Stevens, "'I Don't Grunt, I Do My Stunt,' Mrs. Pat Says to Stevens," *Chicago Examiner*, April 3, 1910, clipping, vol. 98, 63, RLC. In addition, Alan Dale quipped: "She said she had always heard that vaudeville audiences were the finest in America, though she didn't say who had told her" ("Mrs. Campbell Makes 'Expiation' in Vaudeville," *Los Angeles Examiner*, February 23, 1910, clipping, vol. 98, 58, RLC). Another critic suggested that Campbell's praise for vaudeville was tied to her salary: "Besides her being so fondly in love with her audiences in vaudeville, Mrs. Campbell receives the highest salary of any actress in vaudeville" ("Not Afraid of Vaudeville Stage," *Indianapolis Star*, March 20, 1910, clipping, vol. 98, 60, RLC).

24. Tracy C. Davis provides an excellent discussion of these issues in her *Actresses as Working Women*: "Actresses had to overcome the perception that they 'de-classed' themselves by acting and that they schemed to social climb through the self-advertising vehicle of the stage before the upper classes could sympathize or respect them" (71).

25. "The Matinee Girl," *New York Dramatic Mirror*, May 11, 1901, 2.

26. "A Rising Young Actress," *Theatre* 3, no. 29 (July 1903): 178–79.

27. Claudia Johnson, *American Actress*.

28. Tracy C. Davis, *Actresses as Working Women*, 100. Although Davis acknowledges different levels of respectability between low-paid, largely anonymous lines of work and stardom, she also notes that the aspersions cast on the lower echelons

of actresses ultimately affected all female players: "Female performers, regarded as a single class by the dominant culture, received the stigma uniformly in spite of their professional specialities and socioeconomic diversity" (ibid.). This examination of performers' crossing from legitimate theater to vaudeville suggests, however, that categories of high and low culture were important in defining performers' respectability.

29. "Miss Harned's Play Tame," *Baltimore American*, n.d., clipping, vol. 263, 39, RLC.

30. "Hammerstein's," *Variety*, October 10, 1908, clipping, vol. 263, 39, RLC. Woods notes that such "conspicuous display" was prominent in other actresses' vaudeville tours. Mrs. Patrick Campbell, according to Woods, explained that she had "an effective play and a 'beautiful dress'" in negotiating her salary with vaudeville theater administrators, and *Variety* drew further attention to her "wonderful gown of black satin" ("Sarah Bernhardt and the Refining of American Vaudeville," 18).

31. McArthur, *Actors and American Culture*, 29–30.

32. Edmonds, "Princess Hamlet," 73. See also Moore, *Drag!*, chap. 2.

33. Garber, *Vested Interests*, 37–38. In addition, Edmonds explains that these parts were not seen as "innovatory or experimental" in the late nineteenth century ("Princess Hamlet," 60).

34. Cross-dressing, according to Garber, connects with, intensifies, and, at other times, displaces various "categories of crisis" (*Vested Interests*, 16). Although Garber demonstrates cross-dressing's connections to the transgressions of race and class categories, Julia Arthur's transvestism also reveals the confusions of young/old and public/private, along with high/low. But cross-dressing does not appear to be the primary factor in these "categories of crisis" since other actresses who did not cross-dress in vaudeville faced similar dilemmas. It appears to be the move to vaudeville in a particular phase of these women's lives that incited the controversies, not the cross-dressing in and of itself.

35. "This Week's New Bills," *New York Times*, October 31, 1897, 11.

36. "Julia Arthur Here Again," n.d., clipping, *A Lady of Quality*—Boston Folder, Newspaper Clippings Box, JAC.

37. In the midst of Arthur's success as Clorinda Wildairs from 1897 to 1899, she addressed the question of her personal success and artistic integrity: "To speak of my private fortune in connection with my stage work is to do, I think, even greater injustice to my work as an actress" (clipping, n.d., vol. 26, 12, RLC).

38. "Julia Arthur Has Ambition: Beautiful Actress Will Now Play Shakespearean Roles," *New York Telegraph*, October 9, 1898, clipping, Julia Arthur Scrapbook (August 1898–November 1899), JAC.

39. Ibid.

40. Ibid.

41. "Miss Arthur Will Continue," May 22, 1898, clipping, vol. 26, 34, RLC.

42. "Miss Arthur Loses," January 11, 1899, clipping, vol. 26, 42, RLC.

43. "Now Ain't Dat Scand'lous," n.d., clipping, vol. 297, 90, RLC.

44. "Julia Arthur Is Going to Play Hamlet," *New York Journal*, July 12, 1899, clipping, Julia Arthur Scrapbook (August 1898–November 1899), JAC. The same day, the *New York Herald* was equally excited about the vision of Julia Arthur in men's at-

tire, reminding readers that "Miss Arthur had opportunity to show that she looked extremely well in knickerbockers in *A Lady of Quality*" ("Miss Arthur as Hamlet," *New York Herald*, July 12, 1899, clipping, Julia Arthur Scrapbook [August 1898–November 1899], JAC).

45. *Kansas City Journal*, August 20, 1899, clipping, Julia Arthur Scrapbook (August 1898–November 1899), JAC. The *New York Daily News* reported that in a dozen U.S. publications "allusion has been made to the exquisitely moulded limbs Julia Arthur will have to support her when she dons the ebon hose and cloak of the tragic hero. The legs of Hamlet, for sooth!" (*New York Daily News*, July 30, 1899, clipping, Julia Arthur Scrapbook [August 1898–November 1899], JAC).

46. *Broadway Magazine*, September 1899, clipping, Julia Arthur Scrapbook (August 1898–November 1899), JAC.

47. *Boston Herald*, July 13, 1899, clipping, Julia Arthur Scrapbook (August 1898–November 1899). The *Denver Republican* shared this view: "[T]he rumor of Miss Arthur's aspirations might be classed with the press agent tales that are always hatched in vacation season" ("Hamlets That Threaten Us," *Denver Republican*, July 17, 1899, clipping, Julia Arthur Scrapbook [August 1898–November 1899], JAC).

48. *New London (Conn.) Telegram*, July 25, 1899, clipping, Julia Arthur Scrapbook (August 1898–November 1899), JAC.

49. "Hamlets That Threaten Us," *Denver Republican*, July 18, 1899, clipping, Julia Arthur Scrapbook (August 1898–November 1899), JAC. Although it is important to note that Bernhardt's artistic reputation appears to have sheltered her from some criticism of her cross-dressing and that Arthur was frequently characterized as a degraded follower of Bernhardt's achievement, we should not conclude that Bernhardt's Hamlet was unproblematically accepted, as Garber suggests (*Vested Interests*, 37–40). Some critics, for example, vilified all cross-cast Hamlets, and some observers of Arthur's intentions looked back negatively on Bernhardt's efforts. One reviewer held that "of [Bernhardt's] Hamlet the laudatory critics could only say that it was a clever attempt of a great actress to present Hamlet as a woman" (*Kansas City Journal*, August 20, 1899, clipping, Julia Arthur Scrapbook [August 1898–November 1899], JAC).

50. *Dramatic News*, July 22, 1899, clipping, Julia Arthur Scrapbook (August 1898–November 1899), JAC.

51. Clipping, July 18, 1899, and "Hamlets That Threaten Us," *Denver Republican*, July 17, 1899, clipping, Julia Arthur Scrapbook (August 1898–November 1899), JAC.

52. "Hamlets That Threaten Us," *Denver Republican*, July 17, 1899, clipping, Julia Arthur Scrapbook (August 1898–November 1899), JAC.

53. "The Usher," *New York Dramatic Mirror*, August 8, 1896, 13.

54. McArthur, *Actors and American Culture*, 89.

55. Ibid., 216.

56. A. M. Palmer and Edward H. Sothern, "An Endowed Theatre," *Theatre* 1, no. 4 (June 1901): 14.

57. Wilton Lackaye, "Endowed Theatre and the Actor," *Theatre* 1, no. 6 (August 1901): 14. Lackaye concluded that an actor's success "will be measured by the extent to which he merges himself in the intent of the author, and not by the continual forcing of his personality, his private peculiarities, domestic virtues."

58. "The Matinee Girl," *New York Dramatic Mirror*, August 22, 1903, 2.

59. Albert L. Parkes, "A Reminiscence," *New York Dramatic Mirror*, December 22, 1900, 19. Ironically, Parkes pointed to vaudeville's recruitment of legitimate actors and actresses as evidence of the appeal of high-quality acting: "That the public will patronize good acting is attested by the eagerness of vaudeville managers to pay large salaries to capable actors." Parkes's praise for good acting certainly conflicts with many vaudeville managers' assessments of the success of these performers and overlooks the extent to which legitimate performers' names and their flashy appearance (not "good" acting) were their primary attraction for vaudeville managers and patrons.

60. In January 1902, Arthur denied rumors of her return to the stage: "I am happy and contented and there is no desire to take up the care and arduousness of professional life" ("Julia Arthur Denies Yarn," *Chicago Tribune*, January 4, 1902, clipping, Return to the Stage Folder, Newspaper and Clippings Box, JAC). Over a year later, reporters described Arthur's dedication to her home. "She is the same Julia Arthur — beautiful and queenly, fascinating," concluded one reporter, "[b]ut above all she is the matron of her own home. . . . She is absorbed in her house" ("They Live Like Monarchs," *New Yorker*, August 5, 1903, clipping, Return to the Stage Folder, Newspaper Clippings Box, JAC).

61. Evans, *Born for Liberty*, 156–57. She also writes that 50.1 percent of employed women were domestic workers in 1870, 29.4 percent in 1900, and 16.2 percent in 1920. See also Cott, *Grounding of Modern Feminism*, 183. More married black women have historically been employed than white women. In 1900, for example, 26 percent of black wives were employed, as opposed to 3 percent of white wives. See Evans, *Born for Liberty*, 157.

62. Cott, *Grounding of Modern Feminism*, 182.

63. Ibid., 190–91.

64. Ibid., 179.

65. "Why Can't an Actress Quit the Stage and Be Happy in Home?," *Chicago Herald*, August 15, 1915, clipping, vol. 27, 195, RLC.

66. Ibid.

67. Harleigh Schultz, "Will Again See Noted Actress," *Boston Mass American*, October 17, 1914, clipping, Return to the Stage Scrapbooks, vol. 1, JAC.

68. "Julia Arthur's Double-Sacrifice for Love," 1917, clipping, unidentified scrapbook, JAC.

69. "Noted Boston Actress Returns to Stage," *National Magazine*, April 1923, clipping, Julia Arthur Scrapbook (January 1923–May 1924), JAC.

70. Dudden, *Women in the American Theatre*, 30–31.

71. "Julia Arthur Acts to Recoup Fortune," *Boston Mass American*, n.d., Return to the Stage Scrapbooks, vol. 4, JAC.

72. "Julia Arthur," *Variety*, December 22, 1916, clipping, vol. 27, 35, RLC.

73. "It is not likely, in fact it is certain, that Miss Arthur would not now be in the midst of rehearsals, had not Mr. Cheney finally been induced to withdraw his opposition and give her his consent" ("Julia Arthur Glad to Be Back in Harness," *Springfield [Mass.] News*, October 14, 1915, clipping, Return to the Stage Scrapbooks, vol. 2, JAC).

74. Ibid. "My husband," said Arthur, "is the wisest as well as the most thoughtful of men. He has a faculty of understanding me. And when the 'call' came and I said I was 'coming back'; he protested, as a loving husband should, and then, when I persisted, promptly proceeded to help me all he could" ("The Presence Aids in Julia Arthur Interview," *Post*, March 31, 1916, clipping, unidentified scrapbook, JAC).

75. "Mother Cheney" to Julia Arthur, November 10, 1915, Return to the Stage Scrapbooks, vol. 1, JAC.

76. "*Eternal Magdalene* Is Cheap Melodrama," *Cincinnati Times Star*, March 28, 1916, and "Julia Arthur in *Eternal Magdalene* at Grand," *Cincinnati Commercial Tribune*, March 28, 1916, clippings, unidentified scrapbook, JAC. One reviewer for the *Boston Evening Transcript* wrote: "She deserved . . . a piece that by the nature of the subject matter and the treatment should not be distasteful to not a few of the public that cherishes her as one of the ornaments of our stage on the romantic, the poetic, and the Shakespearean side" (H. T. P., "Julia Arthur Actress," *Boston Evening Transcript*, February 2, 1916, clipping, unidentified scrapbook, JAC).

77. "Julia Arthur Actress," *Boston Transcript*, February 2, 1916, clipping, vol. 27, 15, RLC.

78. Salita Solano, "Knighthood Flowers Hardily—But It's Not a Stageland Annual," *Journal*, February 15, 1917, clipping, *Seremonda* I Scrap Album, JAC.

79. "Julia Arthur at Palace," May 29, 1917, clipping, vol. 27, 50, RLC. Also noting that *Liberty Aflame* appealed to the audience mainly because of its patriotism, a reporter for the *Kansas City Times* concluded that "as to the spectacle itself, for no other word seems so aptly to describe it, opinion of its appropriateness on a program made up of several rather mediocre vaudeville numbers, inevitably must be prejudiced favorably because of its patriotic appeal" (E. B. G., "Julia Arthur at the Orpheum," *Kansas City Times*, September 12, 1917, clipping, unidentified scrapbook, JAC).

80. "*Liberty Aflame* Is Feature at Keith's," *Philadelphia Ledger*, May 15, 1917, clipping, vol. 27, 50, RLC. *Liberty Aflame* "seemed like a pretty cheap attempt to capitalize on patriotism and quite unworthy of Miss Arthur's ability either as an elocutionist or an artist" ("Julia Arthur at the Palace," *New York World*, May 29, 1917, clipping, Julia Arthur Scrapbook [*Liberty Aflame*], JAC). Alan Dale, in addition, argued that in vaudeville "patriotism is out of place. . . . [I]t loses its dignity, its reverence. It seems like a mere bid for applause" ("Alan Dale Praises Julia Arthur's Diction," *Toledo Blade*, June 4, 1917, clipping, vol. 27, 51, RLC).

81. J. O. L., "Three Arts," *Baltimore Evening Sun*, n.d., clipping, Julia Arthur Scrapbook (January 1923–May 1924), JAC.

82. Ibid. One audience member, William Muldoon, wrote to Arthur: "It seemed to me that some of your speakings were delivered too rapidly, you did not leave room for the clever acting which you are so capable of doing." He concluded by asserting simply: "You belong in Shakespeare" (William Muldoon to Julia Arthur, January 31, 1923, Julia Arthur Scrapbook [January 1923–May 1924], JAC).

83. Anna Marie Jungman to Julia Arthur, February 5, 1923, Julia Arthur Scrapbook (January 1923–May 1924), JAC.

84. "Seals, Shakespeare, and Trixie Friganza Headliners on Maryland's Current Bill," *Baltimore American*, February 27, 1923, clipping, Julia Arthur Scrapbook (January 1923–May 1924), JAC.

85. Monroe Lathrop, "Topics in Stageland," *Los Angeles Sunday Tribune*, August 12, 1917, clipping, Julia Arthur Scrap Album (clippings and playbills from *Liberty Aflame, Out There, The Woman the Germans Shot, The Common Cause, Victory Loan,* and *Salvation Army Testimonial*), JAC. William Morris, for example, noted in 1909 that "the same audience who on Monday nights patronize a two dollar Broadway opening" also attended a vaudeville performance on Tuesday "with considerable pleasure" ("Vaudeville—Past and Present," *Billboard*, December 11, 1909, quoted in Nasaw, *Going Out*, 29).

86. Hamilton, *Queen of Camp*, 2. My thanks to Leigh Woods for encouraging me to think more about the content of Arthur's act and the context of other female criminals on the vaudeville stage.

87. Green and Laurie, *Show Biz*, 18.

88. Alan Dale, "Julia Arthur in Hamlet Role at Palace," *New York American*, February 6, 1923, clipping, Julia Arthur Scrapbook (January 1923–May 1924), JAC.

89. Horace Ellis to Julia Arthur, March 21, 1923, Julia Arthur Scrapbook (January 1923–May 1924), JAC.

90. Bland Johnson, "The Two-a-Day: Bland Johnson's Review of the Virtues and Villainies of Vaudeville," *Theatre*, April 1923, clipping, Julia Arthur Scrapbook (January 1923–May 1924), JAC.

91. "Rush," "Julia Arthur and Company," n.d., clipping, Julia Arthur Scrapbook (January 1923–May 1924), JAC. Another critic wrote: "In between the joke about crude oil, which the comedian couldn't tell because it wasn't refined, and the dreariest feature of the screen, 'Topics of the Day,' vaudeville did its bit for Shakespeare" ("Julia Arthur's Hamlet," *Boston Globe*, February 6, 1923, clipping, Julia Arthur Scrapbook [January 1923–May 1924], JAC).

92. "Hamlet in Vaudeville," *Drama League Review*, n.d., clipping, Julia Arthur Scrapbook (January 1923–May 1924), JAC.

93. Alan Dale, "Julia Arthur in Hamlet Role at Palace," *New York American*, February 6, 1923, and "Julia Arthur's Hamlet," *Boston Globe*, February 6, 1923, clippings, Julia Arthur Scrapbook (January 1923–May 1924), JAC. The *Baltimore News*, for example, joked about Hamlet's being caught between "a trained seal and Vaughn Comfort, tenor. There is no chance offered to prepare the audience for blank verse, the mental suffering of Hamlet and the like. . . . Mr. Comfort finishes singing a little ditty about papa kissing the maid in the kitchen and—whisk Hamlet is stabbing Polonius in the Queen's closet" ("Hamlet Gets a Chance on Vaudeville Bill," *Baltimore News*, February 27, 1923, clipping, Julia Arthur Scrapbook [January 1923–May 1924], JAC).

94. Letter to Mrs. Benjamin Cheney, February 8, 1923, Julia Arthur Scrapbook (January 1923–May 1924), JAC. A *Variety* review echoed this observation: "There was nothing to separate Miss Arthur from a preceding comedy turn but a short arrangement of musical setting. It requires a good deal of adaptability for an audience to plunge from one extreme to another" ("Rush," "Julia Arthur and Company," n.d., clipping, Julia Arthur Scrapbook [January 1923–May 1924], JAC).

95. J. O. L., "Three Arts," *Baltimore Evening Sun*, n.d., clipping, Julia Arthur Scrapbook (January 1923–May 1924), JAC.

Chapter Five

1. "A Decade of Vaudeville," December 14, 1908, clipping, Clipping Book (February 28, 1908–February 19, 1909), KAC.

2. "Ye Olde Timers' Number," *Keith News*, December 11, 1911, clipping, Clipping Book (March 17, 1911–January 28, 1912), 216, KAC.

3. The male domination of the minstrel show is reflected in the title of Edwin L. Rice's book, *1,000 Men of Minstrelsy and One Woman*, HRHRC.

4. Rogin, "Making America Home," 1068.

5. Toll, *Blacking Up*, 79–80.

6. Thurber, "Development of the Mammy Image," 108. See also Jewell, *From Mammy to Miss America*, chap. 3; and White, *Ar'n't I a Woman?*, chap. 1.

7. Rogin, *Blackface, White Noise*, 39.

8. "Phoebe Ann White," *Songs of Kunkel's Nightengale Opera Troupe* (Baltimore, 1854), quoted in Garber, *Vested Interests*, 276.

9. Lott, *Love and Theft*, 161.

10. See, for example, Ostendorf, *Black Literature in White America*, chap. 3, and Toll, *Blacking Up*. Toll has also noted the subthemes of protest against slavery in the minstrel show. Before 1850, according to Toll, the minstrel show sometimes criticized the cruelty of slavery, particularly the breakup of slave families (ibid., 83–84).

11. Roediger, *Wages of Whiteness*, 120. In his analysis of blackface in Hollywood, Rogin similarly argues that "[u]rban parvenues required the myth of the stable countryside" (*Blackface, White Noise*, 114). See also Saxton, *Rise and Fall of the White Republic*, chap. 7. For a broad discussion of past and present in popular culture, see Lipsitz, "Meaning of Memory," 63–64. Mahar has argued that the focus on race as the main feature of the minstrel show misses the full breadth of this entertainment form. He advocates several new directions in the study of the minstrel show, including the analysis of "the nonracial contents of blackface comedy [and] . . . the treatment of nonblack racial groups" ("Ethiopian Skits and Sketches," 241).

12. As cultural critic Susan Gubar has observed, the minstrel show "influenced many art forms not generally associated with it" (*Racechanges*, 55).

13. Rogin, *Blackface, White Noise*, 147.

14. Gubar points to the "tendency of male artists to approach the subject [of race changes] through dramatic forms of impersonation, while women of letters for the most part remain more absorbed by issues of lineage and inheritance" (*Racechanges*, 43).

15. Ibid., 57.

16. Spear, *Black Chicago*. Spear notes, for example, that Chicago's black population grew from approximately 6,000 in 1880 to roughly 30,000 in 1900 (ibid., 12). Historians have observed that popular entertainment focused on African Americans as the objects of hostile jokes and created particularly virulent stereotypes of African Americans during the mid-nineteenth century in the minstrel show and around the turn of the century in vaudeville. These escalations of racial animosity in popular culture correspond to periods of intense political debate about race relations. "It is interesting to note," writes historian J. Stanley Lemons, "that the black person as en-

tertainment and comic figure has emerged twice in popular culture, and at both times race relations were extremely bad" ("Black Stereotypes," 104).

17. Report Book 1, 127, KAC. Fletcher notes that "Rosalie" Tyler was a member of the cast in George Walker and Bert Williams's musical comedies, such as *Bandannaland*, in the early twentieth century (*100 Years of the Negro in Show Business*, 236). See also Helen Armstead Johnson, "Blacks in Vaudeville."

18. Report Book 5, 246, KAC.

19. Report Book 14, 58, KAC.

20. Report Book 6, 16, KAC. The Dixie Serenaders apparently pleased the Boston manager because they accepted the limits on African American performances. According to him, they owed "a considerable part of their success to the fact that they never forget they are darkies and never try to do 'white folks' comedy" (Report Book 8, 121, KAC).

21. Report Book 6, 150, KAC.

22. Report Book 7, 64, KAC.

23. Report Book 4, 47, KAC.

24. Report Book 7, 95. Lovenberg remarked that the black woman in the mind-reading act, Joveddah de Rajah, "could pass for a white woman" (Report Book 20, 175, KAC).

25. Report Book 12, 242, KAC.

26. Newman, "'Brightest Star,'" 467. See also Krasner, "Rewriting the Body."

27. Ninety-year-old Shep Edwards explained to Marshall and Jean Stearns in 1968 that "[t]hey did a take-off on the high manners of the white folks in the 'big house,' but their masters, who gathered around to watch the fun missed the point" (Stearns and Stearns, *Jazz Dance*, 22).

28. Stearns and Stearns, *Jazz Dance*, 122; Newman, "'Brightest Star,'" 468.

29. Snyder, *Voice of the City*, 120–21.

30. Ann Douglas, *Terrible Honesty*, 328–29. See also Gilbert, *American Vaudeville*, 284–87.

31. Report Book 16, 169, 50, KAC.

32. Other vaudeville circuits, such as the Theatre Owners Booking Association (TOBA), which promoted black vaudeville in the South and Midwest, seem to have allowed a wider range of performance styles for black women. TOBA, for example, featured the blues queens Ma Rainey, Ida Cox, and Mamie Smith. See Harrison, *Black Pearls*; Carby, "'It Jus Be's Dat Way Sometime'"; and DuCille, "Blues Notes on Black Sexuality."

33. A few black women led pickaninny acts as well. Fletcher, for example, in *100 Years of the Negro in Show Business* mentions that Belle Davis had her own pickaninny troupe.

34. Bogle, *Toms, Coons, Mulattoes*, 7. Bogle notes that a 1904 Edison film, *Ten Pickaninnies*, featured anonymous black children running around on-screen.

35. Typescript, June 10, 1905, Josephine Gassman/Phina clippings, Envelope 1751, RLC.

36. Goings, *Mammy and Uncle Mose*, 27.

37. Dormon, "Shaping the Popular Image of Post-Reconstruction American Blacks," 451; Lemons, "Black Stereotypes." Dennison also concludes that "[s]ongs

about the black were more brutally insulting than at any time following the advent of minstrelsy" (*Scandalize My Name*, 423).

38. Dormon, "Shaping the Popular Image of Post-Reconstruction American Blacks"; Cothern, "Coon Song."

39. "Hartford Theater," n.d., 6, clipping, Ethel Whiteside Clipping Folder, BRTC.

40. "Avon Theater: Vaudeville," *Rochester Post Express*, n.d., clipping, Envelope 1874, RLC.

41. "At the Broadway," *Columbus Journal*, n.d., clipping, Envelope 1874, RLC.

42. Report Book (1902–3), 204, KAC.

43. Report Book 20, 247, KAC.

44. Report Book (1902–3), 70, KAC.

45. Ibid., 92. Another review stated that the "two negro boys . . . have outgrown the pickaninny class and [their] work consists of making discordant noises on a cornet, a trombone and shouting at the top of their voices in a way that would blast rocks" (ibid., 55).

46. Report Book 6, 41, KAC.

47. Report Book 3, 201, KAC.

48. "Actress-Teacher," October 22, 1911, clipping, Envelope 2352, RLC.

49. Typescript, ca. 1905, Josephine Gassman/Phina clippings, Envelope 1751, RLC.

50. Report Book 7, 249, KAC.

51. "Mayme Remington," n.d., clipping, Envelope 1874, RLC.

52. "How a Sister Act Gained Fame and Local Color," *New Jersey Telegram*, October 24, 1907, clipping, Envelope 1614, RLC.

53. "Rare Plants of the Vaudeville Field," n.d., clipping, Envelope 1614, RLC.

54. Fred Fischer, "If the Man in the Moon Were a Coon" (Chicago: Will Rossiter, 1905), Minstrel Show Collection, Theatre Arts Collection, HRHRC.

55. *South Bend Tribune*, March 18, 1913, clipping, Envelope 1614, RLC.

56. Hillman and Perrin, "Mammy's Little Pumpkin Colored Coons" (M. Witmark and Sons, 1897), and Lee Johnson, "Mammy's Carolina Twins" (San Francisco: Lee Johnson, 1899), HC.

57. Report Book 8, 220, KAC.

58. Morton, *Disfigured Images*, 35.

59. Ibid.

60. Thurber, "Development of the Mammy Image"; Woodward, *Origins of the New South*, 154–58. Woodward describes reunions of Confederate soldiers and Jefferson Davis's emergence from seclusion as examples of a nostalgic trend—longing for the Old South—that emerged along with visions of a New South.

61. Clinton, *Plantation Mistress*, 202.

62. Ibid.

63. Turner, *Ceramic Uncles and Celluloid Mammies*, 47.

64. Morton, *Disfigured Images*, 36.

65. Turner, *Ceramic Uncles and Celluloid Mammies*, 52.

66. She received one negative review from Keith's manager in Philadelphia: "Think that the 'regulars' who saw her last week expected more new songs. . . . [W]ith her stiff salary and immense repertoire it does seem as if she should have

given the second week crowd something they had not heard before" (Report Book 7, 172, KAC).

67. "The New Bully" is listed as an encore for two vaudeville appearances in 1907 and one in 1908. See ibid., 153. A review in 1907 noted that the "greatest hits were songs she had made the country whistle and sing five eight and ten years ago" ("$2,500-a-Week May Irwin Leads Sortie in Vaudeville War of Dollars," ca. 1907, clipping, vol. 297, 69, RLC).

68. Gilbert, *American Vaudeville*, 96.

69. Charles E. Trevathan, "Honey on My Lips" (Boston: White-Smith Music Publishing Company, 1896), HC. "Her first 'ragtime' was 'The Bully' in which she made great sport by bringing a little coloured boy on stage with her" ("Famous Actresses of the Day," n.d., clipping, vol. 297, 52, RLC). See also the photographs captioned "May Irwin and the New Bully," May Irwin Clipping File, Theatre Arts Collection, HRHRC.

70. "May Irwin, the Jolly," *Criterion*, December 25, 1897, clipping, vol. 297, 20, RLC.

71. "May Irwin," n.d., clipping, ser. 5, pt. 2, reel 38, 373, DBS.

72. "Courted into Court," ca. 1897, clipping, vol. 297, 11, RLC.

73. Quoted in Dennison, *Scandalize My Name*, 375–76. There are many versions of "The Bully Song," but the renditions I have read strike a similar tone and create a vengeful black male narrator. See, for example, the 1896 version of the song held at the HC.

74. Charles Trevathan, "Crappy Dan de Spo'tin' Man" (New York: Chas. Shead and Company, 1896), HC.

75. Clipping, ca. 1908, vol. 298, 74, RLC.

76. "May Irwin, Ragtime, and the Cakewalk," February 15, 1902, clipping, vol. 297, 85, RLC.

77. "Chase's—May Irwin Heads Good Bill," *Washington Post*, January 14, 1908, 5.

78. Alan Dale, "Bunches of Good Things in May Irwin's New Play," n.d., clipping, vol. 297, 60, and *Chicago Dramatic Magazine*, May 1898, clipping, vol. 297, 28, RLC.

79. "Even in Coon Songs the Fashions Change," n.d., clipping, vol. 297, 102, RLC.

80. Ibid.

81. Fay Templeton, "Grease Paint and Glory: The Final Installment of the Fascinating Life-Story of the Actress Who Conquered New York and Became a Reigning Star," *Pictorial Review*, November 1926, clipping, Fay Templeton Clipping File, Theatre Arts Collection, HRHRC.

82. Toll, "Sophie Tucker."

83. Tucker, *Some of These Days*, 33.

84. Toll, "Sophie Tucker." By pointing to the popularity of fat white coon shouters, I am not suggesting that they were the only type of coon singers. Artie Hall, Ruth Nelta, and Louise Dresser were thin women who sang coon songs during approximately this same time period.

85. Allen, *Horrible Prettiness*, 282.

86. Report Book 15, 161, KAC.

87. "What! Not a Mash Note Ever Sent May Irwin?," n.d., clipping, vol. 297, 109, RLC.

88. Alan Dale, "Fat Has Come Back to the Stage," ca. 1897, clipping, vol. 297, 17, RLC.

89. "Two Girls Not Afraid of Their Complexions," *Toledo News Bee*, n.d., clipping, vol. 422, RLC.

90. My thanks to Lillian Schlissel for urging me to consider more of the positive aspects of Irwin.

91. "Talk with May Irwin," January 6, 1897, clipping, vol. 297, 8, RLC.

92. "May Irwin, Ragtime, and the Cakewalk," February 15, 1902, clipping, vol. 297, 85, RLC.

93. Clipping, n.d., ser. 5, pt. 2, reel 38, 382, DBS. A black maid was also reportedly significant in Sophie Tucker's career. Tucker learned her famous song, "Some of These Days," from her black maid (Rogin, *Blackface, White Noise*, 109).

94. Sociologist K. Sue Jewell describes the mammy's obesity, particularly her large breasts, as signs of her "maternal nurturance" rather than her "sexual desirability" (*From Mammy to Miss America*, 40).

95. May Irwin, "I Want to Live to Be One Hundred," *Green Book Magazine*, n.d., clipping, ser. 5, pt. 2, reel 38, 430, 435; photograph, ser. 5, pt. 2, reel 38, 412; and Ada Patterson, "Twenty Years a Star," n.d., clipping, ser. 5, pt. 2, reel 38, 435, DBS.

96. "May Irwin—The Model Housewife," n.d., clipping, vol. 298, 2, RLC.

97. Bob Cole and J. W. and Rosamond Johnson, "Louisiana Lize" (New York: Joseph W. Stern and Company, 1899); Bob Cole and J. W. and Rosamond Johnson, "Magdaline My Southern Queen" (New York: Joseph W. Stern and Company, 1900), and "Ma Mississippi Belle" (New York: Joseph W. Stern and Company, 1903), HC.

98. Ann Douglas, *Terrible Honesty*, 370; Furia, *Poets of Tin Pan Alley*, 27–28; Saunders, "Dilemma of Double Identity."

99. Fredrickson, *Black Image in the White Mind*, chap. 7.

100. Dyer, *Heavenly Bodies*, 124.

101. Ibid., 135.

102. "Fie! Fie!—Giddy! Giddy!," *Variety*, March 16, 1908, clipping, vol. 298, 77, and "May Irwin Songs," *Variety*, December 7, 1907, clipping, vol. 297, 73, RLC.

103. "Fie! Fie!—Giddy! Giddy!," *Variety*, March 16, 1908, clipping, vol. 298, 77, RLC.

104. "May Irwin Says That She Will 'Mope No Mo,'" August 31, 1904, clipping, vol. 297, 103, RLC. See also "Even in Coon Songs the Fashions Change," n.d., clipping, vol. 297, 102, RLC.

105. Report Book 7, 180, KAC.

106. Report Book 19, 251, KAC.

107. Report Book 20, 247, and Report Book 21, 6, KAC.

108. "The Vaudeville," *Peoria Evening Times*, October 17, 1896, clipping, Ned Wayburn Scrapbook 21,049, 14, BRTC.

109. "At the Auditorium," n.d., clipping, Ned Wayburn Scrapbook 21,049, 14, BRTC.

110. Program, State Street Theater, Chicago, n.d., Ned Wayburn Scrapbook 21,049, BRTC, quoted in Cohen-Stratyner, *Ned Wayburn and the Dance Routine*, 10.

111. Ned Wayburn, "She's a Thoroughbred," n.d., clipping, ser. 5, pt. 2, reel 38,

399, DBS. For more on Wayburn's early life, see Cohen-Stratyner, *Ned Wayburn and the Dance Routine*, 1–13.

112. Cohen-Stratyner, *Ned Wayburn and the Dance Routine*, chap. 2.

113. Ibid., 26.

114. From 1907 to 1912, the number of headliner acts staged by male producers skyrocketed in vaudeville. Jesse Lasky led the field, presenting ten shows during this period, whereas B. A. Rolfe contributed five. Charles Lovenberg, who started to produce vaudeville acts while continuing to manage Keith's theater in Providence, presented three headliner numbers, and Gus Edwards and Joseph Hart added two and four top acts, respectively. Between 1912 and 1917, the well-known producers lost some of their prominence at the headliner position: Lasky reached the top of Keith's bill in Providence only four times, whereas Rolfe and Hart both produced headliner acts at Keith's twice during this five-year period. Hart contributed fourteen productions between 1907 and 1916.

115. Cohen-Stratyner, *Ned Wayburn and the Dance Routine*, chap. 2.

116. "Ned Wayburn of Stage Fame Dies," *Boston Globe*, September 3, 1942, clipping, Ned Wayburn Clipping File, HTC.

117. Toll, *Blacking Up*, chap. 5. Toll states that these all-female troupes were forerunners of the "girlie show" (ibid., 139). Haverly's Minstrels marketed their extensive scenery, costumes, and casts. One act reportedly featured forty-two people, whereas another included scenery representing a Turkish palace in silver and gold ("Boston Theatre . . . Haverly's United Mastadon Minstrels," *The Bay*, June 16, 1879, 1, Haverly's Minstrels Clippings and Playbills Folder, Minstrel Show Collection, Theatre Arts Collection, HRHRC). In this way, the minstrel show followed the trend established by *The Black Crook* (1866–67), an elaborate musical comedy that included women in skimpy costumes as a primary attraction. For more on *The Black Crook*, see Allen, *Horrible Prettiness*.

118. Neil Harris, *Humbug*, 245; Rubin, *Showstoppers*, 26.

119. Leach, *Land of Desire*, 40.

120. "The Redheads," *Keith News*, November 24, 1913, 2, clipping, Clipping Book (December 29, 1912–December 8, 1913), 242, KAC.

121. Ibid.

122. Allen, *Horrible Prettiness*, 246.

123. This description is taken from excerpts of reviews in *Ned Wayburn's Minstrel Misses* (1903), brochure, Ned Wayburn Clipping File, HTC. "What is worse than a giraffe with a sore neck?," questioned one "end woman." "A centipede with corns," she answered herself.

124. "Midsummer Night's Entertainment," n.d., clipping, vol. 245, 123, RLC.

125. Rogin in *Blackface, White Noise* describes this element in many films, including *The Jazz Singer* and *Holiday Inn* (1942).

126. Roediger, *Wages of Whiteness*, 117.

127. Tucker, *Some of These Days*, 35.

128. Rogin, "'Democracy and Burnt Cork,'" 9.

129. "Wayburn Provides a 'Real Treat,'" *Ned Wayburn's Minstrel Misses* (1903), brochure, Ned Wayburn Clipping File, HTC.

130. Ibid.

131. Report Book 16, 100, KAC.

132. "Ned Wayburn Talks about His Minstrel Misses," *Ned Wayburn's Minstrel Misses* (1903), brochure, Ned Wayburn Clipping File, HTC.

133. "How Ned Wayburn Invented the Minstrel Misses," *Morning Telegraph*, July 5, 1903, clipping, Envelope 2509, RLC.

134. Gubar, *Racechanges*, 79.

135. "Cook Opera House," *Rochester Democrat and Chronicle*, February 23, 1904, 13.

136. Lovenberg wrote in 1903 that "strangely these girls didn't get much applause, although personally I think it is a very strong act" (Report Book [1902–3], 324, KAC).

137. Ibid., 334.

138. Report Book 1, 26, KAC.

139. F. Heiser, "Climbing up de Golden Stairs" (New York: T. B. Harms, 1884), HC; James Bland, "Oh Dem Golden Slippers" (London: C. Sheard, n.d.), HC.

140. Report Book 6, 72, KAC.

141. "Handling Humanity in the Mass," *Theatre*, May 1913, clipping, vol. 305, 178, RLC.

142. Ned Wayburn, "Show Girls Yesterday and Today," *Theatre*, December 1916, clipping, vol. 305, 188, RLC.

143. George Vaux Bacon, "Chorus Girls in the Making," n.d., clipping, Ned Wayburn Clipping File, HTC.

Chapter Six

1. "She Can Carry Ballot to Box," September 25, 1916, clipping, box 1, vol. 7, RBC.

2. Peiss defines the New Woman as "independent, athletic, sexual and modern" (*Cheap Amusements*, 7). See also Smith-Rosenberg, "New Woman as Androgyne."

3. A feature act was second only to the headliner act of the ten to twelve acts on a vaudeville bill.

4. Smith-Rosenberg, "New Woman as Androgyne," 291. Film historians have turned to the anonymous female acrobat in the 1901 Edison film, *Trapeze Disrobing Act*, to describe the gendered power relations in spectatorship. This acrobat has served as an emblem of woman's captivity as a sexual object in popular film in the early twentieth century because she reveals the structure of the male gaze and female spectacle. The film shows two men watching a woman's trapeze act. They become increasingly exuberant as the woman takes off her skirt, blouse, and stockings and then performs a flip in her undergarments. Allen concludes that the acrobat in *Trapeze Disrobing Act* was "silenced, frozen in time and captured within the film's frame" (*Horrible Prettiness*, 271). See also Mayne, "Uncovering the Female Body."

5. Senelick, "Boys and Girls Together," 83–84.

6. *New York Hippodrome Winter Circus*, program, February 11, 1915, box 1, vol. 6, RBC. First opening its doors in 1904, the Hippodrome was a huge theater, accommodating circuses throughout the winter months.

7. Report Book 4, 44, KAC.

8. Report Book (1902–3), 135, KAC.

9. Report Book 1, 6, KAC.

10. Report Book 7, 203, KAC. The Hurleys, another male/female acrobatic team, also capitalized on this gender novelty: "The fact of the woman doing the understanding puts it almost in a class by itself" (ibid., 87). Lovenberg commented on the Schiavoni Troupe on September 6, 1910: "One girl in the act is a wonder for feats of strength particularly" (Report Book 11, 61, KAC). On March 23, 1914, Lovenberg wrote of the Bimbos: "The woman is particularly clever as the understander" (Report Book 16, 182, KAC). See also Report Book 17, 99, KAC.

11. Report Book 16, 126, KAC.

12. Eckley, *American Circus*, 182. To execute a one-armed plange, an acrobat flipped his or her body over, using one arm, which was secured to the rope, as a lever. Thanks to historian Janet Davis for clarifying this for me.

13. Report Book 16, 93, and Report Book 5, 208, KAC. The Sisters Gausch "work exactly as two men would. That is to say, they accomplish everything they attempt with all the finish of male performers and they perform some pretty difficult tricks" (Report Book 1, 137, KAC).

14. For further discussion of the issue of gender inversion, see Natalie Zemon Davis, "Women on Top."

15. In 1914 Ruth Budd wrote that she and her brother had been barred from playing on Sunday in Philadelphia because "[a]ny act working in tights can't work on Sunday" (Ruth Budd to Ray Hanna, November 8, 1914, box 1, vol. 6, RBC). After performing at a Fort Wayne vaudeville theater in 1911, Ruth Budd began a correspondence with one of the theater's stagehands, Ray Hanna. He saved Budd's long series of letters, and when Hanna and Budd were married in 1927, the letters written by Budd became part of her personal collection, now held at the Allen County–Fort Wayne Historical Society, Fort Wayne, Indiana.

16. Report Book 18, 193, KAC. In 1908 the manager of Boston's Keith theater applauded Maybelle Meeker's disrobing: "Opens with a song and acrobatic dance, then strips to tights and does some excellent contortion work. She makes a very attractive stage appearance after she makes her change" (Report Book 8, 133, KAC). Grace DeMar also used this convention in her act. One Keith manager wrote: "The novelty stunt is changing costume while suspended by teeth" (Report Book 15, 162, KAC). Trick bicyclist Lala Selbini stripped to tights in the midst of her athletic display, according to Charles Barnes, Keith manager in Philadelphia: "[She] begins with a song, then proceeds with the well-known disrobing act on the bicycle.... [S]he depends upon her corsetless stunts on the wheel to save the act" (Report Book 7, 68, KAC).

17. Ruth Budd to Ray Hanna, June 17, 1918, box 2, vol. 8, RBC.

18. Steegmuller, "Onward and Upward with the Arts," 135.

19. Report Book 21, 140, KAC.

20. Report Book 16, 164, KAC. In addition, the manager of the Scenic Theatre in Pawtucket revealed that the Silverton Girls were in fact a male/female team: "Man made up as a woman and does all the work that amounts to anything" (Report Book 18, 22, KAC).

21. Senelick cites as examples the Hanlons and the Voltas, who "testified that an admiration for the muscular masculine form and professional reliance on one another's strength and skill made most acrobats and trapezists scornful of women"

("Boys and Girls Together," 84). In addition, Senelick points to a "homosexual undercurrent in circus life" that has appeared in fiction but has not been documented by historians (ibid.).

22. *The Three Budds* (1909?), pamphlet, box 1, vol. 2, RBC.

23. *Colonial Clipper*, September 26, 1914, clipping, box 1, vol. 6, RBC. "The Aerial Budds are beyond doubt the fastest workers . . . in the line," commented one observer; "[t]hey are doing 24 tricks in 5 minutes, presenting the routine so fast that it is almost impossible to count the tricks" ("The Best Show Ever at the Palace Music Hall," n.d., clipping, box 1, vol. 6, RBC).

24. *The Three Budds* (1909?), pamphlet, box 1, vol. 2, RBC.

25. Ibid.

26. Ruth Budd to Ray Hanna, January 31, 1912, box 1, vol. 3, RBC.

27. "Exceeds Speed Limit: Acrobat Act Sixty Miles an Hour Produced at the Gaiety," April 1911, clipping, box 1, vol. 3, RBC.

28. "Sylvester Schaffer Astounds Beholders," *Philadelphia Record*, n.d., clipping, box 1, vol. 3, RBC.

29. Ruth Budd to Ray Hanna, October 9, 1913, box 1, vol. 5, RBC.

30. Ruth Budd to Ray Hanna, September 22, 1913, box 1, vol. 5, RBC.

31. Ruth Budd to Ray Hanna, June 13, 1915, box 1, vol. 6, RBC.

32. Lovenberg wrote that the LaBelle Trio, occupying the first position on January 7, 1907, was "about as bad an affair as we have had. . . . [T]he best I can do is bury them" (Report Book 5, 220, KAC).

33. Ruth Budd to Ray Hanna, December 4, 1914, box 1, vol. 6, RBC.

34. Ruth Budd to Ray Hanna, June 14, 1916, box 1, vol. 7, RBC.

35. Ruth Budd to Ray Hanna, December 2, 1911, box 1, vol. 3, RBC. See also Ruth Budd to Ray Hanna, October 30, 1913, box 1, vol. 5, and April 23, 1912, box 1, vol. 3, RBC.

36. Lovenberg reflected on October 9, 1903, that the Althea Twins' six-minute act was "alright . . . but too short to be of value" (Report Book 4, 57, KAC). He commented on December 21, 1914: "To my mind an act that cannot fill ten minutes, no matter how clever the work is, is hardly worth consideration" (Report Book 17, 131, KAC).

37. Eckley, *American Circus*, 142. Hippisley Coxe explains: "Little shows—such as Quick and Mead's, which in 1826 had no more than four wagons, nine horses, a fifty foot big top and an orchestra which consisted of one hurdy gurdy—eventually became gigantic combines in which a thousand people produced simultaneous spectacles in three rings and four stages for an audience of 16,000" (*Seat at the Circus*, 36).

38. In 1914 one manager wrote that the "yokels" laughed at the Chadwick Trio, "the roughest kind of a rough slapstick act, absolutely devoid of merit" (Report Book 16, 144, KAC). The Cleveland manager found that "the rubes of Northern Ohio . . . applauded anything and everything from the entrance of the musicians to the raising and lowering of the olio" (Report Book 14, 147, KAC).

39. Report Book 9, 249, KAC.

40. Report Book 17, 119, KAC. Budd also wrote that managers in London had told her that the Budds "worked too fast" (Ruth Budd to Ray Hanna, December 8, 1912, box 1, vol. 3, RBC).

41. Report Book 17, 147, KAC.

42. Ruth Budd to Ray Hanna, September 25, 1915, box 1, vol. 6, RBC.

43. A 1917 review offers some clues to the type of verbal comedy she added to her act: "'Nothing like knowing the ropes,' she says merrily, and comes spinning head-first from the wings. . . . 'Now I've put my foot in it,' she laughs and goes whirling into space" ("Vaudeville Reviews," *Green Room*, n.d., clipping, box 2, vol. 8, RBC).

44. Using only the front section of the stage was called working "in one."

45. Ruth Budd to Ray Hanna, October 15, 1915, box 1, vol. 6, RBC.

46. Song typescript, box 1, vol. 6, RBC.

47. Ruth Budd to Ray Hanna, August 24, 1916, box 1, vol. 7, RBC.

48. Dolly Dalrymple, "Little Miss Ruth Budd Is a Physical Pastel, a Graceful Little Reed with Shapely Little Pipe-Stem Limbs, a Fascinating Smile and the Serious Face of a Little Child," *Birmingham Age-Herald*, December 3, 1918, clipping, box 2, vol. 9, RBC.

49. "Ruth Budd," *Variety*, June 22, 1917, clipping, box 1, vol. 7, RBC.

50. "Bill Is Superb from End to End," June 11, 1916, clipping, box 1, vol. 7, RBC. Although her single act changed over the years, she maintained the element of surprise by concealing her acrobatic segment until she changed from full dress to tights. By 1922 Budd had added a piano player to her act, and she began to spend the first part of the act singing on top of the piano, but she retained her trademark of disrobing in midact: "After a catchy song or two she reappeared in fleshings prepared for the remainder of her act. This included everything known to the experts of the aerial rings and trapeze" ("Ruth Budd at Keith's," *Boston Post*, May 23, 1922, clipping, box 2, vol. 12, RBC).

51. Lenskyj, *Out of Bounds*, 68.

52. Rabinovitz, "Temptations of Pleasure."

53. Ibid., 83.

54. Cahn, *Coming On Strong*, 47–50; Lenskyj, *Out of Bounds*, 59–64.

55. Report Book (1902–3), 329, KAC.

56. Report Book 6, 234, KAC.

57. Report Book 7, 11, KAC.

58. "St. Havens Tops Bill," *Morning Oregonian*, June 3, 1918, clipping, box 2, vol. 8, RBC.

59. Anonymous fan to Ruth Budd, October 30, 1917, box 2, vol. 8, RBC.

60. Green, *Fit for America*, 222.

61. Margaret Sanger, "Why Not Birth Control in America?," *Birth Control Review*, May 1919, quoted in Gordon, *Birth Control in America*, 281.

62. Report Book 6, 228, KAC.

63. Ruth Budd to Ray Hanna, March 14, 1919, box 2, vol. 9, RBC.

64. "*A Scream in the Night*," *Exhibitors' Campaign Book* (1919), 8, box 1, vol. 9, RBC.

65. Ibid.

66. Ibid.

67. Ibid.

68. "*A Scream in the Night*," *Variety*, October 24, 1919, quoted in *Variety's Film Reviews*, n.p.

69. Ibid.

70. "Man's Power of Reason," *Exhibitors' Campaign Book* (1919), 6, box 1, vol. 9, RBC.

71. W. Stephen Bush, "*A Scream in the Night*," *Billboard*, October 18, 1919, 82.

72. Ibid.

73. Ibid.

74. "Movies Made Ruth Budd Real 'Monkey,'" n.d., clipping, box 2, vol. 9, RBC.

75. Keith program, October 25, 1909, Clipping Book (February 20, 1909–November 15, 1909), KAC.

76. Report Book 15, 114, KAC. One trainer had a monkey perform on a swinging trapeze and the rings (Report Book 5, 136, KAC).

77. Vogt, *Lectures on Man*, quoted in Russett, *Sexual Science*, 56.

78. Russett, *Sexual Science*, 195.

79. Ibid., 205.

80. Bederman, *Manliness and Civilization*, 25.

81. Sargent, "How Can I Have a Graceful Figure?," quoted in Cahn, *Coming On Strong*, 19–20.

82. Ruth Budd to Ray Hanna, January 25, 1916, box 1, vol. 7, RBC.

83. Green, *Fit for America*, 257.

84. "Ruth Budd Is Perfect Specimen of Womanhood," *Exhibitors' Campaign Book* (1919), 8, box 1, vol. 9, RBC.

85. "A Bit of Budd," *Variety*, December 26, 1919, 30.

86. "Women Are Not the Weaker Sex, Says This Movie Star," *Exhibitors' Campaign Book* (1919), 6, box 1, vol. 9, RBC.

87. Letter to Ruth Budd, n.d., box 5, miscellaneous letter folder, RBC.

88. Chauncey, *Gay New York*, 55–56. See also Ullman, "'Twentieth Century Way.'"

89. Faderman, *Odd Girls and Twilight Lovers*, 46. See also Katz, "Invention of Heterosexuality." Julien Chevalier, a French sexologist, connected women's participation in "masculine" sports and politics to female sexual inversion in his 1893 *Inversion sexuelle*.

90. For more on the famous sexologists, see Faderman, *Odd Girls and Twilight Lovers*, chap. 2.

91. "Why the Strangest of Engagements Has Been Broken Off," 1922, clipping, box 2, vol. 12, RBC.

92. Ibid.

93. Karl K. Kitchen, "Cancel of a Wedding 'Booking,'" *New York World*, August 13, 1922, box 2, vol. 12, RBC.

94. "Ex-Fiancée Describes Wreck of 'Fashion Plate's' Romance," July 4, 1922, clipping, box 2, vol. 12, RBC. This certainly would have been a plausible explanation to the public by 1931, when other male entertainers associated with femininity, female impersonation, and the gay subculture set up faux marriages. Chauncey recounts the marriage of Gene Malin, a performer who had been a female impersonator and then became a "pansy." His marriage to Christine Williams and their quick divorce led reporters to contemplate whether or not he was a homosexual. The *New York Daily News* asked, "Is he ——?" (quoted in *Gay New York*, 314–18).

95. Letter to Ruth Budd, n.d., box 5, miscellaneous letter folder, RBC.

96. "$8,000 Mends Broken Heart," *Zit's Theatrical Newspaper*, May 23, 1925, clipping, box 2, vol. 14, and "He'll Wed, Sure, but Get Heart Balm, Try and Get It," *New York Daily News*, July 1, 1922, clipping, box 2, vol. 12, RBC.

97. The most graphic mother-in-law jokes drew the censure of managers. In 1903 Carl Lothrop, manager of Keith's theater in Boston, instructed Mr. and Mrs. Robyns to "cut that portion of [your] opening song in which the coffin full of cheese is mistaken for the remains of a mother-in-law" (Report Book [1902–3], 282, KAC).

98. Karl K. Kitchen, "Cancel of a Wedding 'Booking,'" *New York World*, August 13, 1922, box 2, vol. 12, RBC.

99. "Ex-Fiancée Describes Wreck of 'Fashion Plate's' Romance," *Baltimore American*, July 4, 1922, clipping, box 2, vol. 12, RBC.

100. Ibid.

101. Ullman, "'Twentieth Century Way,'" 590–91.

102. Senelick, "Lady and the Tramp," 37–38. Senelick has written about the gay subculture surrounding female impersonators in "Boys and Girls Together."

103. Slide, "Karyl Norman," 374.

104. Chauncey, *Gay New York*, 4.

105. Ibid., chap. 11.

106. Report Book 11, 22, KAC.

107. Senelick, "Boys and Girls Together," 90–93.

108. Faderman, *Odd Girls and Twilight Lovers*, chap. 3.

Chapter Seven

1. "The White Rats of America," *New York Dramatic Mirror*, July 21, 1900, 7.

2. These other labor unions also had roots in fraternal societies. Uriah S. Stephens, a tailor who was a member of several fraternal orders (including the Masons), founded the Knights of Labor in 1869. Under the direction of Terence Powderly, the Knights adopted more aggressive tactics in labor struggles, although elements of Masonic rituals endured, despite Powderly's objections. See Carnes, *Secret Ritual and Manhood*, 9.

3. The White Rats Actors' Union staged walkouts and pickets at several theaters around Chicago after managers canceled acts there at the last minute. It was able to force managers to reinstate acts or at least pay the salary of the canceled acts. See "Triple Victor for White Rats," *The Player*, March 31, 1911, 22, and "Two More Victories," *The Player*, May 19, 1911, 9.

4. Clawson, *Constructing Brotherhood*, 172–77.

5. Bederman, *Manliness and Civilization*, 15. Jeffries came back from his retirement to fight black boxer Jack Johnson (then heavyweight champion) in 1910. Jeffries lost this widely publicized match in a rout. See Bederman's introduction for an overview of the transformations in masculinity in this period. According to Gorn, "[t]oughness, ferocity, prowess, honor, these became the touchstones of maleness and boxing along with other sports upheld this alternative definition of manhood" (*Manly Art*, 141). See also Kaster, "Labor's True Man," and Dabakis, "Douglas Tilden's *Mechanics Fountain*."

6. "White Rats Win Their Point," *New York Dramatic Mirror*, February 16, 1901, 20.

7. "The White Rats of America," *New York Dramatic Mirror*, July 21, 1900, 7.

8. Ibid.

9. Clawson, *Constructing Brotherhood*, 154. In addition, historian David Montgomery explains that the control the nineteenth-century craftsman had over his work was tied, in part, to a code of manliness: "dignity, respectability, defiant egalitarianism, and patriarchal male supremacy" (*Workers' Control in America*, 13).

10. James W. Fitzpatrick, "Fitzpatrick Tells What the Actors Really Have to Do with Stage World," *The Player*, 2d ser., February 9, 1917, 14. Berk Saukman shared this position, concluding that "the artist makes the money for them all [i.e., managers, agents, theater owners]. Without him the show is nil. I predict that when his alarm clock goes off . . . the artist will jointly own the theatres; that he will have his own booking offices and self-appointed managers" ("The Vaudevil [*sic*] Performer," *The Player*, December 30, 1910, 26).

11. James W. Fitzpatrick, "Fitzpatrick Tells What the Actors Really Have to Do with Stage World," *The Player*, 2d ser., February 9, 1917, 14.

12. Brody, "American Worker in the Progressive Age," 8. See also Montgomery, "New Tendencies in Union Struggles."

13. Ruth Budd to Ray Hanna, March 14, 1924, box 2, vol. 12, RBC.

14. One observer noted: "This is getting down to department store and commercial business methods" ("Time Clock on Performers," *The Player*, December 24, 1909, 1). One performer complained about a manager who ordered him to "go on and sing one song and tell one gag and get off" (James Fitzpatrick testimony, box 71, 1885, *FTC v. VMPA*.

15. Kaster, "Labor's True Man," 39.

16. "White Rats and Unionists at Variance over Agents," *Variety*, June 18, 1910, 5; "Application by White Rats Made to Federation of Labor," *Variety*, September 24, 1910, 5. Through the merger with the International Actors' Union (IAU), which was affiliated with the AFL, the White Rats received an AFL charter to represent all performers. Several newspaper reports indicate that in 1910 the IAU was far more militant than the White Rats. The White Rats, for example, protested the attempt by the IAU to declare a closed shop in Chicago and establish a minimum wage for acts.

17. Max Leo Corrigan, "The Awakening," *The Player*, January 3, 1911, 8.

18. J. Aldrich Libbey, "Art and Labor," *The Player*, June 2, 1911, 8.

19. Addison, introduction to *Arts and Crafts in the Middle Ages*, quoted in Boris, *Art and Labor*, 28.

20. Boris, *Art and Labor*, 12.

21. Ibid., 28–29.

22. Ibid., 193.

23. Harry De Veaux, "Vaudeville Artists' Progress v. Legitimate Actors' Indifference," *The Player*, March 31, 1911, 41.

24. Harry Mountford, "Questions and Answers," *The Player*, February 24, 1911, 5.

25. "Sensible and Plucky Vaudevillers," *New York Dramatic Mirror*, February 23, 1901, 18.

26. A.A.A. [member] no. 278, "To the Legitimate Actor," *The Player*, March 10, 1911, 23.

27. "The Question of Art," *New York Dramatic Mirror*, July 14, 1900, 12.

28. McArthur, *Actors and American Culture*, 216–18.

29. "Seek Actors' Equity Aid," *New York Times*, October 28, 1915, 11. In addition, vaudeville managers threatened to bring in dramatic actors to break the threatened White Rats' strike in 1911: "It is said the booking office has been planning to fill the vaudeville theatres with dramatic and musical attractions in case the strike takes place, and to simply stop presenting vaudeville" ("Suits in White Rats' War," *New York Times*, June 16, 1911, 9).

30. Actors' Equity faced off against the United Managers' Protective Association (UMPA), an alliance of theater owners, booking agents, and producing managers around the country. The actors' organization tried to win the UMPA's approval of several aspects of a standard contract, including a clause mandating two weeks' notice of the closing of a show and a guarantee of extra pay for actors who performed more than the regular eight shows per week. When the UMPA refused these provisions, Actors' Equity began to consider affiliation with the AFL. Not surprisingly, some players spoke up against such a move, like actress Blanche Bates, who reasoned that "[w]e are not in the condition of capital and labor . . . because we do not work with our hands" (quoted in McArthur, *Actors and American Culture*, 226). In this debate about unionization, however, Bates and her followers lost. Partly because of members' frustration with the lack of progress on the contract and partly because they could see that the White Rats were strongly opposing the VMPA, Actors' Equity voted in 1916 to affiliate with the AFL. The association with the AFL was complicated by the fact that the vaudevillians held the charter for the whole "amusement field," and members of Actors' Equity were reluctant to hand over control of their organization to vaudevillians, whom some viewed as beneath them. Finally, in 1917 the UMPA agreed to accept the Actors' Equity contract. With this achievement, Actors' Equity set aside affiliation with the AFL until 1919. See ibid., 213–36.

31. Raymond Williams, *Culture and Society*, 43–44.

32. Franklyn Gale, "Our Woman Correspondent Still in Chicago," *The Player*, February 24, 1911, 21.

33. J. Aldrich Libbey, "Art and Labor," *The Player*, June 2, 1911, 8. Other articles also chided legitimate actors for being cowards. See, for example, "It's Your Own Fault," *The Player*, April 28, 1911, 13.

34. "Well, Dramatic Boys and Girls," *The Player*, June 2, 1911, 28.

35. Bert Saukman, "The Vaudivil [*sic*] Performer," *The Player*, December 30, 1910, 26.

36. "The Real Thing," *The Player*, December 9, 1910, 95.

37. Leo Donnelly, "From the Audience Side," *The Player*, December 17, 1909, 12. Douglas Gilbert explains that George Fuller Golden, one of the founders of the White Rats, fought against "the freak, polite and hammy legit acts that were to make anemic the vigorous, lusty, kick-in-the-belly-and-lima-beans vaudeville, which for all its grossness, was virile and forthright (*American Vaudeville*, 234).

38. Frank Conroy, "Vaudeville (Variety) Past and Present," *The Player*, December 9, 1910, 94.

39. "The Unmasked Marvel," *The Player*, February 23, 1917, 2.

40. "White Rats to Admit Women," *New York Dramatic Mirror*, January 26, 1901, 18. Other accounts describe the female members as "White Stars." *White Rats Bulletin*, July 9, 1901.

41. Mattie Keene, "A Woman's View," *The Player*, June 10, 1910, 29.

42. "Billiken," "Skirts and Rats," *The Player*, April 8, 1910, 6.

43. Clawson, *Constructing Brotherhood*, chap. 5.

44. Harry Mountford, "The Associated Actresses of America and Some of Its Advantages," *The Player*, September 16, 1910, 7.

45. "Application for Membership: Associated Actresses of America," *The Player*, September 16, 1910, 8.

46. Franklyn Gale, "Our Woman Correspondent Visits the Club Room," *The Player*, May 26, 1911, 21.

47. Harry Mountford, "The Associated Actresses of America and Some of Its Advantages," *The Player*, September 16, 1910, 7.

48. Gilbert, *American Vaudeville*, 234. Labor organizations, in particular, often maintained the secrecy of their initiations to protect their members from being placed on blacklists, but their rituals, like those of other groups, also helped affirm the masculinity of the members.

49. Dumenil, *Freemasonry and American Culture*, 35.

50. Clawson, *Constructing Brotherhood*, 129–30.

51. Carnes, *Secret Ritual and Manhood*, 125.

52. Daisy Browner, letter to the editor, *The Player*, January 20, 1911, 32.

53. Franklyn Gale, "Our Woman Correspondent Returns to Chicago," *The Player*, December 16, 1910, 33.

54. Harry Mountford, "The Associated Actresses of America and Some of Its Advantages," *The Player*, September 16, 1910, 7.

55. Mountford, for example, referred to the "sufferings undergone by the struggling women of the profession" to argue that "every self-respecting, every honest woman in the theatrical profession would become a member of the A. A. A." ("The Woman's Need of Protection," *The Player*, September 30, 1910, 7).

56. Franklyn Gale, "A Woman's View," *The Player*, July 22, 1910, 8.

57. Franklyn Gale, "Our Woman Correspondent Tells Us Some News from Chicago," *The Player*, August 12, 1910, 36.

58. "News of the Order and Associated Actresses," *The Player*, September 23, 1910, 12.

59. Meyerowitz, *Women Adrift*.

60. "Protect Girls, White Rats Ask," *The Player*, March 10, 1911, 4.

61. Daisy Browner, letter to the editor, *The Player*, January 20, 1911, 32.

62. "White Rats News," *Variety*, August 18, 1916, 14. As the strike wore on, union leaders continued to emphasize the vulnerability of female performers to ignite support for the strike. James Fitzpatrick, president of the White Rats, in a letter to *Variety* described "a negro manager's . . . disgraceful [treatment] of a mother and daughter [team]" (letter to the editor, *Variety*, November 24, 1916, 13).

63. "White Rats Strike," *The Player*, 2d ser., February 9, 1917, 4. During this strike, the managers, on the other hand, argued that the White Rats had shunned the mothers and widows of impoverished actors; they noted that these destitute women re-

ceived aid from the National Vaudeville Association (the union sponsored by the managers) ("Agitator's Goldbrick," *Variety*, September 22, 1916, 23).

64. Murphy, *Ten Hours' Labor*, 191.

65. *La Grange (Ga.) Graphic*, February 14, 1916, quoted in MacLean, "Leo Frank Case Reconsidered," 940.

66. *Journal of Labor*, May 2, 1913, quoted in Hall, "Private Eyes, Public Women," 265.

67. Kessler-Harris, *Out to Work*, 188–89. See also Cobble, *Dishing It Out*.

68. James Fitzpatrick to J. J. Murdock, January 11, 1917, in Fitzpatrick testimony, box 71, 1946, *FTC v. VMPA*.

69. "A Lesson to Chorus Girls," *The Player*, September 16, 1910, 9.

70. Murphy, *Ten Hours' Labor*, 209.

71. Hall, "Private Eyes, Public Women," 264. See also Meyerowitz, *Women Adrift*; Peiss, *Cheap Amusements*; and Tracy C. Davis, *Actresses as Working Women*.

72. "Lady Artist Resents Slur on Profession," *The Player*, February 10, 1911, 20.

73. Franklyn Gale, "A Woman's View," *The Player*, April 8, 1910, 18.

74. "Agitator's Goldbrick," *Variety*, September 22, 1916, 23.

75. Franklyn Gale, "A Woman's View," *The Player*, April 15, 1910, 18.

76. Franklyn Gale, "A Woman's View," *The Player*, April 1, 1910, 17. See also Franklyn Gale, "A Woman's View," *The Player*, March 18, 1910, 18.

77. "Discontent amongst Actresses: Why Not Join the A.A.A.?" *The Player*, October 21, 1910, 8.

78. "Oklahoma City Strike Quiet," *Variety*, November 17, 1916, 6.

79. "Union Pickets Arrested," *Daily Oklahoman*, August 3, 1916, 1. T. H. Boland, manager of the Empress theater, and a striker, R. F. Shumaker, scuffled on the picket line in late September. After Shumaker called Boland a "dirty scab," Boland struck him in the face ("Arbitration Board Counsels Reinstatement of Strikers," *Variety*, September 29, 1916, 6). See also "Strikers Picket Theaters," *Daily Oklahoman*, July 31, 1916, 2.

80. "Odorous Bombs Halt Show," *New York Times*, March 15, 1917, 9.

81. Harry Mountford, "White Rats News," *Variety*, August 18, 1916, 15.

82. Norwood, *Labor's Flaming Youth*, 4.

83. Ibid.

84. Ibid., 118, chap. 5.

85. Albert Fenyvessy testimony, box 70, 695, *FTC v. VMPA*.

86. "Cora Youngblood Corson Abroad," *New York Telegraph*, January 20, 1913, clipping, vol. 349, 190, RLC. During the strike, Corson was singled out by managers as an "outside agitator." Both theater managers and strikers attempted to cast their opponents as outsiders. The theater managers, in their July 30, 1916, statement, vilified Corson: "A woman claiming to be a vaudeville actress, but who admits that she has been blacklisted for several years by reputable booking agents because of violations of her contract, comes to Oklahoma City, assumes control . . . and by pretense of authority directs what shall or shall not be done by Oklahoma theater managers in their own houses" ("Theater Owners Make Statement," *Daily Oklahoman*, July 30, 1916, 8A).

87. "Judge Dismisses Chicago Pickets," *The Player*, 2d ser., April 13, 1917, 13.

88. "Pantages Has 'Lung' Champion," n.d., clipping, vol. 349, 191, RLC.

89. A 1909 article again presented her as "abnormal": "[T]hough weighing only 145 pounds, she has development in her breathing apparatus equal to that of any man" ("Too Much Lung Expansion," *Variety*, October 2, 1909, clipping, vol. 349, 197, RLC).

90. Al Harvey ("Dr. Joy's Sanitarium"), letter to the editor, *Variety*, August 11, 1916, 8.

91. Ibid.

92. Managers on the West Coast who were affiliated with the UBO announced that they would not book any performer who refused to play in Oklahoma City. Such performers were labeled "undesirable" by many agents and managers ("Protecting Oklahoma City Aim of Chicago Association," *Variety*, October 6, 1916, 6). To be reinstated into the powerful booking offices of the managers' association, "canceled Rats" had to be approved by a managers' committee ("Canceled Rats Passed Upon by Managers' Committee," *Variety*, November 17, 1916, 5). Such roadblocks to the vaudevillians' unionization efforts were commonplace during this period. Beginning around the turn of the century, trade associations provided strikebreakers, hired industrial spies, and maintained central "blacklists," helping turn back many union challenges. Throughout the early twentieth century as well, courts regularly intervened to protect employers from union pickets and boycotts by declaring that union members were restraining trade. Despite the 1914 Clayton Act's guarantee that unions were no longer subject to the Sherman Anti-Trust Act, judges sympathetic to employers continued to issue injunctions against labor activism. Finally, company unions increased following World War I. Controlled by management and guided by the assumption that management and labor were not opposed, company unions hindered many employee-controlled unions' efforts in the late 1910s and 1920s.

93. "Do Not Blame the Agitators," *Variety*, November 24, 1916, 2; "Managers Say 'Blacklist' for Any Striking Actor," *Variety*, December 8, 1916, 1. In *Variety* on November 10, 1916, performer Jessie Haywood published an obsequious letter to the VMPA stating his resignation from the White Rats ("An Open Letter," *Variety*, November 10, 1916, 39).

94. "Oklahoma City Strike," *Variety*, November 3, 1916, 6. Also, on October 27, 1916, *Variety* reported that "business at the Empress is also good, while the Majestic generally is crowded" ("Oklahoma City Strike," *Variety*, October 27, 1916, 6).

95. Pat Casey testimony, box 70, 270, *FTC v. VMPA*.

96. Valerie Bergere testimony, box 72, 2694–95, *FTC v. VMPA*.

97. Elizabeth Murray testimony, box 72, 2724–25, *FTC v. VMPA*.

98. Ibid., 2725.

99. Fred Schanberger testimony, box 72, 2913, *FTC v. VMPA*.

100. Pat Casey testimony, box 70, 351, *FTC v. VMPA*.

101. Nan Halperin testimony, box 72, 2884, *FTC v. VMPA*.

102. Valerie Bergere testimony, box 72, 2703, *FTC v. VMPA*.

103. *Brief for Respondents*, 58, box 69, *FTC v. VMPA*. This offered further proof of their assertion that "the public has not been affected by any of the alleged practices or conduct" (ibid., 3).

104. Emma Carus testimony, box 72, 2958, *FTC v. VMPA*.

105. See Pat Rooney's testimony, box 72, 2480, *FTC v. VMPA.*

106. *Brief for Respondents,* 83, box 69, *FTC v. VMPA.* See *Federal Trade Commission v. Gratz,* 258 Fed. 314 (1919). After the U.S. Circuit Court of Appeals reversed the FTC's decision in the Gratz case, the FTC appealed to the Supreme Court. Justice McReynolds's majority opinion stated that the Court had the final authority to decide the parameters of unfair trade and thus destroyed the FTC's "administrative discretion" (Kelly and Harbison, *American Constitution,* 678–79).

107. Dawley, *Struggles for Justice,* 145.

108. "Federal Trade Decision: Week's Most Discussed Topic," *Variety,* April 19, 1920, 5.

109. *Brief for Respondents,* 90, box 69, *FTC v. VMPA.*

110. Ibid., 91.

111. "Discovers No Trust of Vaudeville Houses," *New York Times,* April 1, 1920, 9. The *Washington Post* also wrote that "the controversy arose originally over a difference between an actors' organization . . . and the vaudeville managers. The White Rats demanded that no one be engaged as actors other than members of their organization" ("Vaudeville Trust Dismissed," *Washington Post,* April 1, 1920, 9).

112. "Federal Trade Decision: Week's Most Discussed Topic," *Variety,* April 19, 1920, 5.

113. Bernheim, "The Facts of Vaudeville," *Equity* 8 (September 1923): 11. For further discussion of U.S. policy toward trusts and labor unions, see Forbath, *Law and the Shaping of the American Labor Movement.* Considering the social context of the hearing, the FTC's decision was not unusual. Since the 1890s, the rise of industrial combinations and the concentration of wealth resulting from company mergers had caused public concern and antipathy. In 1914 President Woodrow Wilson decided to handle the debate about trusts by creating a five-person commission to receive complaints, hold hearings, gather evidence, call witnesses, and issue cease-and-desist orders. This approach struck a middle ground between those who advocated absolute free enterprise, including the abolition of "reasonable" trusts, and those who fought for socialist programs. Trade unionists were particularly interested in the development of trust legislation around the turn of the century because they were well aware that antitrust statutes could be used against unions. Many union tactics had been declared violations of antitrust laws in the early twentieth century, including consumer boycotts in conjunction with strikes and the publication of lists of unfair employers. Labor leaders such as Samuel Gompers celebrated the Clayton Anti-Trust Act, passed in 1912, for protecting labor unions from antitrust prosecutions and injunctions. But this act, which asserted the legality of labor unions (an already accepted legal axiom) and allowed injunctions in struggles between employers and employees when they were "necessary to prevent irreparable injury to property," did not stem the tide of injunctions against unions (ibid., 157). In fact, the number of injunctions against labor unions rose after the passage of the Clayton Anti-Trust Act. In this light, we can see that although antitrust sentiment shaped the atmosphere of the 1919–20 FTC case discussed here, the period was also marked by the government's compromising approach to business (in which "reasonable" trusts were protected) and by the continued use of injunctions against labor unions based on antitrust laws (ibid., 155–56).

Chapter Eight

1. Frank Fogarty testimony, box 71, 1226, *FTC v. VMPA.*
2. Gilbert, *American Vaudeville,* 392.
3. "Keith Opens in Syracuse," *Variety,* January 31, 1920, 6.
4. "New Keith's Toledo," *Variety,* March 29, 1923, 6; Gilbert, *American Vaudeville,* 392.
5. Report Book 23, 87, KAC.
6. In 1920, for example, *Variety* reported "apathetic" audiences for vaudeville ("Inside Stuff—On Vaudeville," *Variety,* April 16, 1920, 7).
7. "Orpheum Billing Pictures above Its Vaudeville Acts," *Variety,* September 1, 1926. Keith's Palace Theatre in Cleveland also announced this policy in 1926. See "Fifteen 2-a-Day Vaudeville Houses Left in All America," *Variety,* August 18, 1926, 67.
8. "No Drum Crashes for Sleep Drive in Keith-Albee Vaudeville," *Variety,* October 23, 1926, 28.
9. Spitzer, *The Palace,* 132–33.
10. Quoted in ibid., 137–38, 145.
11. Laurie, *Vaudeville,* 498.
12. Hansen argues that amusement parks and vaudeville "lacked the technology of representation that would make the cinema a model of mass-cultural consumption" (*Babel and Babylon,* 62).
13. Snyder, *Voice of the City,* 159.
14. Jenkins, *What Made Pistachio Nuts?,* 88.
15. Ibid., 97–98.
16. "Vaudeville Invades Comic Opera," *New York Telegraph,* November 13, 1910, clipping, vol. 444, 69, RLC.
17. Obituary, *Variety,* January 7, 1925, in *Variety Obituaries,* n.p.
18. Charles P[?] to Mrs. Benjamin Cheney, November 25, 1924, Julia Arthur/*St. Joan* Book (1924–25), vol. 2, 96, JAC.
19. *Toronto Daily Star,* October 6, 1924, clipping, Julia Arthur/*St. Joan* Book (1924–25), vol. 1, JAC.
20. Slide, "May Irwin."
21. Obituary, October 28, 1938, clipping, ser. 5, pt. 2, reel 38, 456, DBS.
22. "Barbette in Amazing Feats at the Palace," n.d., clipping, Barbette Clipping File, BRTC. For more on Barbette, see Steegmuller, "Onward and Upward with the Arts." Someone noted Barbette's replacement of Budd in the margin of *Zits Theatrical Magazine,* October 15, 1927, clipping, box 3, vol. 18, RBC.
23. Ruth Budd to Ray Hanna, October 17, 1928, box 3, book 19, RBC.
24. "Vaudeville," *Variety,* November 11, 1925, 19.
25. "Present Headline Scarcity Due to Timidity of Bookers," *Variety,* September 6, 1923, 4. See also Staples, *Male-Female Comedy Teams,* 193–96, and "Too Much Spotlight and Bunk," *Variety,* September 20, 1923, 5.
26. Lears, "Mass Culture and Its Critics," 591.
27. Ann Douglas, *Terrible Honesty,* 246, 135. See also Huyssen, "Mass Culture as Woman."

28. Rourke, *American Humor*, quoted in Ann Douglas, *Terrible Honesty*, 42–43.

29. For an excellent examination of this transformation, see Butsch, "Bowery B'hoys and Matinee Ladies."

30. Walter Prichard Eaton, "Women as Theater-Goers," *Woman's Home Companion*, October 1910, quoted in Butsch, "Bowery B'hoys and Matinee Ladies," 397; Ann Douglas, *Terrible Honesty*, 380.

31. Ann Douglas, *Terrible Honesty*; Taylor, *In Pursuit of Gotham*, chap. 8.

32. James Fitzpatrick testimony, box 71, 1918, *FTC v. VMPA*.

33. Frank Conroy, "Vaudeville (Variety) Past and Present," *The Player*, December 9, 1910, 94. Other voices joined the White Rats' condemnation of the fake female star. A letter to the editor in *Variety* stated: "It is understood that one alleged weak voiced prima donna who has been touring the local vaudeville houses as a headliner in gorgeous gowns (where her talent ends) will find things a little more difficult in the future" (letter to the editor, *Variety*, December 23, 1905, 5). Another author hoped that "spangled fleshings, thinly draped nudity and women with odorous pasts are doomed to the warehouse of oblivion" (W. R. Dailey, "Melodrama in Vaudeville," *The Player*, January 21, 1910, 20).

34. James Fitzpatrick testimony, box 71, 1929–30, *FTC v. VMPA*.

35. Roberts, *Papa Jack*.

36. James Fitzpatrick testimony, box 71, 1931, *FTC v. VMPA*.

37. Slide, *Vaudevillians*, 149–51.

38. "Evelyn Nesbit and Jack Clifford," *Keith News*, March 8, 1915, 2, clipping, Clipping Book (October 25, 1914–August 9, 1915), KAC.

39. "It Certainly Makes a Difference," *The Player*, March 25, 1910, 18.

40. "The Bookseller," *Saturday Review of Literature*, quoted in Radway, *Feeling for Books*, 211.

41. Ibid., 189–90. For Radway's full discussion of gender in the controversy surrounding the book clubs, see ibid., 205–17.

42. *Petticoat* (1967), quoted in Frith and McRobbie, "Rock and Sexuality," 389.

43. Gilbert, *American Vaudeville*, 393.

44. Short, *Fifty Years of Vaudeville*, 242.

45. Staples, *Male-Female Comedy Teams*, 194.

46. Kennedy, "We've Forgotten How to Fight," 42.

BIBLIOGRAPHY

◆ ——————————————— ◆

Manuscript Collections

Austin, Texas
  University of Texas, Harry Ransom Humanities Research Center
    Theatre Arts Collection
      May Irwin Clipping File
      Minstrel Show Collection
      Fay Templeton Clipping File
Cambridge, Massachusetts
  Harvard University, Houghton Library
    Harvard Theatre Collection
      Julia Arthur Collection
      Sarah Bernhardt Clipping File
      Clipping File, "Boston Theatres"
      Ned Wayburn Clipping File
Fort Wayne, Indiana
  Allen County–Fort Wayne Historical Society
    Ruth Budd Collection
Iowa City, Iowa
  University of Iowa Library, Special Collections Department
    Keith/Albee Collection
Madison, Wisconsin
  Wisconsin State Historical Society
    Daniel Blum Scrapbooks
New York, New York
  New York Public Library for the Performing Arts
    Robinson Locke Collection
    Billy Rose Theatre Collection
Providence, Rhode Island
  Brown University, John Hay Library, Special Collections
    Harris Collection
Rochester, New York
  University of Rochester Library, Department of Rare Books and Special Collections
    Elinore Sisters' Vaudeville Act Papers

Suitland, Maryland
   National Records Center
      Federal Trade Commission v. Vaudeville Managers' Protective Association et al.,
         Docket 128, Record Group 122
Washington, D.C.
   Library of Congress
      Manuscript Division
         Drama Deposits
      Motion Picture, Broadcasting, and Recorded Sound Division
         The Finish of Bridget McKeen (Edison, 1901)
         Rubes in the Theater (Edison, 1901)
         Two Knights of Vaudeville (Ebony Films, 1916)

Newspapers and Magazines

Daily Oklahoman, July–September 1916
New York Dramatic Mirror, January–December 1896, October 1899–November
   1904, July–November 1910
The Player, December 1909–September 1910, December 1916–April 1917
Theatre, May 1901–November 1910
Variety, December 1905–May 1906, March 1909–April 1911, July 1916–January 1917
White Rats Bulletin, June 1901–February 1902

Books

Abelson, Elaine. *When Ladies Go A-Thieving: Middle-Class Shoplifters in the Victorian Department Store*. New York: Oxford University Press, 1989.

Allen, Robert C. *Horrible Prettiness: Burlesque and American Culture*. Chapel Hill: University of North Carolina Press, 1991.

Aron, Cindy. *Ladies and Gentlemen of the Civil Service: Middle-Class Workers in Victorian America*. New York: Oxford University Press, 1987.

Auster, Albert. *Actresses and Suffragists: Women in the American Theater, 1880–1920*. New York: Praeger, 1984.

Baron, Ava. *Work Engendered: Toward a New History of American Labor*. Ithaca: Cornell University Press, 1991.

Bederman, Gail. *Manliness and Civilization: A Cultural History of Gender and Race in the United States, 1880–1917*. Chicago: University of Chicago Press, 1995.

Benson, Susan Porter. *Counter Cultures: Saleswomen, Managers, and Customers in American Department Stores, 1890–1930*. Urbana: University of Illinois Press, 1986.

Blair, Karen J. *The Torchbearers: Women and Their Amateur Art Associations in America, 1890–1930*. Bloomington: Indiana University Press, 1994.

Blumin, Stuart. *The Emergence of the Middle Class: Social Experience in the American City, 1760–1900*. Cambridge: Cambridge University Press, 1989.

Bogle, Donald. *Toms, Coons, Mulattoes, Mammies, and Bucks: An Interpretive History of Blacks in American Films*. New York: Viking Press, 1973.

Boris, Eileen. *Art and Labor: Ruskin, Morris, and the Craftsman Ideal in America*. Philadelphia: Temple University Press, 1986.

Brett, Roger. *Temples of Illusion: The Golden Age of Theaters in an American City*. Bristol, R.I.: Brett Theatricals, 1976.

Bright, Brenda Jo, and Liza Bakewell, eds. *Looking High and Low: Art and Cultural Identity*. Tuscon: University of Arizona Press, 1995.

Butsch, Richard, ed. *For Fun and Profit: The Transformation of Leisure into Consumption*. Philadelphia: Temple University Press, 1990.

Caffin, Caroline. *Vaudeville*. New York: M. Kennerie, 1914.

Cahn, Susan. *Coming On Strong: Gender and Sexuality in Twentieth Century Women's Sport*. New York: Free Press, 1994.

Carnes, Mark. *Secret Ritual and Manhood in Victorian America*. New Haven: Yale University Press, 1989.

Chapin, Robert Coin. *The Standard of Living among Workingmen's Families in New York City*. New York: Charities Publishing Committee, 1909.

Chauncey, George. *Gay New York: Gender, Urban Culture, and the Making of the Gay Male World, 1890–1940*. New York: Basic Books, 1994.

Clawson, Mary Ann. *Constructing Brotherhood: Class, Gender, and Fraternalism*. Princeton: Princeton University Press, 1989.

Clinton, Catherine. *The Plantation Mistress: Woman's World in the Old South*. New York: Pantheon Books, 1982.

Cobble, Dorothy Sue. *Dishing It Out: Waitresses and Their Unions in the Twentieth Century*. Urbana: University of Illinois Press, 1991.

Cohen, Lizabeth. *Making a New Deal: Industrial Workers in Chicago, 1919–1939*. Cambridge: Cambridge University Press, 1990.

Cohen-Stratyner, Barbara Naomi. *Ned Wayburn and the Dance Routine: From Vaudeville to the "Ziegfeld Follies."* Studies in Dance History, no. 13. Madison: Society for Dance History Scholars, 1996.

Cott, Nancy. *The Bonds of Womanhood: "Woman's Sphere" in New England, 1780–1835*. New Haven: Yale University Press, 1977.

———. *The Grounding of Modern Feminism*. New Haven: Yale University Press, 1987.

Davis, Michael. *The Exploitation of Pleasure: A Study of Commercial Recreations in New York City*. New York: Russell Sage Foundation, 1911.

Davis, Susan. *Parades and Power: Street Theatre in Nineteenth Century Philadelphia*. Berkeley: University of California Press, 1986.

Davis, Tracy C. *Actresses as Working Women: Their Social Identity in Victorian Culture*. London: Routledge, 1991.

Dawley, Alan. *Struggles for Justice: Social Responsibility and the Liberal State*. Cambridge: Harvard University Press, 1991.

Dennett, Andrea Stulman. *Weird and Wonderful: The Dime Museum in American Culture*. New York: New York University Press, 1997.

Dennison, Sam. *Scandalize My Name: Black Imagery in American Popular Music*. New York: Garland, 1982.

Diner, Hasia. *Erin's Daughters in America: Irish Immigrant Women in the Nineteenth Century*. Baltimore: Johns Hopkins University Press, 1983.

Douglas, Ann. *The Feminization of American Culture.* New York: Knopf, 1977.

————. *Terrible Honesty: Mongrel Manhattan in the 1920s.* New York: Farrar, Straus and Giroux, 1995.

Dudden, Faye E. *Women in the American Theatre: Actresses and Audiences, 1790–1870.* New Haven: Yale University Press, 1994.

Dulles, Foster Rhea, and Melvyn Dubofsky. *Labor in America: A History,* 4th ed. Arlington Heights: Harlan Davidson, 1984.

Dumenil, Lynn. *Freemasonry and American Culture, 1880–1930.* Princeton: Princeton University Press, 1984.

Dyer, Richard. *Heavenly Bodies: Film Stars and Society.* New York: St. Martin's Press, 1986.

Eckley, Wilton. *The American Circus.* Boston: Twayne Publishers, 1984.

Erenberg, Lewis. *Steppin' Out: New York Nightlife and the Transformation of American Culture, 1890–1930.* Chicago: University of Chicago Press, 1981.

Evans, Sara. *Born for Liberty: A History of Women in America.* New York: Free Press, 1989.

Faderman, Lillian. *Odd Girls and Twilight Lovers: A History of Lesbian Life in Twentieth Century America.* New York: Columbia University Press, 1991.

Fletcher, Tom. *100 Years of the Negro in Show Business.* New York: Da Capo Press, 1984.

Forbath, William. *Law and the Shaping of the American Labor Movement.* Cambridge: Harvard University Press, 1991.

Fredrickson, George. *The Black Image in the White Mind: The Debate on Afro-American Character and Destiny, 1817–1914.* New York: Harper and Row, 1971.

Furia, Philip. *The Poets of Tin Pan Alley: A History of America's Great Lyricists.* New York: Oxford University Press, 1990.

Garber, Marjorie. *Vested Interests: Cross-Dressing and Cultural Anxiety.* New York: Routledge, 1992.

Gilbert, Douglas. *American Vaudeville: Its Life and Times.* New York: Whittlesey House, 1940.

Gilkeson, John S., Jr. *Middle-Class Providence, 1820–1940.* Princeton: Princeton University Press, 1986.

Goings, Kenneth. *Mammy and Uncle Mose: Black Collectibles and American Stereotyping.* Bloomington: Indiana University Press, 1994.

Golden, George Fuller. *My Lady Vaudeville and Her White Rats.* New York: Broadway Publishing, 1909.

Gordon, Linda. *Birth Control in America: Woman's Body, Woman's Right.* New York: Penguin, 1976.

Gorn, Elliott. *The Manly Art: Bare-Knuckle Prize Fighting in America.* Ithaca: Cornell University Press, 1986.

Green, Abel, and Joe Laurie Jr. *Show Biz: From Vaude to Video.* New York: Holt, 1951.

Green, Harvey. *Fit for America: Health, Fitness, Sport, and American Society.* New York: Pantheon Books, 1986.

Grossman, Barbara. *Funny Woman: The Life and Times of Fanny Brice.* Bloomington: Indiana University Press, 1991.

Gubar, Susan. *Racechanges: White Skin, Black Face in America.* New York: Oxford University Press, 1997.

Hamilton, Marybeth. *The Queen of Camp: Mae West, Sex, and Popular Culture.* London: Pandora, 1996.

Hansen, Miriam. *Babel and Babylon: Spectatorship in American Silent Film.* Cambridge: Harvard University Press, 1991.

Harris, Neil. *Humbug: The Art of P. T. Barnum.* Boston: Little, Brown, 1973.

Harrison, Daphne DuVal. *Black Pearls: Blues Queens of the 1920s.* New Brunswick: Rutgers University Press, 1988.

Hippisley Coxe, Antony. *A Seat at the Circus.* Hamden, Conn.: Archon Books, 1980.

Jenkins, Henry. *What Made Pistachio Nuts?: Early Sound Comedy and the Vaudeville Aesthetic.* New York: Columbia University Press, 1992.

Jewell, K. Sue. *From Mammy to Miss America and Beyond: Cultural Images and the Shaping of U.S. Social Policy.* London: Routledge, 1993.

Johnson, Claudia. *American Actress: Perspectives on the Nineteenth Century.* Chicago: Nelson Hall, 1984.

Kasson, John. *Amusing the Million: Coney Island at the Turn of the Century.* New York: Hill and Wang, 1978.

—. *Rudeness and Civility: Manners in Nineteenth-Century Urban America.* New York: Hill and Wang, 1990.

Kelly, Alfred, and Winnifred Harbison. *The American Constitution: Its Origins and Development.* 5th ed. New York: W. W. Norton, 1963.

Kessler-Harris, Alice. *Out to Work: A History of Wage-Earning Women in the United States.* New York: Oxford University Press, 1982.

Kimmel, Michael. *Manhood in America: A Cultural History.* New York: Free Press, 1996.

Lamont, Michèle, and Marcel Fournier, eds. *Cultivating Differences: Symbolic Boundaries and the Making of Inequality.* Chicago: University of Chicago Press, 1992.

Lane, Roger. *Roots of Violence in Black Philadelphia, 1860–1890.* Cambridge: Harvard University Press, 1986.

Laurie, Joe, Jr. *Vaudeville: From the Honky-Tonks to the Palace.* New York: Henry Holt, 1953.

Leach, William. *Land of Desire: Merchants, Power, and the Rise of a New American Culture.* New York: Vintage Books, 1993.

Lenskyj, Helen. *Out of Bounds: Women, Sport, and Sexuality.* Toronto: Women's Press, 1986.

Levine, Lawrence. *Highbrow/Lowbrow: The Emergence of Cultural Hierarchy in America.* Cambridge: Harvard University Press, 1988.

Lott, Eric. *Love and Theft: Blackface Minstrelsy and the American Working Class.* New York: Oxford University Press, 1993.

McArthur, Benjamin. *Actors and American Culture, 1880–1920.* Philadelphia: Temple University Press, 1984.

McLean, Albert F. *American Vaudeville as Ritual.* Lexington: University of Kentucky Press, 1965.

Marston, William H., and John H. Feller. *F. F. Proctor: Vaudeville Pioneer.* New York: Richard R. Smith, 1943.

Meyerowitz, Joanne. *Women Adrift: Independent Wage-Earners in Chicago, 1880–1930.* Chicago: University of Chicago Press, 1988.

Miller, Kerby. *Emigrants and Exiles: Ireland and the Irish Exodus to North America.* New York: Oxford University Press, 1985.

Montgomery, David. *Workers' Control in America: Studies in the History of Work, Technology, and Labor Struggles.* Cambridge: Cambridge University Press, 1979.

Moore, F. Michael. *Drag!: Male and Female Impersonators on Stage, Screen, and Television—An Illustrated World History.* Jefferson, N.C.: McFarland, 1994.

More, Louise Bolard. *Wage-earners' Budgets: A Study of Standards and Cost of Living in New York City.* New York: Henry Holt, 1907.

Morton, Patricia. *Disfigured Images: The Historical Assault on Afro-American Women.* Contributions in Afro-American and African Studies, no. 114. New York: Greenwood Press, 1991.

Moskow, Michael H. *Labor Relations in the Performing Arts: An Introductory Survey.* New York: Associated Council of the Arts, 1969.

Murphy, Teresa. *Ten Hours' Labor: Religion, Reform, and Gender in Early New England.* Ithaca: Cornell University Press, 1992.

Musser, Charles. *The Emergence of Cinema: The American Screen to 1907.* New York: Scribner, 1990.

Nasaw, David. *Going Out: The Rise and Fall of Public Amusements.* New York: Basic Books, 1993.

Norwood, Stephen. *Labor's Flaming Youth: Telephone Operators and Worker Militancy, 1878–1923.* Urbana: University of Illinois Press, 1990.

Ohmann, Richard. *Selling Culture: Magazines, Markets, and Class at the Turn of the Century.* London: Verso, 1996.

Ostendorf, Berndt. *Black Literature in White America.* Totowa, N.J.: Barnes and Noble Books, 1982.

Peiss, Kathy. *Cheap Amusements: Working Women and Leisure in Turn-of-the-Century New York.* Philadelphia: Temple University Press, 1986.

Poggi, Jack. *Theater in America: The Impact of Economic Forces, 1870–1967.* Ithaca: Cornell University Press, 1968.

Rabinovitz, Lauren. *For the Love of Pleasure: Women, Movies, and Culture in Turn-of-the-Century Chicago.* New Brunswick: Rutgers University Press, 1998.

Radway, Janice. *A Feeling for Books: The Book-of-the-Month Club, Literary Taste, and Middle-Class Desire.* Chapel Hill: University of North Carolina Press, 1997.

Renton, Edward. *The Vaudeville Theatre: Building, Operation, Management.* New York: Gotham Press, 1918.

Roberts, Randy. *Papa Jack: Jack Johnson and the Era of White Hopes.* New York: Free Press, 1983.

Roediger, David. *The Wages of Whiteness: Race and the Making of the American Working Class.* London: Verso, 1991.

Rogin, Michael. *Blackface, White Noise: Jewish Immigrants in the Hollywood Melting Pot.* Berkeley: University of California Press, 1996.

Rosen, Ruth. *The Lost Sisterhood: Prostitution in America, 1900–1918.* Baltimore: Johns Hopkins University Press, 1982.

Rowe, Kathleen. *The Unruly Woman: Gender and the Genres of Laughter*. Austin: University of Texas Press, 1995.

Rubin, Martin. *Showstoppers: Busby Berkeley and the Tradition of Spectacle*. New York: Columbia University Press, 1993.

Russett, Cynthia Eagle. *Sexual Science: The Victorian Construction of Womanhood*. Cambridge: Harvard University Press, 1989.

Russo, Mary. *The Female Grotesque: Risk, Excess, and Modernity*. New York: Routledge, 1995.

Ryan, Mary P. *Cradle of the Middle Class: The Family in Oneida County, New York, 1790–1865*. Cambridge: Cambridge University Press, 1981.

Saxton, Alexander. *The Rise and Fall of the White Republic: Class, Politics, and Mass Culture in Nineteenth-Century America*. London: Verso, 1996.

Scanlon, Jennifer. *Inarticulate Longings: "The Ladies Home Journal," Gender, and the Promises of Consumer Culture*. New York: Routledge, 1995.

Short, Ernest. *Fifty Years of Vaudeville*. Westport, Conn.: Greenwood Press, 1946.

Slide, Anthony. *Selected Vaudeville Criticism*. Metuchen, N.J.: Scarecrow Press, 1988.

———. *The Vaudevillians: A Dictionary of Vaudeville Performers*. Westport, Conn.: Arlington House, 1981.

Smith, Judith. *Family Connections: A History of Italian and Jewish Immigrant Lives in Providence, Rhode Island, 1900–1940*. Albany: State University of New York Press, 1985.

Snyder, Robert W. *The Voice of the City: Vaudeville and Popular Culture in New York*. New York: Oxford University Press, 1989.

Spear, Allan. *Black Chicago: The Making of a Negro Ghetto, 1890–1920*. Chicago: Chicago University Press, 1967.

Spitzer, Marian. *The Palace*. New York: Atheneum, 1969.

Stallybrass, Peter, and Allon White. *The Politics and Poetics of Transgression*. Ithaca: Cornell University Press, 1986.

Staples, Shirley. *Male-Female Comedy Teams in American Vaudeville, 1865–1932*. Ann Arbor: UMI Research Press, 1984.

Stearns, Marshall, and Jean Stearns. *Jazz Dance: The Story of American Vernacular Dance*. New York: Macmillan, 1968.

Studlar, Gaylyn. *This Mad Masquerade: Stardom and Masculinity in the Jazz Age*. New York: Columbia University Press, 1996.

Taylor, William R. *In Pursuit of Gotham: Culture and Commerce in New York*. New York: Oxford University Press, 1992.

Todd, Ellen Wiley. *The "New Woman" Revised: Painting and Gender Politics on Fourteenth Street*. Berkeley: University of California Press, 1993.

Toll, Robert. *Blacking Up: The Minstrel Show in Nineteenth Century America*. New York: Oxford University Press, 1974.

———. *On with the Show: The First Century of Show Business in America*. New York: Oxford University Press, 1976.

Tompkins, Jane. *Sensational Designs: The Cultural Work of American Fiction, 1790–1860*. New York: Oxford University Press, 1985.

Tucker, Sophie. *Some of These Days: The Autobiography of Sophie Tucker*. Garden City, N.Y.: Doubleday, Doran, 1945.

Bibliography

Turner, Patricia. *Ceramic Uncles and Celluloid Mammies: Black Images and Their Influence on Culture*. New York: Anchor Books, 1994.

Ullman, Sharon. *Sex Seen: The Emergence of Modern Sexuality in America*. Berkeley: University of California Press, 1997.

Uricchio, William, and Roberta Pearson. *Reframing Culture: The Case of the Vitagraph Quality Films*. Princeton: Princeton University Press, 1993.

Variety Obituaries, 1905–1923. Vol. 1 of *Variety Obituaries*. New York: Garland, 1988.

Variety's Film Reviews, 1907–1920. Vol. 1 of *Variety's Film Reviews*. New York: R. R. Bowker, 1983.

Waller, Gregory. *Main Street Amusements: Movies and Commercial Entertainment in a Southern City, 1896–1930*. Washington, D.C.: Smithsonian Institution Press, 1995.

White, Deborah Gray. *Ar'n't I a Woman?: Female Slaves in the Plantation South*. New York: W. W. Norton, 1985.

Wiebe, Robert. *The Search for Order*. New York: Hill and Wang, 1967.

Williams, Raymond. *Culture and Society, 1780–1950*. New York: Harper Torchbooks, 1958.

Woodward, C. Vann. *The Origins of the New South, 1877–1913*. Baton Rouge: Louisiana State University Press, 1951.

Articles and Book Chapters

Allen, Robert C. "B. F. Keith and the Origins of American Vaudeville." *Theatre Survey* 21 (1980): 105–15.

Bernheim, Alfred. "The Facts of Vaudeville." *Equity* 8 (September 1923): 9–37; (October 1923): 13–37; (November 1923): 33–41; (December 1923): 19–47.

———. "The Facts of Vaudeville." *Equity* 9 (January 1924): 15–47; (February 1924): 19–45; (March 1924): 17–44.

Brody, David. "The American Worker in the Progressive Age: A Comprehensive Analysis." In *Workers in Industrial America: Essays on the Twentieth Century Struggle*, 3–47. New York: Oxford University Press, 1980.

Brown, Victoria Bissell. "The Fear of Feminization: Los Angeles High Schools in the Progressive Era." *Feminist Studies* 16, no. 3 (Fall 1990): 493–517.

Burdette, Robert. "Have Women a Sense of Humor?" *Harper's Bazaar*, July 1902, 597–98.

Butsch, Richard. "Bowery B'hoys and Matinee Ladies: The Re-gendering of Nineteenth-Century American Theater Audiences." *American Quarterly* 46, no. 3 (September 1994): 374–405.

———. "Introduction: Leisure and Hegemony in America." In *For Fun and Profit: The Transformation of Leisure into Consumption*, 3–27. Philadelphia: Temple University Press, 1990.

Carbine, Mary. "'The Finest outside the Loop': Motion Picture Exhibition in Chicago's Black Metropolis, 1905–1928." *Camera Obscura* 23 (1990): 9–41.

Carby, Hazel. "'It Jus Be's Dat Way Sometime': The Sexual Politics of Women's Blues." In *Unequal Sisters: A Multicultural Reader in U.S. Women's History*, edited by Ellen Carol Dubois and Vicki Ruiz, 238–49. New York: Routledge, 1990.

Collins, Randall. "Women and the Production of Status Cultures." In *Cultural Differences: Symbolic Boundaries and the Making of Inequality*, edited by Michèle Lamont and Marcel Farnier, 213–31. Chicago: University of Chicago Press, 1992.

Coquelin, Constant. "Have Women a Sense of Humor?" *Harper's Bazaar*, January 1901, 67–69.

Cott, Nancy. "Passionlessness: An Interpretation of Victorian Sexual Ideology, 1790–1850." In *A Heritage of Her Own*, edited by Nancy Cott and Elizabeth Pleck, 162–81. New York: Simon and Schuster, Touchstone, 1979.

Dabakis, Melissa. "Douglas Tilden's *Mechanics Fountain*: Labor and the 'Crisis of Masculinity' in the 1890s." *American Quarterly* 47, no. 2 (June 1995): 204–35.

Davis, Natalie Zemon. "Women on Top." In *Society and Culture in Early Modern France*, 124–51. Palo Alto: Stanford University Press, 1975.

Davy, Kate. "Fe/Male Impersonation: The Discourse of Camp." In *Critical Theory and Performance*, edited by Janelle Reinelt and Joseph Roach, 231–47. Ann Arbor: University of Michigan Press, 1992.

de Cordeva, Richard. "Ethnography and Exhibition: The Child Audience, the Hays Office, and Saturday Matinees." *Camera Obscura* 23 (1990): 91–106.

Denning, Michael. "The End of Mass Culture." *International Labor and Working-Class History* 37 (Spring 1990): 4–18.

DiMaggio, Paul. "Cultural Boundaries and Structural Change: The Extension of the High Culture Model to Theater, Opera, and the Dance, 1900–1940." In *Cultivating Differences: Symbolic Boundaries and the Making of Inequality*, edited by Michèle Lamont and Marcel Fournier, 21–57. Chicago: University of Chicago Press, 1992.

———. "Cultural Entrepreneurship in Nineteenth Century Boston: The Creation of an Organizational Base for High Culture in America." *Media, Culture, and Society* 4, no. 1 (1982): 33–50.

———. "Cultural Entrepreneurship in Nineteenth Century Boston, Part II: The Classification and Framing of American Art." *Media, Culture, and Society* 4, no. 4 (1982): 303–22.

Distler, Paul Antonie. "Exit the Racial Comics." *Educational Theatre Journal* 18 (October 1966): 247–54.

Dormon, James. "American Popular Culture and the New Immigrant Ethnics: The Vaudeville Stage and the Process of Ethnic Ascription." *American Studies/Amerika Studien* 36, no. 2 (1991): 179–93.

———. "Ethnic Cultures of the Mind: The Harrigan and Hart Mosaic." *American Studies* 33, no. 2 (Fall 1992): 21–41.

———. "Shaping the Popular Image of Post-Reconstruction American Blacks: The 'Coon Song' Phenomenon of the Gilded Age." *American Quarterly* 40, no. 4 (December 1988): 450–71.

Douglas Wood, Ann. "'The Fashionable Diseases': Women's Complaints and Their Treatment in Nineteenth Century America." In *Clio's Consciousness Raised: New Perspectives on the History of Women*, edited by Mary S. Hartman and Lois Banner, 1–22. New York: Harper Colophone Books, 1974.

DuCille, Ann. "Blues Notes on Black Sexuality: Sex and the Texts of Jessie Fauset and Nella Larsen." *Journal of the History of Sexuality* 3, no. 3 (1993): 418–44.

Edmonds, Jill. "Princess Hamlet." In *The New Woman and Her Sisters: Feminism and Theatre, 1850–1914*, edited by Vivien Gardner and Susan Rutherford, 59–76. Ann Arbor: University of Michigan Press, 1992.

Enstad, Nan. "Dressed for Adventure: Working Women and Silent Movie Serials in the 1910s." *Feminist Studies* 21, no. 1 (Spring 1995): 67–91.

Fanning, Charles. "The Short Sad Career of Mr. Dooley in Chicago." *Ethnicity* 8 (1981): 169–88.

Fox, Richard Wightman. "The Discipline of Amusement." In *Inventing Times Square: Commerce and Culture at the Crossroads of the World*, edited by William R. Taylor, 83–98. New York: Russell Sage Foundation, 1991.

Frith, Simon. "The Good, the Bad, and the Indifferent: Defending Popular Culture from the Populists." *diacritics* 21, no. 4 (Winter 1991): 102–15.

Frith, Simon, and Angela McRobbie. "Rock and Sexuality." In *On Record: Rock, Pop, and the Written Word*, edited by Simon Frith and Andrew Goodwin, 371–89. New York: Pantheon Books, 1990.

Glenn, Susan. "'Give an Imitation of Me': Vaudeville Mimics and the Play of the Self." *American Quarterly* 50, no. 1 (March 1998): 47–76.

Gorn, Elliott. "Sports through the Nineteenth Century." In *The Encyclopedia of American Social History*, edited by Elliott Gorn, Mary Kupie Cayton, and Peter W. Williams, 3:1627–42. New York: Charles Scribner's Sons, 1993.

Hall, Jacqueline Dowd. "Disorderly Women: Gender and Labor Militancy in the Appalachian South." *Journal of American History* 73 (September 1986): 354–82.

———. "Private Eyes, Public Women: Images of Class and Sex in the Urban South, 1913–1915." In *Work Engendered: Toward a New History of American Labor*, edited by Ava Baron, 243–72. Ithaca: Cornell University Press, 1991.

Hansen, Miriam. "Pleasure, Ambivalence, Identification: Valentino and Female Spectatorship." *Cinema Journal* 25, no. 4 (Summer 1986): 6–32.

Harris, Geraldine. "Yvette Guilbert: *La Femme Moderne* on the British Stage." In *The New Woman and Her Sisters*, edited by Viv Gardner and Susan Rutherford, 115–36. New York: Harvester Wheatsheaf, 1992.

Harris, Neil. "Four Stages of Cultural Growth." In *Cultural Excursions: Marketing Appetites and Cultural Taste in Modern America*, 12–28. Chicago: University of Chicago Press, 1990.

Huyssen, Andreas. "Mass Culture as Woman: Modernism's Other." In *After the Great Divide: Modernism, Mass Culture, Postmodernism*, 44–64. Bloomington: Indiana University Press, 1986.

Johnson, Claudia. "That Guilty Third Tier: Prostitution in Nineteenth Century American Theaters." In *Victorian America*, edited by Daniel Walker Howe, 111–20. Philadelphia: University of Pennsylvania Press, 1976.

Johnson, Helen Armstead. "Blacks in Vaudeville: Broadway and Beyond." In *American Popular Entertainment: Papers and Proceedings of the Conference on the History of American Popular Entertainment*, edited by Myron Matlaw, 77–86. Westport, Conn.: Greenwood Press, 1979.

Joyrich, Lynn. "Critical and Textual Hypermasculinity." In *Logics of Television: Essays in Cultural Criticism*, edited by Patricia Mellencamp, 156–73. Bloomington: Indiana University Press, 1990.

Katz, Jonathan. "The Invention of Heterosexuality." *Socialist Review* 90, no. 1 (1990): 7–34.

Kennedy, John B. "We've Forgotten How to Fight." *Colliers*, May 1929, 42.

Kibler, M. Alison. "Nothing Succeeds Like Excess: Lillian Shaw's Comedy and Sexuality on the Keith Vaudeville Circuit." In *Performing Gender and Comedy: Theories, Texts, and Contexts.* Studies in Humor and Gender, no. 4, edited by Shannon Hengen, 59–80. Amsterdam: Gordon and Breach, 1998.

Kimmel, Michael. "Consuming Manhood: The Feminization of American Culture and the Recreation of the Male Body, 1832–1920." *Michigan Quarterly Review* 33, no. 1 (Winter 1994): 7–36.

———. "Men's Response to Feminism at the Turn of the Century." *Gender and Society* 1, no. 3 (September 1987): 261–83.

Kirby, Lynne. "Gender and Advertising in American Silent Film: From Early Cinema to the Crowd." *Discourse* 13, no. 2 (Spring/Summer 1991): 3–20.

Krasner, David. "Rewriting the Body: Aida Overton Walker and the Social Formation of Cakewalking." *Theatre Survey* 37, no. 2 (November 1996): 66–92.

Leach, William. "Transformations in Culture: Women and Department Stores, 1890–1925." *Journal of American History* 71 (September 1984): 319–42.

Lears, T. J. Jackson. "From Salvation to Self-Realization: Advertising and the Therapeutic Roots of the Consumer Culture, 1880–1930." In *The Culture of Consumption: Critical Essays in American History, 1880–1980*, edited by T. J. Jackson Lears and Richard Wightman Fox, 3–38. New York: Pantheon Books, 1983.

———. "Mass Culture and Its Critics." In *The Encyclopedia of American Social History*, edited by Elliott Gorn, Mary Kupie Cayton, and Peter W. Williams, 3:1591–1609. New York: Charles Scribner's Sons, 1993.

Lemons, J. Stanley. "Black Stereotypes as Reflected in Popular Culture, 1880–1920." *American Quarterly* 29, no. 1 (Spring 1977): 102–16.

Lenox, Jean. "I Don't Care." In *Favorite Songs of the Nineties*, edited by Robert Fremont, 131. New York: Dover Publications, 1973.

Lenz, Guenter. "'Ethnographies': American Cultural Studies and Postmodern Anthropology." *Prospects* 16 (1991): 1–40.

Levine, Lawrence. "The Folklore of Industrial Society: Popular Culture and Its Audience." *American Historical Review* 97 (December 1992): 1369–99.

Lipsitz, George. "The Meaning of Memory: Family, Class, and Ethnicity in Early Network Television." In *Time Passages: Collective Memory and American Popular Culture*, 39–76. Minneapolis: University of Minnesota Press, 1990.

McGovern, James R. "The American Woman's Pre–World War I Freedom in Manners and Morals." *Journal of American History* 55 (September 1968): 315–33.

McLean, Albert F. "Genesis of Vaudeville: Two Letters from B. F. Keith." *Theatre Survey* 1 (1960): 82–95.

———. "U.S. Vaudeville and the Urban Comics." *Theatre Quarterly* 1, no. 4 (October–December 1971): 50–57.

MacLean, Nancy. "The Leo Frank Case Reconsidered: Gender and Sexual Politics in the Making of Reactionary Populism." *Journal of American History* 78 (December 1991): 917–48.

Mahar, William. "Black English in Early Blackface Minstrelsy: A New Inter-

Bibliography

pretation of the Sources of Minstrel Show Dialect." *American Quarterly* 37, no. 2 (Summer 1985): 260–85.

———. "Ethiopian Skits and Sketches: Contents and Contexts of Blackface Minstrelsy, 1840–1890." *Prospects* 16 (1991): 241–79.

Maschio, Geraldine. "Ethnic Humor and the Demise of the Russell Brothers." *Journal of Popular Culture* 26, no. 1 (Summer 1992): 81–92.

———. "A Prescription for Femininity: Male Interpretation of the Feminine Ideal at the Turn of the Century." *Women and Performance* 4, no. 1 (1988/89): 43–49.

Maurice, Arthur Bartlett. "Feminine Humorists." *Good Housekeeping*, January 1910, 39.

Mayne, Judith. "Uncovering the Female Body." In *Before Hollywood: Turn of the Century American Film*, edited by John Fell, 63–67. New York: Hudson Hills Press, 1987.

Meagher, Timothy. "Introduction." In *From Paddy to Studs: Irish-American Communities in the Turn-of-the-Century Era, 1880–1920*, edited by Timothy Meagher, 1–26. Westport, Conn.: Greenwood Press, 1986.

———. "Sweet Good Mothers and Young Women out in the World: The Roles of Irish American Women in Late Nineteenth and Early Twentieth Century Worcester, Massachusetts." *U.S. Catholic Historian* 5 (Summer/Fall 1986): 325–43.

Merish, Lori. "'The Hand of Refined Taste' in the Frontier Landscape: Caroline Kirkland's *A New Home, Who'll Follow?* and the Feminization of American Consumerism." *American Quarterly* 45, no. 4 (December 1993): 485–523.

Modleski, Tania. "Femininity as Mas(s)querade." In *Feminism without Women: Culture and Criticism in a "Postfeminist" Age*, 23–34. New York: Routledge, 1991.

Montgomery, David. "New Tendencies in Union Struggles and Strategies in Europe and the United States." In *Work, Community, and Power: The Experience of Labor in Europe and America, 1900–1925*, edited by James E. Cronin and Carmen Sirianno, 88–116. Philadelphia: Temple University Press, 1983.

Newman, Richard. "'The Brightest Star': Aida Overton Walker in the Age of Ragtime and Cakewalk." *Prospects* 18 (1993): 465–81.

Oberdeck, Kathryn J. "Contested Cultures of American Refinement: Theatrical Manager Sylvester Poli, His Audiences, and the Vaudeville Industry, 1890–1920." *Radical History Review* 66 (1996): 40–91.

———. "Religion, Culture, and the Politics of Class: Alexander Irvine's Mission to Turn-of-the-Century New Haven." *American Quarterly* 47, no. 2 (June 1995): 236–79.

Peiss, Kathy. "Commercial Leisure and the 'Woman Question.'" In *For Fun and Profit: The Transformation of Leisure into Consumption*, edited by Richard Butsch, 105–17. Philadelphia: Temple University Press, 1990.

Petro, Patrice. "Mass Culture and the Feminine: The 'Place' of Television in Film Studies." *Cinema Journal* 25, no. 3 (Spring 1986): 5–21.

Rabinovitz, Lauren. "Temptations of Pleasure: Nickelodeons, Amusement Parks, and the Sights of Female Sexuality." *Camera Obscura* 23 (Summer 1991): 71–88.

Radway, Janice. "The Book-of-the-Month Club and the General Reader: On the Uses of 'Serious' Fiction." *Critical Inquiry* 14 (Spring 1988): 516–38.

———. "On the Gender of the Middlebrow Consumer and the Threat of the Culturally Fraudulent Female." *South Atlantic Quarterly* 93, no. 4 (Fall 1994): 871–93.

———. "Reception Studies: Ethnography and the Problems of Dispersed Audiences and Nomadic Subjects." *Cultural Studies* 2, no. 3 (1988): 359–77.

———. "The Scandal of the Middlebrow: The Book-of-the-Month Club, Class Fracture, and Cultural Authority." *South Atlantic Quarterly* 89, no. 4 (Fall 1990): 703–37.

Rogin, Michael. "'Democracy and Burnt Cork': The End of Blackface, the Beginning of Civil Rights." *Representations* 46 (Spring 1994): 1–34.

———. "Making America Home: Racial Masquerade and Ethnic Assimilation in the Transition to Talking Pictures." *Journal of American History* 79 (December 1992): 1050–77.

Rowe, Kathleen. "Roseanne: Unruly Woman as Domestic Goddess." *Screen* 31 (Winter 1990): 408–19.

Rupp, Leila. "Feminism and the Sexual Revolution in the Early Twentieth Century: The Case of Doris Stevens." *Feminist Studies* 15, no. 2 (Summer 1989): 289–309.

Russo, Mary. "Female Grotesques: Carnival and Theory." In *Feminist Studies/ Critical Studies*, edited by Teresa De Lauretis, 213–29. Bloomington: Indiana University Press, 1986.

Saunders, James Robert. "The Dilemma of Double Identity: James Weldon Johnson's Artist Acknowledgment." *Langston Hughes Review* 8, nos. 1 and 2 (Spring/Fall 1989): 68–75.

Scott, Joan. "Gender: A Useful Category of Historical Analysis." *American Historical Review* 91 (December 1986): 1053–76.

Senelick, Laurence. "Boys and Girls Together: Subcultural Origins of Glamour Drag and Male Impersonation on the Nineteenth Century Stage." In *Crossing the Stage: Controversies on Cross-dressing*, edited by Lesley Ferris, 80–95. London: Routledge, 1993.

———. "The Lady and the Tramp: Drag Differentials in the Progressive Era." In *Gender in Performance: The Presentation of Difference in the Performing Arts*, edited by Laurence Senelick, 26–45. Hanover, N.H.: University Press of New England, 1992.

———. "Variety into Vaudeville: The Process Observed in Two Manuscript Gagbooks." *Theatre Survey* 19 (1978): 1–15.

Sholle, David. "Reading the Audience, Reading Resistance: Prospects and Problems." *Journal of Film and Video* 43, nos. 1 and 2 (Spring/Summer 1991): 80–89.

Singer, Stan. "Vaudeville in Los Angeles, 1910–1926: Theatres, Management, and the Orpheum." *Pacific Historical Review* 61, no. 1 (February 1991): 103–14.

Slide, Anthony. "E. F. Albee," "Blacks in Vaudeville," "May Irwin," and "Karyl Norman." In *The Encyclopedia of Vaudeville*, 5–7, 49–52, 262–63, 374–75. Westport, Conn.: Greenwood Press, 1994.

Smith-Rosenberg, Carroll. "The New Woman as Androgyne: Social Order and

Gender Crisis, 1870–1936." In *Disorderly Conduct: Visions of Gender in Victorian America*, 245–96. New York: Oxford University Press, 1985.

————. "Puberty to Menopause: The Cycle of Femininity in Nineteenth Century America." In *Clio's Consciousness Raised: New Perspectives on the History of Women*, edited by Mary S. Hartman and Lois Banner, 23–37. New York: Harper Colophone Books, 1974.

Snyder, Robert. "Big Time, Small Time, All Around the Town: New York Vaudeville in the Early Twentieth Century." In *For Fun and Profit: The Transformation of Leisure into Consumption*, edited by Richard Butsch, 118–35. Philadelphia: Temple University Press, 1990.

Sochen, June. "Slapsticks, Screwballs, and Bawds: The Long Road to the Performing Talents of Lucy and Bette." In *Women's Comic Visions*, 141–57. Detroit: Wayne State University Press, 1991.

Steegmuller, Frances. "Onward and Upward with the Arts: An Angel, a Flower, a Bird." *New Yorker*, September 1969, 130–41.

Thurber, Cheryl. "The Development of the Mammy Image and Mythology." In *Southern Women: Histories and Identities*, edited by Virginia Bernhard, Betty Brandon, Elizabeth Fox-Genovese, and Theda Perdue, 87–108. Columbia: University of Missouri Press, 1992.

Toll, Robert. "Sophie Tucker." In *Notable American Women: The Modern Period*, edited by Barbara Sicherman, Carol Hurd Green, Ilene Katrov, and Harriette Walker, 699–700. Cambridge: Harvard University Press, 1980.

Ullman, Sharon. "'The Twentieth Century Way': Female Impersonation and Sexual Practice in Turn-of-the-Century America." *Journal of the History of Sexuality* 5, no. 4 (1995): 573–600.

Walsh, Francis. "Lace Curtain Literature: Changing Perceptions of Irish American Success." *Journal of American Culture* 2, no. 1 (1979): 139–46.

Woods, Leigh. "Ethel Barrymore and the Wages of Vaudeville." *New England Theatre Journal* 4 (1993): 79–95.

————. "'The Golden Calf': Noted English Actresses in American Vaudeville, 1904–1916." *Journal of American Culture* 15 (Fall 1992): 61–71.

————. "Sarah Bernhardt and the Refining of American Vaudeville." *Theatre Research International* 18, no. 1 (1993): 16–24.

————. "Two-a-Day Redemptions and Truncated Camilles: The Vaudeville Repertoire of Sarah Bernhardt." *New Theatre Quarterly* 10, no. 37 (February 1994): 11–23.

Unpublished Material

Cothern, Leah. "The Coon Song: A Study of American Music, Entertainment, and Racism." M.A. thesis, University of Oregon, 1990.

Distler, Paul. "The Rise and Fall of the Racial Comics in Vaudeville." Ph.D. dissertation, Tulane University, 1963.

Kaster, Greg. "Labor's True Man." Paper presented at National Endowment for the Humanities Summer Seminar, "Ethnicity, Race, and Gender in U.S. Labor History," 1996.

Oberdeck, Kathryn J. "Labor's Vicar and the Variety Show: Popular Theatre, Popular Religion, and Cultural Class Conflict in Turn-of-the-Century America." Ph.D. dissertation, Yale University, 1992.

Williams, William H. A. "Green Again: Re-Immigration and Gender Themes in Irish-American Lace Curtain Satire." Unpublished paper, 1997.

INDEX

◆ ———————————————— ◆

Barrymore, John, 227 (n. 122)
Baseball, 10, 217 (n. 39)
Basque Quartette, 45
Batty's Bears, 47
Beck, Martin, 19, 82
Bederman, Gail, 162, 218 (n. 57), 250 (n. 5)
Bell, Archie, 28, 32
Benson, Susan Porter, 221 (n. 13)
Bentley, Gladys, 169
Bergere, Valerie, 194, 195
Bernhardt, Sarah, 79, 82, 89, 95–96, 195, 235 (n. 49)
Bicycle craze, 156–57
Bimbos, 246 (n. 10)
Birth of a Nation, 125
Bisexuality, 169
Black, Violet, 232 (n. 3)
Blackburn, Billie, 124
Blackface, 36, 80, 111–15; and white women, 112–13, 120–21, 123, 129–31, 137–42
Blake, Marion, 184
Bogle, Donald, 119
Book-of-the-Month-Club, 209–10
Boris, Eileen, 176
Boxing, 7, 50–51, 172, 250 (n. 5)
Breen, Harry, 225 (n. 69)
Brody, David, 174–75
Brown, Harris, and Brown, 38
Brown, Victoria Bissell, 218 (n. 57)
Budd, Giles, 149–51
Budd, Ruth, 143–44, 147, 148–58, 175, 203–4, 246 (n. 15); and *Building Up the Health of a Nation*, 163–64; and gender reversal, 149–51, 154, 167–68; and "Girl with the Smile," 154; and race suicide, 158–64; and *Scream in the Night*, 159–64; and sexuality, 156–58, 164–69
Building Up the Health of a Nation, 163–64
"Bully Song," 126, 128, 131, 132, 242 (n. 73)
Burdette, Robert, 59
Burlesque, 130

Burnett, Frances Hodgson, 81; *Lady of Quality*, 81, 90–93, 104
Burroughs, Edgar Rice: *Tarzan of the Apes*, 162–63
Butsch, Richard, 52

Caffin, Caroline, 42, 60
Cahill, W. P., 40
Cakewalk, 117–18, 128, 131–32, 240 (n. 27)
Campbell, Mrs. Patrick, 79, 86, 233 (n. 23), 234 (n. 30)
Capitol Theatre, 200
Carnes, Mark, 182–83
Caron and Herbert, 37, 224 (n. 62)
Carter, Mrs. Leslie, 80, 99–100
Carus, Emma, 40, 194, 196
Case, Charlie, 226 (n. 85)
Casey, Pat, 191–93
Castanos, 46
Chadwick, Ida, 231–32 (n. 70)
Chapin, Benjamin, 220 (n. 83)
Chapin, Robert, 27
Chauncey, George, 165, 168–69, 249 (n. 94)
Cheney, Benjamin, 81, 90, 92, 101
Chevalier, Albert, 45
Chevalier, Julien, 249 (n. 89)
Chorus girls, 123, 126–27, 134–36, 137, 141–42, 188, 204–5, 211
Circus, 135–36, 148, 151–53, 247 (n. 37)
Civil War, 124
Clayton Anti-Trust Act, 197, 255 (n. 92), 256 (n. 113)
"Climbing Up de Golden Stairs," 141
Cline, Maggie, 62
Clinton, Catherine, 125
Clipper Quartette, 169
Coakley and McBride, 38, 224 (n. 66)
Cohan, George M., 48, 63
Cole, Robert, 132; "Louisiana Lize," 132; "Magdaline My Southern Queen," 132; "Ma Mississippi Belle," 132
Coley, Clarence, and Hattie Coley, 130–31

Index

International Ladies' Garment Workers' Union, 191
Irish, Annie, 4
Irish Americans: representation of, 60–61, 67–68, 72–76; social status of, 74–76; women, 58, 74–76
Irish 400, 64–65, 72
Irving, Washington, 29
Irwin, May, 92–93, 95–96, 126–34; and black masculinity, 128, 132–34; and "Crappy Dan de Spo'tin' Man," 128, 132; and *Kiss*, 203; and "I'm Afraid to Go Home in the Dark," 128; as mammy, 131–32; large size of, 128–31, 133; and *Swell Miss Fitzwell*, 93, 134; and *Widow Jones*, 126, 203
"I Want You, Ma Honey," 129

Jazz Singer, 115, 138, 201
Jeffries, Jim, 172, 250 (n. 5)
Jenkins, Henry, 37–38, 63, 83, 202, 230 (n. 37)
Johnson, Honey, 117
Johnson, J. Rosamond, 132; "Louisiana Lize," 132; "Magdaline My Southern Queen," 132; "Ma Mississippi Belle," 132
Johnson, Jack, 208
Johnson, James Weldon, 132; "Louisiana Lize," 132; "Magdaline My Southern Queen," 132; "Ma Mississippi Belle," 132

Kasson, John, 217 (n. 20)
Kate Kip, Buyer, 134
Kean, Richard, 44
Keene, Mattie, 181
Keith, A. Paul, 15
Keith, Benjamin F., 15, 23–24, 196
Keith circuit: decline of, 199, 202, 211–13; growth of, 15–20, 219 (n. 67); as monopoly, 194–97; and White Rats, 171–72, 193–97, 206–9
Keith theaters, 17; admission prices, 25–27, 221–22 (nn. 16, 17); in Boston, 15, 20, 28; in Cleveland, 28,

32, 35; demasculinization of, 32; domestication of, 31–32; in New York City, 15, 26; in Philadelphia, 1, 15; in Providence, 15, 23–24, 26; in Syracuse, 200
Kennedy, Joseph P., 201
Kiernan, James A., 40
Kimball, Moses, 219 (n. 65)
Kimmell, Michael, 218 (n. 57)
Kiss, 203
Kitchen, Karl K., 167–68
Klaw, Marc, 19
Knights of Labor, 250 (n. 2)
Knotts, Mrs. Everett, 189
Kreisel's animal act, 47

LaBelle Trio, 247 (n. 32)
Labor legislation, protective, 187–88
Labor unions. *See* White Rats of America
Lackaye, Wilton, 97
Lady Betty, 160
Lady of Quality, 81, 90–93, 104
Lady of the Green Veil, 31
Lafayette, the Great, 47
Langtry, Lily, 43–44, 80, 226 (n. 87)
La Pierre, Irma, 190
Larsen, Robert, 223 (n. 42), 225 (n. 84)
Lasky, Jesse, 136–37, 244 (n. 114); *At the Waldorf*, 136–37
Laurie, Joe, Jr., 201
Leach, William, 136
Leach and Wallen, 148
Legitimate stage. *See* Theater, legitimate
Leitzel, Lillian, 146
Lemons, J. Stanley, 239–40 (n. 16)
Lenglen, Suzanne, 157
Le Page, Collis, 184
LePage and Florence, 146
Lesbians, 144, 165–69
Levey, Ethel, 48
Levine, Lawrence, 30
Levinsky at the Wedding, 56
Lewisohn, Ludwig, 205
Libbey, J. Aldrich, 175–76, 179

Index

Index

Index

Weber, Joe, 56

"When You Ain't Got No Money," 126

White Rats of America, 171–72, 206–9; and African Americans, 173–74, 179; and American Federation of Labor, 173, 177, 197; and cultural hierarchy, 4, 173, 174, 177–80, 193–95, 197; decline of, 193, 196–98, 199–200; and *Federal Trade Commission v. Vaudeville Managers' Protective Association et al.*, 193–97; and legitimate performers, 174–76, 177–79; and managers, 175, 183–87, 193; masculinity of, 4, 172–75, 179–80, 182–83, 185; and strikes, 20, 172, 186, 190–93, 250 (n. 3), 255 (n. 92); and union shop, 193–95; and women, 173–74, 180–93

Whiteside, Ethel, 120

Widow Jones, 126, 203

Willard, Frances, 156

Williams, Bert, 35, 117–18; and *In Dahomey*, 118

Williams, Percy, 19

Williams, Raymond, 178

Williams, Sam, 202

Wilson, Jack, 2

Wilson, Tony, and Mademoiselle Heloise, 146

Wilson, Woodrow, 256 (n. 113)

Winter, Winona, 33

Women: "women adrift," 184–85; and art, 31–32, 86–88, 90–92; as civilizers, 62–66, 71–76; differences among, 13–14, 115–17, 143–44, 156–57, 188–89; employment of, 12, 27, 98–99, 184–90; and evolution, 160–64; and labor activism, 190–92; and morality, 5, 86–88, 188; and sexuality, 13–14, 50–52, 62, 87–88, 125, 137, 156–57, 165–69, 184–85, 189; and sport, 156–57, 163–64; as theater patrons, 6–7, 30–32, 46–54, 205; unruly, 13–14, 62–65, 229–30 (nn. 36, 37); as victims, 183–88, 253 (n. 62); Victorian, 13–14. *See also* Performers, female

"Women adrift," 184–85

Woods, Leigh, 82, 234 (n. 30)

World's Trio, 47

Xenophobia, 158–59

Yeamans, Annie, 84

Ziegfeld, Florenz, 118, 135, 137, 212

Ziegfeld Follies, 118, 135, 139, 201–2. *See also* Chorus girls; Girl acts

Zukor, Adolph, 200

Gender and American Culture

Labor and Desire: Women's Revolutionary Fiction in Depression America,
 by Paula Rabinowitz (1991)
*Community of Suffering and Struggle: Women, Men, and the Labor
 Movement in Minneapolis, 1915–1945,* by Elizabeth Faue (1991)
All That Hollywood Allows: Re-reading Gender in 1950s Melodrama,
 by Jackie Byars (1991)
*Doing Literary Business: American Women Writers in the Nineteenth
 Century,* by Susan Coultrap-McQuin (1990)
*Ladies, Women, and Wenches: Choice and Constraint in Antebellum
 Charleston and Boston,* by Jane H. Pease and William H. Pease (1990)
The Secret Eye: The Journal of Ella Gertrude Clanton Thomas, 1848–1889,
 edited by Virginia Ingraham Burr, with an introduction by
 Nell Irvin Painter (1990)
*Second Stories: The Politics of Language, Form, and Gender in Early
 American Fictions,* by Cynthia S. Jordan (1989)
*Within the Plantation Household: Black and White Women of the Old
 South,* by Elizabeth Fox-Genovese (1988)
*The Limits of Sisterhood: The Beecher Sisters on Women's Rights and
 Woman's Sphere,* by Jeanne Boydston, Mary Kelley, and Anne
 Margolis (1988)